What Kind of God Do I Serve?

Endorsements

Keith Drury Professor Emeritus Indiana Wesleyan University
"Masterful and immensely practical."

Tim Keep Bible Methodist Missions Director
"Thoughtful, relevant, and engaging."

Kristina Clemens Author of *After Nathaniel*
"Useful, practical, and desperately needed."

Melvin Adams President of Renewanation
"Clear, biblical, and very useful!"

Mark Cravens Pastor and College Professor
"Practical and thought-provoking."

Troy Keaton Pastor at Eastlake Community Church
"An excellent and easy to use tool."

Samuel McConkey United Methodist Pastor
"A compelling call to be wholeheartedly God's."

Mark Bird Theology Professor and author of *Defending Your Faith*
"An effective tool for discipling Christians new to the faith."

Titus Byer Bible Methodist Pastor
"A needed foundation for new believers."

David Duncombe Teacher and PhD. Student at Regent University
"An admirable guide for an individual or small group."

Josh Stobart Nazarene Worship Leader
"Practical, challenging, and effective for discipleship."

WHAT KIND OF
GOD
DO I SERVE?

Ezra Byer

What Kind of God Do I Serve?

ISBN: 978-1-934447-59-8

All scripture references are from the ESV unless stated otherwise.

Interior design by Wilma Albright

Cover design by Brandon Hilligoss

Printing by Country Pines Printing of Shoals, Indiana

Printed in the United States of America

Dedication

I dedicate this book to my incredible wife Janan. It was because of her continued support, many hours of proofreading, and overall encouragement that this book came to completion. I have found it true that at the end of the day, being popular with God and being popular at home is what matters most in life. Thank you, Janan, for being the greatest girl a guy could hope for!

I also want to thank the church I had the opportunity to serve with for three years, Eastlake Community Church. They have been an incredible blessing to me, and their continued support has been phenomenal.

Finally, I want to thank my alma mater, God's Bible School and College. The contents of this book stand on the shoulders of the teaching and training I received from my great teachers and heroes at this tremendous school.

CONTENTS

I Serve Someone Who...

Week 1 ...Wants to Know Me

Week 2 ...Created Me to Glorify and Enjoy Him

Week 3 ...Wants to Give Me Total Freedom

Foreword

Trying to grow spiritually without understanding God's plan for transforming your life is like trying to put together a jigsaw puzzle without looking at the picture on the front of the box. *What Kind of God Do I Serve?* helps eliminate the guesswork by providing the reader with a biblical portrait of what spiritual transformation looks like, while at the same time, offering a simple process for learning and living that transformed life. This book is a welcomed resource for a church that is struggling to produce men and women who fit the biblical standard of spiritual maturity.

New believers do not develop into deep Christians on their own any more than a little boy playing soldier becomes a great general on his own. We know this from church history and from personal experience. More importantly, we know this because the Bible gives us examples of how God himself develops deep people. The Gospels provide a front row seat to watch how Jesus reshaped the spiritual character of his disciples in a way that would prepare them to live, suffer, and die for his Kingdom. At its very core, *What Kind of God Do I Serve?* is doing just that—training new believers to be "Kingdom" people.

What Kind of God Do I Serve? doesn't purport to be a theology or even a catechism, but every question and every answer is under-pinned with sound biblical exegesis and upheld by solid theological thought.

I am grateful to Ezra for offering the Church this wonderful resource. Every new convert that is offered the opportunity to use it will at the same time be placed on a deliberate trajectory toward spiritual maturity, scriptural living, sacrificial loving and giving—all traits of the mature Christian.

Dr. Michael Avery
President of God's Bible School & College

Introduction

I believe you are a seeker after truth. Hopefully, the reason you have picked up this book is because you want to know more about what God is like. You have a desire to understand how he chooses to reveal himself to you. This excites me!

As you read this book, picture yourself on an ocean journey, your ship only scratching the surface of a vast depth below. In each of the topics covered in this book, there is an ocean's depth amount of study and research that could be done. In fact, each topic could rightly deserve its own separate book! My hope and prayer is you will view each section as a primer that will motivate you to expand your knowledge of God in each of these areas.

Approach this read as a journey. Download a QR code scanner on your phone or tablet and watch the videos that can be found at the start of every day. Let the words of each daily section sink into your life. Stop if you are feeling challenged. Take some time to think about how you can apply these words to your Christian walk.

As you will soon discover, I am a big believer in the Bible. I believe it is the greatest book of all time, and it serves as the foundational starting point for all I have written. In the Bible, Romans 15:18 to be precise, a man named the apostle Paul stated these profound words: "I will not speak of anything except what Christ has accomplished through me." I have adapted this statement as my motto for writing. In all that I write, I want to be certain it comes from not only my head, but also my heart.

My bold prayer for you as you read is that your mind and your heart will be transformed. I want the thoughts and concepts of this book to make a radical change in your life because they have made an incredible impact in mine!

Finally, let me just say this. I believe the highest form of learning comes through sharing. If you really want the words of this book to affect you, immediately begin sharing its contents with others. Find someone to go through this book with you. Make a decision to not walk this journey alone. I can assure you it will make a huge difference!

That being said, let me say a brief prayer for you before we begin:

"Dear God, help us as we embark on this six-week journey into some important truths about you. We need your help to guide us. Help us not to get bogged down in mere information, but let us experience radical transformation. Keep our hearts and minds humble, open, and eager to learn all that you have for us. You are an awesome God, and we long to serve you better! Amen."

Week 1

I Serve Someone Who Wants to Know Me

—•◦•— Day 1 —•◦•—
You Become Like the One You Serve

"How you picture God will determine how you serve him."

How you picture God will ultimately determine how you choose to serve him.

This should cause us to ask ourselves some very important questions such as: Is the God I serve worth serving? Is he actually real? Does he care about who I am or who I become? If I died today and came face to face with the one I picture God to be like, would this excite or disappoint me?

Author A.W. Tozer states, "The most portentous fact about any man is not what he at a given time may say or do, but what he in his deep heart conceives God to be like." In other words, if you don't get your concept of God right, every action in your life will reflect this faulty understanding.

You will go through your spiritual journey saying you love God, while living contrary to his desires for your life. This will lead to frustration and confusion in your service of him. Each day you may get up with a desire to do God's will, but your faulty picture of God messes everything up!

Knowing Impacts Serving

For several years, I worked for Pastor Troy Keaton at Eastlake Community Church in Moneta, Virginia. If there is one thing I learned during my time there, it was the value of communication. Understanding what was expected of me made all the difference between failing and succeeding.

To be honest, getting this down was a big learning curve for me. At first, it felt like I would often fail to live up to Pastor Troy's expectations. Not because they were so high, but because I needed to grow in some areas of maturity. (No, I was not paid to write this!) Because I did not understand him, I would often wrongly interpret his intentions, and I am sure I must have driven him crazy at times!

Here is something I realized though. The more I began to understand Pastor Troy as a person, the more I understood what was expected. Just hearing what he said was one thing, but understanding what he was like made all the difference.

When it comes to serving God, my mental understanding of him makes all the difference in the world. I have found *the more I understand what God is like, the easier it has become to do what he says.*

Do you want to serve God effectively? Then it is important to take some time, do some hard work, and understand what he is like.

We Are Called to Be Bondservants

For most people, being a servant brings a negative image to their mind. They have been so conditioned to think that serving necessarily means a step down. What about you? What comes to your mind when you think of service? Before you answer, just remember service was at the heart of everything God's Son, Jesus Christ, did when he came to earth. In fact, Matthew 20:28 says Jesus did not come to be served but to serve.

The Bible talks about service a lot. It is mentioned hundreds of times in the pages of Scripture. From these passages, we see it is impossible to serve two masters (Matt. 6:24), and we are commanded to serve God alone (Luke 4:8).

One of the most beautiful images of service we see is the idea of a bondservant. The concept of this word can be found a dozen or so times in the New Testament by a writer named the apostle Paul.

Although we seldom use this word in today's culture, it holds a rich truth for the way God intended for us to serve him.

To be a bondservant is different from our modern day concept of service or slavery. A bondservant was one who willfully sold himself in service to another. It was not a forced relationship but one rooted in choice. A man or woman chose to become a bondservant of another because they valued what their master had to offer.

So in our lives, we are invited to be bondservants of God. Far from being drudgery, this invitation is the greatest opportunity and privilege ever offered to mankind!

God Does Not Need You

Trying to define God is like trying to define the smell of green. We can try, but even our best efforts fall far short of the intended goal. That being said, one of the best definitions I have heard comes from Theologian A.H. Strong. He offers a broad definition of God as the "infinite and perfect spirit in whom all things have their source, support, and end." This is certainly a good starting point. God does not need anyone. He is entirely self-sustaining.

God does not need you and me to serve him. He needs no person and no thing since he is the originator of all. This is hard for me to wrap my mind around. However, the more I try, the more I am humbled to understand that the very God who needs no one offers me an opportunity to serve him.

Serving Is a Pleasure

Picture a person you would love to meet. Maybe it is a famous athlete, movie star, or political figure. For me, I would love to spend a few minutes with the Prime Minister of Canada. Let's just imagine for a minute that you would as well. Now say one day, out of the blue, you get a phone call from the Prime Minister's office.

The message you receive offers you an opportunity to accompany the Prime Minister on a journey overseas.

On this trip, you are expected to fulfill certain requirements that he assigns you to do. Some days you are helping him set up PowerPoint slides for his United Nations address. Other days, you work to set up his speaking engagements. All the while, he is right by your side, working with you and coaching you through the process.

I cannot speak for you, but if I were in that position, I would think quite a few times before ever voicing a complaint. Serving the Prime Minister of Canada in this way would be a tremendous privilege and honor.

In the same way that this type of service for the Prime Minister would be a privilege, how much more it is an honor to serve the very God who created this universe!

Serving God Changes Everything

Serving God is a huge deal. How you perceive God will dramatically affect the way you live and portray him to others!

What we believe to be true about God formulates what we believe to be true of this world. Theologian James Torrance stated, "Our doctrine of God reflects our understanding of humanity, and conversely, our understanding of the human being reflects our view of God."

On a radio interview I held with him several years ago, Dr. Jeff Myers of Summit Ministries stated, "Where you start spiritually will determine where you end up in every other area of life." Start with an improper view of God, and you end with a distorted view of life. Start with a proper understanding of God, and then you get a proper understanding of reality.

When we serve God in the way he intended, life takes on a fresh sense of purpose and meaning. There is new clarity and focus. Daily choices such as what we watch, how we talk, and how we act understandably matter! We have an objective standard for what is right versus what is wrong.

Gradually, the more we serve him, the more we become like him. *The more we become like him, the greater our life will become!*

Action Points

1. Describe in a sentence or two what you picture God to be like.
2. Does service bring a negative or positive image to your mind? Explain.
3. How does serving God as described in Day 1 change everything?

⸺ Day 2 ⸺
Everything Starts With Knowing Jesus

"Jesus Christ is not valued at all until He is valued above all."
—Saint Augustine

Making a decision to serve God always requires a starting point. It may not be a time of cake, ice cream, and parties, but it is a time when we definitively make a decision to switch allegiances. We go from serving Satan, the ultimate corrupter, to serving God, the life-giving Creator.

This starting point always begins through an encounter with Jesus. One of the most profound yet simple books I have read was Dennis Kinlaw's work, *Let's Start with Jesus*. In a nutshell, Kinlaw points out that it is only when we start with Jesus that things begin to be clear. By starting with an understanding of who Jesus is, we are then able to move towards understanding how God wants us to serve him.

However, before we start with Jesus, let's back up and ask ourselves this question: Why do we need him?

You Are Broken from Birth

The simple answer for why we need Jesus is because we are broken without him. At the beginning of creation, mankind's relationship with God was clear. Adam and Eve were the first two people on earth and enjoyed perfect fellowship with God. This is where God's arch-rival, Satan, came into the mix. Because of his hatred and jealousy towards God, he took it upon himself to deceive the hearts and minds of men and women. Sadly, through his deception and the disobedience of the first man, Adam, sin was brought into the world. Our relationship with God was broken. As a result, every child born into this world begins with an inward bent to sin (Psa. 51:5).

Romans 3:23 says all have sinned and fallen short of the glory of God. Because of our sin, a barrier is placed in between us and our relationship with God. There is a disconnect, and our fellowship with him is broken. Romans 6:23 goes on to say that because of our sin we deserve death. While that may sound extreme by human standards, by God's perfect system of justice this is the proper price to pay for rebellion against him.

Sin is the direct antithesis of God's very nature. To sin against the God of this universe is the highest form of treason. We will discuss this in more detail when we get to week three, but it is important for us to understand sin is no joking matter. It always leads to separation from God.

Jesus Came to Offer Re-Connection

Because we are broken, Jesus offers us the only way to be restored to relationship with him. In John 14:6, Jesus tells us that he is that way. He comes as our Savior and is our only means of salvation (2 Tim. 2:10), for he is the very author of salvation (Heb. 2:10). This salvation is offered by grace through faith in Jesus Christ (Eph. 2:8-9).

Salvation came to us through Jesus' death on the cross. Through his death, he took the weight of our sins upon his shoulders. He suffered as no man or woman has ever suffered because the weight of sin was heavier than all of the physical suffering he endured.

To the world, Christ's death makes little sense. It even sounds barbaric. In 1 Corinthians 1:18, the apostle Paul points out that the message of the cross is foolishness to those who refuse to accept it. On the flip side of the equation, to those who receive, it is powerful! It is freely offered, and it is God's great desire that all men and women come to repentance (2 Pet. 3:9).

When Jesus died and arose from the dead, he became the mediator between God the Father and mankind. Our connection with God that was once broken by sin can now be restored!

Connection Is a Two-Way Street

God does not force anyone to be connected to him. Restoration only happens one way. There are not multiple formulas or schemes.

However, because Jesus offers us a relationship with him, there is an opportunity to accept or reject this gracious offer. God sovereignly chooses not to enter the hearts of those who do not accept him. Connection is a two-way street. God promises to do his part, but we have the choice whether or not to do ours.

What do we do to connect to Jesus? It is very straightforward. Jesus asks that every man and woman take three steps to restore their relationship with him. Without taking them, all is lost.

Step 1 – Genuine Repentance

You cannot enter into relationship with Jesus Christ without repentance. Jesus taught in Luke 13:3 that unless we repent, we will all surely perish. Without repentance, we will die in sin and suffer eternal separation from God.

Repentance in Jesus' day meant much more than turning one's back on sin. A key contributing factor that enraged the religious leaders and eventually led to Christ's death on the cross was the form of repentance Jesus preached. Biblical scholar N.T. Wright points out that repentance in Jesus' day took on a highly political and life-changing message. It called for a Jewish nation, one who largely longed for freedom through means of social uprising, to lay down their arms and commit themselves to Jesus' way of living. This was no trivial "Pray, and tell Jesus you are sorry for your sins" prayer. It was an active and aggressive change in lifestyle!

In Matthew 4:17, Jesus preached: Repent for the Kingdom of God is at hand. As he spoke these words, he was addressing a primarily Jewish audience. Most were familiar with the Old Testament and probably lived decent lives. And yet, in order for them to receive eternal life, Jesus made it clear that repentance was expected of all – regardless of how good they may have been. Acts 17:30 goes on to support this position and reiterates that all men and women must repent.

True repentance involves turning from sin and turning to God. It is a purposeful change in direction! It is saying to God, "I am going to quit pursuing my own dreams and ambitions, and I am going to take up your pursuits and your plans for my life." Without repen-

Everything Starts With Knowing Jesus

tance, we will all come to ruin (Ezek. 18:30). True repentance is not a quick fix apology. It is a decisive change of lifestyle. As Acts 3:19 boldly affirms, we must repent so our sins may be blotted out.

A repentant heart manifests itself in different ways. Maybe there are many tears or maybe there are few tears. This is not what is important. *The critical factor in repentance is not the outward posture of the body but the inward change of heart.*

Step 2 – Authentic Belief

In Mark 1:15, Jesus stated that after repentance we must believe in the gospel. *The true gospel is the great message that Jesus Christ is the Savior of the world and is the only hope for the human race.*

Belief in Christ must always follow repentance (Acts 16:31). Belief in Jesus is not just acknowledging his existence. It is a decision to submit to his lordship as Master of our life! It is recognizing who Jesus is and deciding we want to become like him.

Authentic belief accepts that Jesus is able to do in your life what he did for those in the Bible. It gives us boldness and is anything but shameful. In Romans 1:16, the apostle Paul lets us know we have no reason to be ashamed of the gospel because it is the power of God to salvation for all who believe.

True belief does not just accept Jesus is A way to eternal life, it decides that he is THE way.

Step 3 – Willing Obedience

In 1 Samuel 15:22, God points out that he longs for obedience above any sacrifice we can offer to him. Jesus said it plainly in Luke 6:46 when he stated, "Why do you call me 'Lord, Lord' and not do what I tell you?"

God loves it when we obey him. Obedience to him is in our best interest. He knows what is best. This should cause us to serve him with a willing spirit and not one of drudgery.

When we commit to obey Jesus we are committing to walk as he wants us to walk. In the Bible, the word "light" is used to refer to knowledge. Each time God shines light upon our lives with a new area of knowledge, we should willingly commit to walk in that light (1 John 1:7).

When we accept God's gift of salvation, we are turning the YES sign on in our heart. When God reveals new areas of truth to us, we obey!

Are You a Servant of Jesus?

It was Saint Augustine who said these words many years ago: "Jesus Christ is not valued at all until He is valued above all." Before you move on to the next section, it is vitally important you answer this question with honesty: "Is Jesus Christ the Master of my life?" Does your entire life start and end with him or is there something keeping you from making this decision?

Oftentimes, I get the opportunity to talk to people who speak very vaguely about their relationship with Jesus. They claim to have the "salvation tattoo" stamped on their shoulder, but know nothing of having a genuine relationship with him. I certainly do not want to cause you to question any work God has done in your heart. If you know for certain that you are a follower of Jesus Christ, rejoice and be glad!

On the other hand, if you have doubts or you know Jesus is not your Master, take a few moments and speak this simple prayer:

Jesus, I admit that I am a sinner who is in desperate need of a Savior. For too long, I have tried to run my life my way. Today I want things to be different. I acknowledge my need for you and repent of the sins I have committed against you. I believe you are the only one who can save me from my sins. I no longer want to be a servant of sin, but I want to be a servant of you. From this day forward, I commit to obeying your voice. This very moment, I call out to you in faith, asking you to come into my life and change me. I worship you, Jesus. Amen.

Action Points

1. How does "Starting With Jesus" change the way we approach life?
2. Has there been a time in your life when you have made a decision to serve Jesus Christ? If so, when?
3. How has your understanding of repentance, belief, and obedience grown through this reading today?

Day 3
Service Calls for Discipleship

"Discipleship can tolerate no conditions which might come between Jesus and our obedience to him."
—Dietrich Bonhoeffer

God's act of salvation in your life goes far beyond your initial conversion experience. He does not just get you to "say the prayer" and leave you abandoned. No, Christ's radical appeal to repentance, belief, and obedience calls for immediate action.

One of the great problems with believers who come to faith in Christ is they fail to fully engage. They have signed up for the benefits of being a Christian but have no interest in paying the cost.

In Luke 14, Jesus said that just as a builder counts the cost before starting a project, so we should count the cost in making our decision to be his disciple. In fact, Jesus says that anyone who does not renounce all they have cannot be his disciple.

You Are Called to Be Christ's Disciple

Serving Jesus and being his disciple run hand in hand. At the end of Jesus' final great commission to his followers in Matthew 28, he challenged them to go out into all the world and make disciples. He did not say, "Make all men like you." He did not call them to get everyone to join a church. He called them, and he is calling us, to make disciples!

A disciple in those days was someone who would become a student of their teacher. Greek and Roman literature gives us different examples of leaders who would have disciples. To say you were a disciple of someone meant you were declaring that you wanted to be molded and shaped by their life. It was a teacher and apprentice relationship. John the Baptist had disciples (Mark 2:18), and Moses had disciples (John 9:28). *Being a disciple of Jesus means it is your desire to become like him.*

Jesus' words in Matthew 16:24 laid down the parameters for being his disciple. He said, "If any man will come after me, let him deny himself, and take up his cross, and follow me." To deny our self is to deny all that is sinful and self focused. By taking up our cross, we identify with Christ in his sufferings and willingly choose to be in union with him. Through following Jesus, we commit to living as he wants us to live and walking as he wants us to walk.

One of my heroes and martyrs of the Christian faith is German theologian Dietrich Bonhoeffer. Sentenced to hang by the Nazi regime for his commitment to truth, Bonhoeffer never wavered in his faith. In his book, *The Cost of Discipleship*, he made this statement: "Discipleship can tolerate no conditions which might come between Jesus and our obedience to him." For Bonhoeffer, obedience to Jesus meant eventual death.

In connection with repentance, to be a disciple of Jesus, you are making a personal statement of faith that says, "I will do whatever it takes to become more like my teacher Jesus … even if it means I may die in the process."

Discipleship Leads to Baptism

Following our commitment to being Christ's disciple, we are urged to be baptized. Baptism is subsequent to salvation. It is much more than just being a member of a church.

Baptism is the greatest outward symbolism of the inward work Jesus Christ has done in your heart. This happens when a new believer is submerged or sprinkled with water to symbolize the work Christ has done in their life.

In baptism, we say to the world that we are dead to sin when we go under the water and alive to Christ when we rise from the water (Col. 2:12). It symbolizes we have made a transition from death to life (Rom. 6:4). Baptism does not save us. (The thief on the cross was not baptized, and yet Jesus said that day he would be in Paradise.) But baptism is a critical step forward in our Christian journey.

To be baptized is to say you identify with your teacher and master. For example, John the Baptist had many followers who were baptized. They declared their allegiance to his teaching. To be baptized in Christ means you believe what he says. You believe that you are a sinner and in need of a Savior. You publicly commit to living as Jesus wants you to live and to obey his every command.

Jesus set the standard in Matthew 3 when he was baptized and the Holy Spirit descended upon him. Jesus commands us to go out into all the world and baptize in the name of the Father, Son, and Holy Spirit (Matt. 28:19). Baptism is an obedience issue. When we are baptized, we are tangibly demonstrating before God and others our level of commitment to Jesus.

All throughout the New Testament, baptism is shown as the natural next step after salvation for a new believer (Acts 2:38). Baptism is necessary for rich or poor, young or old. It brings us together as believers. While there may be many different flavors of Christianity, there is ultimately only one baptism (1 Cor. 12:13).

Because baptism is one of the boldest statements a believer can make, the devil fights it with a vengeance. Max Lucado is right on when he says, "Baptism separates the tire kickers from the car buyers." It brings to light people who are really serious about serving God! It is what Chinese missionary Watchman Nee called "faith in action."

Commonly, when a new believer is about to be baptized, I sense tremendous opposition. Maybe the fear wells up in their heart that they will not be able to keep their commitment. Truth be told, at the core of this fear is a heart that is not certain if it wants to really do all that Jesus wants it to do.

If you have given your heart to Jesus Christ, you need to be baptized.

You Should Have a Personal Testimony

If Jesus has done a work in your life, you should have a testimony to share. A genuine testimony is a statement of what you know in your heart to be true. It is saying, "Jesus has done great things in my life and he longs to do the same in yours if you will let him!"

In Acts 22, the apostle Paul gives us several ideas for how we should share our personal testimony. (It might be a good idea to read that passage right now.) Keep in mind he is addressing Jews who were very hostile to his message. They were so against him that they wanted to kill him. But even in the midst of this pressure, Paul kept his cool and gave us four helpful points for sharing our personal testimony.

First, he builds a point of connection. He lets them know he was a Jew who was taught under Gamaliel – a famous Jewish teacher. This helped them see he was not randomly speaking from ignorance. *Second,* he sympathizes with his audience by showing how he, too, once sought to destroy believers. *Third,* he talks about what Jesus has done for him. *Most important and fourth,* he confronts the key issue preventing his audience from accepting Jesus as their personal Savior. It was the fact that any Gentile who believed in Jesus could be saved.

When we share our personal testimony with others, we should attempt to do these four things. *A good testimony builds a point of connection, sympathizes with our hearer, makes much of Jesus, and confronts what is holding people back from making a commitment.*

If you are a disciple and servant of Jesus, it is critical that you have a personal testimony prepared to share with others. A good place to start is by using this threefold outline: 1) What I was before Jesus, 2) How I met Jesus, and 3) What has happened since I met Jesus. Fill these answers out on a note card. Memorize them. Ultimately, your purpose is to make it very natural to share with others while you are on the go.

Most times, we only get very short windows of time to share the gospel with others, sometimes 90 seconds or less. Because of this, we should have a core outline of our testimony committed to memory and adjust it on the fly as we interact with others. When we do this, it is important to keep it simple. Less is more! Stay out of the weeds. The more detailed you get, the quicker your listener will tune you out. Keep it quick, punchy, and make much of Jesus!

How Much Do You Value Becoming Like Jesus?

Okay, I have a feeling that after reading this section, maybe you have grown a little discouraged. Maybe you are thinking, "Man, I did not realize being a follower of Jesus would cost me something!"

If this is your case, could I suggest you may be looking at this from the wrong vantage point? Let's take a modern day sport's analogy. Wayne Gretzky is arguably the best skater who has ever played the game of hockey. Imagine, by some fortunate twist of fate, you had the opportunity to be coached and to be mentored by him. (I'm making the unlikely assumption you would want to take up my favorite sport of hockey!)

Day in and day out, he runs you through drills, places you on a heavy workout program, and has you eating only certain types of foods. The list feels like it goes on forever! Oh, and his only promise to you is that if you follow through with this program, you will become like him. How would you respond? My guess is your response would be determined by how much you valued being like him. Think about that.

Likewise, in your relationship with Jesus, your commitment to do what he says is determined by the value you place on becoming like him. Do you really mean it when you say that you want to become like the Jesus you serve? If so, there is going to be some hard work involved. There will be some tough days. But all of this pales in comparison to the over-arching realization that – hey – his goal is to make you like him!

Action Points

1. How has your understanding of being a disciple expanded?
2. Have you ever been baptized? If not, what is holding you back?
3. Take some time to write out your personal testimony using the three step formula: 1) What I was before Jesus, 2) How I met Jesus, and 3) What has happened since I met Jesus.

Day 4
We Speak to God Through Prayer

"Prayer is the difference between the best you can do and the best God can do!"
—Mark Batterson

There is no source of power more available to a disciple of Jesus, yet as seldom used, than prayer. I am tempted to repeat this sentence several times for emphasis, but I will refrain. If I were preparing a sermon manuscript, this is where I would scribble the words "emphasize point strongly" in the margins of my text. Bottom line: Prayer changes everything!

You may have seen the bumper sticker, "When all else fails, pray." In other words, when you have tried everything humanly possible, then it is time to get on your knees before God in prayer. But in my opinion this is a sad way to live! Shouldn't our view of prayer be just the opposite? Shouldn't prayer be our first option, rather than a final alternative when we are in a jam? A better way of saying it might be, "Before all else fails, pray!"

Author Mark Batterson likes to say, "Prayer is the difference between the best we can do and the best God can do!" Prayer is not mystical. It is powerful. Prayer warrior Watchman Nee once said, "Our prayers lay the track down on which God's power can come. Like a mighty locomotive, his power is irresistible, but it cannot reach us without rails." Like an engine without fuel, so is a believer without prayer. *A prayerless life always leads to a powerless life, and a powerless life always leads to a sinful life.*

It was sometime around the fall of 2005 that I picked up a copy of a book by Jim Cymbala called *Fresh Wind, Fresh Fire.* This book changed my life forever. Through it, God placed within me a desire to pray as never before. He gave me a greater burden for knowing him more intimately and sharing him with other people. Cymbala writes, "The devil is not terribly frightened of our human efforts and credentials. But he knows his kingdom will be damaged when we begin to lift up our hearts to God."

I step into this day about prayer hesitantly and with humility. I feel far from being an expert in the school of prayer. I admit that in my own strength, I have no knowledge of how to communicate with God. Yet through God's graciousness and mercy, it is something I have grown to develop with him over time. I can now truthfully say that along with the study of his Word, communicating with God in prayer has become the most enjoyable and fulfilling part of my day.

That being said, let's dig into what it means to pray.

Prayer Can Only Be Taught By One

The disciples came to Jesus and said, "Lord, teach us to pray." They did not say, "Lord teach us to preach, teach us to sing, or teach us to read eloquently." They said, "Teach us to pray." Books, sermons, and discussions about prayer are fantastic. But at the end of the day, true prayer can only be taught through sitting at the feet of the one to whom we pray.

This is difficult. I for one find it far easier to talk about prayer than to actually pray. This is why many "prayer meetings" today consist of everything but prayer. We would rather talk about God than commune with him. But just as it is an enormous waste of time to speak about a wonderful well, yet we never draw any water from the well, so it is a waste of time when we only talk of what God can do rather than going to him directly and asking!

Five Characteristics of True Prayer

To pray as God desires, an internal change must take place in our demeanor. Ecclesiastes 5 gives us a model for how we approach God. Read this passage. It is convicting! From this passage and others, here are a few characteristics of what Scripture indicates our prayer lives should look like.

1) Reverent – God is not our big buddy and high-five man up in the sky. He is the sovereign Creator of the universe, and we must treat him with respect. Our reverence for God should grow as we develop in our understanding of who he is. By reverence, I do not mean formal. It is not as if kneeling on your knees in a straight back position is somehow holier. But the way you approach God says a lot about how you will hear his voice.

2) Dependent – I love these words from one of my spiritual heroes, Pastor Mark Cravens. He says, "True prayer is the daily, honest confession of the believer that there is only one who can truly help him, one upon whom he is totally depending, his Heavenly Father." Our help comes only from the Lord (Psa. 121:2) and we can take joy knowing our Father in Heaven knows what we need even before we ask (Matt. 6:8)!

3) Fervent – There should be an urgency about our prayers. This does not mean panic. But fully understanding the reality of our time on earth should motivate us to pray with a fervency and motivation to see others saved. Fervency often leads to lengthier and deeper prayers. I have noticed that the more we become passionate about the burdens God places on our hearts, the longer we persist in praying for them.

4) Consistent – It is better to start small and be consistent than it is to start big and only pray once a week. If you are new to prayer, start with five minutes a day. From that, continue to expand and consistently increase your time and quality of communication with

God. Set some goals for where you would like to be, and ask God in prayer to help you move towards them.

5) Expectant – Prayer without expectancy is lack of faith. To pray without expecting God to answer your prayers reveals what you really feel about your relationship with him. I have stopped praying what I call "timid prayers." Prayers that I know I can answer in my own power and strength. I have replaced these with God-sized petitions. Prayers that I know will not come to pass unless God intervenes. I expect him to do greatness!

A Simple Four-Step Prayer Model

When it comes to prayer, there are many different "methods." The formula and method is not the answer. But a good place to start is with a simple process called the A-C-T-S model. It is simple but it helps to provide a framework when we pray to God. By taking a few minutes in each of these categories, you will be aided in establishing a balanced and consistent prayer pattern.

Adoration – The A in ACTS stands for adoration. To adore is to esteem and worship God for who he is. In this step we acknowledge God's sovereign, holy, and loving character. We praise him for attributes such as his mercy, justice, and faithfulness. A great place to start is by reading the book of Psalms in the Old Testament. Every time you observe an attribute of God, write it down and add it to your prayer list. This will give you a much greater appreciation for who God is and will deepen your confidence in whom you serve.

Confession – C stands for confession. Each day we should ask God to search our lives and confess to him any areas that are not surrendered to his control. The surest way to starve a prayer life is to leave areas of sin dormant in our heart. Before going to God and asking him to touch the lives of others, first ask him to clean out the clutter in your own heart.

Thanksgiving – To be thankful is to recognize how God is working in your life and to give him praise for it. Journaling and writing down ways God has worked in your life is instrumental in developing a thankful spirit. Read Joshua 4. In this chapter, Joshua commands the tribes of Israel to erect twelve stones as a way to remember what God had done for them. The message we can take from this is to be intentional about being thankful. Write down and celebrate what God has done for you in prayer.

Supplication – Another word for supplication is plea. It involves intercession to God on behalf of a situation in your life or in the life of another. This type of praying can be physically draining. Maybe your child is not a believer as you are, or perhaps a crisis has arisen, and you desperately need God's help. God wants us to know we can call out to him for every need we have.

Prayer Requires Persistence

It has been said that in order to get to the Spirit, sometimes we have to walk through the flesh. Sometimes, we rush the Spirit. We get down on our knees for a few minutes and feel, hear, and sense nothing from God and so we quit! But in order to encounter spiritual breakthroughs in prayer, we must be persistent.

Why did Jesus spend all night in prayer? Why did he take forty days to fast before he began his public ministry and picked the disciples? If anyone could have prayed a simple token prayer and been done with things, it should have been Jesus. Yet, he did not, and there must be a reason why.

Persistence in prayer develops us spiritually in a way that nothing else can do. *Persistent praying weeds out the passive from the serious believers.* Persistent praying wears down our obsession of self-control. The more we pray, the more we stop trying to fix our problems in the flesh.

I think of my mom as I write this. She is the most persistent prayer warrior I have ever known. Consistently, every morning, she is on her knees asking God to bless her family. And I am convinced that it is largely through her persistence in prayer that each one of her kids is serving the Lord today.

Prayer Brings Power

Prayer does not suddenly inject us with a spiritual steroid. It does not magically increase our personal strength and self-esteem. It actually weakens it. But through the Holy Spirit, we gain a fresh new power. A power that is so much greater than anything we can do in our personal strength.

If you have not experienced the power of God through prayer, determine in your heart that today will be a fresh new start. Prioritize your schedule, set aside distractions, and get alone with God. As you do this, it may seem slow at times. You may get frustrated. But do not stop. Make the decision that your life will have the fuel and the power of God pumping through it every moment of every day!

Prayer is the greatest privilege we have in this world!

Action Points

1. How does it feel to you to picture praying to God? Does it seem natural or does it feel a little bit strange?
2. Discuss the ACTS model of prayer. How will you try to incorporate this practice into your life?
3. Using the ACTS model, take several moments right now and talk to God in prayer.

Day 5

We Listen to God Through Scripture

"Put your nose into the Bible every day. It is your spiritual food. And then share it. Make a vow not to be a lukewarm Christian."
—Kirk Cameron

Jesus did not just call us to be like him. He gave us an instruction manual that walks us step by step through the process. This instruction manual is the Bible – God's written Word to us.

The simplest and most concrete step you can take to becoming more like the God you serve is by committing to study his Word. Understanding God's Word is the key to understanding who Jesus is. If you doubt the Bible, you will doubt Jesus.

Think about these Scriptures. In John 8:31-32, Jesus shows us that knowing his Word is equal to knowing truth. 2 Peter 3:1-2 says the Old Testament and the New Testament writers have equal authority in their writing. Jesus himself, in John 10:35, said Scripture cannot be broken. *If Jesus is truth, the Bible is truth.*

This is why it is critical that we as Christians understand the truth about the Bible, God's written Word to us. We will go into greater detail about this in section four, but it is important that we get the issue of God's Word settled in the early stage of our Christian journey.

If Satan can get us to doubt the words of Jesus, he will unquestionably lead us to doubting Jesus himself.

Telephone and Accuracy

Kid moment! Have you ever played the game telephone? As a young boy, I remember different times when we would all sit around the room in a circle. One of us would make up a message

37

such as, "The toy train moved sluggishly down the track." (I didn't say the messages were always profound.) This message would then be passed along from kid to kid around the circle through whispering into each other's ears. Usually, by the tenth whisper or so, the message was hopelessly lost! We would move from talking about "toy trains" to something like "eggs in Japan."

When it comes to the Bible, skeptics bring up this same "telephone logic." They say, "How on earth can we have the same message today from when it was written nearly two thousand years ago?" Didn't the message get lost, or at the very least confused, somewhere along the way?

This is a good question, but I believe there are some even better answers. We start with the historical reliability of the second portion of our Bible, the New Testament. The New Testament makes a lot of bold claims. Its writers affirm repeatedly that the Old Testament was accurate and inspired by God. Thus if we can affirm that the New Testament is correct, we can take great confidence in the totality of Scripture.

There are three factors to consider when assessing whether or not the New Testament is accurate.

Time Span Is Short

The first of these is the time span. The New Testament was written within a period of sixty years, most of them within thirty years, of the death of Christ (AD 30). This is significant because this means the authors wrote from eyewitness testimony or spoke to others who had an eyewitness encounter with Jesus. They weren't just shooting from the hip!

Also, early church fathers such as Clement and Ignatius were quoting many of the New Testament books by around AD 100. Clearly these writings about Jesus were already in circulation.

It is true that we do not have any "original" manuscripts of the New Testament. However, this is the norm for a work that is this old. That being said, we do have copies of the original manuscripts that were written very close to the same time. Author Mark Bird notes, "The time span (between the originals and the earliest existing copies) for most classical Greek works is about 1,000 years. The time span for most books in the New Testament is around 90 years (by AD 150)." Very significant!

Christian apologist Norman Geisler writes, "Most scholars (conservative and critical) believe the New Testament was completed by 100 AD. And the earliest undisputed manuscript fragment is the *John Ryland Fragment* (100-150 AD) which contains five verses from John 18. This would leave less than a 50 year gap to the original which most scholars believe was written by 90 AD."

The time span for the New Testament writing adds a lot of credibility and helps to assure us that we have an accurate copy of God's Word in our hands.

Number Is High

Second, the sheer number of manuscripts we have available to us today is overwhelming! Since no original manuscripts of the Bible exist in our current age, this means we have to rely on the copies of the original manuscripts we have in our possession. Again, this is common for every piece of ancient literature.

If we add up the total number of New Testament manuscripts we have available today, from differing languages such as Syriac, Arabic, Ethiopic, Latin, Coptic, Greek and so forth, we get a stunning amount of roughly 24,000 manuscripts available.

According to latest data, there are about 5,800 Greek manuscripts available to us today. That may not sound impressive until we contrast it with the nearest competitors. For many ancient writers such as Plato, Caesar, and Tacitus we have only a dozen or so early copies of their work. The largest number of manuscripts available, outside of Scripture, is Homer's *Iliad* that claims just under 1,800 early copies.

Manuscript expert Dan Wallace gives us a tremendous imagery. He points out that the total thickness from manuscript copies of the average ancient author would only pile four feet in height. Compare that to the New Testament manuscripts that would be roughly a mile in height! That is a lot of writing!

The sheer volume of manuscripts we have available to us today is not just interesting, it is extraordinary! And it aids greatly to solidifying our confidence in God's Word to us.

Quality Is Superb

Third, the quality of our manuscripts is incredible. When it comes to ancient writings, most great works have a wide discrepancy between the various manuscripts. For instance, by piecing together various copies of Homer's *Iliad*, we can determine that it is roughly 95% pure. This is extremely good.

What I find amazing is that when it comes to the New Testament, we find there is an even greater reliability. Like any ancient manuscript, there are small discrepancies between copies. A word was left off or a sentence structured slightly different. These instances are relatively minor and hold little significant impact on the overall meaning of the text.

For instance, say I hand you two separate messages. One says, "John ran to store." The other said, "To the store ran John." The wording is different in each example, but the meaning is clear: "John ran to the store." When it comes to the New Testament, biblical scholars Ezra Abbott and A.T. Robertson showed that between 99.75% and 99.9% of the New Testament manuscripts were free of any distinction in meaning. German theologian Philip Schaff pointed out there is not one doctrinal discrepancy in question among all of the New Testament manuscripts available to us today. Simply astounding!

The quality of God's Word handed down to us is superb!

Translation Is Solid

When it comes to translating the Bible into the English language, translators and scholars have gone to great lengths. By and large, the English translations you hold in your hand are excellent representations of the Word of God.

That being said, every translation has its own particular style. Because the Greek language of the original New Testament and the Hebrew language of the original Old Testament use different sentence and grammar structure, the way that scholars translate can vary ever so slightly. There are two basic ends of the spectrum when it comes to translation.

First, there is the *word for word* translation method. In this process, great diligence is taken to get the precise meaning of the original text. While sometimes these translations can appear a little more choppy in sentence structure, they are very accurate and extremely helpful in Bible study. Examples of some of these translations include the *New American Standard Bible*, the *King James Bible*, the *Interlinear Bible*, the *Amplified Bible*, and several others.

Second, other scholars lean more towards a *thought for thought* translation. These tend to focus on making the text very readable and fluid. They are generally still very accurate but may not provide as much depth of meaning as other more literal translations would. Examples of thought for thought translations include versions like the *New International Version*, the *Living Bible*, and numerous others.

My personal favorite that I use the most is the *English Standard Version*. I have found it does a great job of being very literal in message while smooth in translation.

We Have an Accurate Picture of God's Word Today

The culmination of all of these points listed is the reason why we can boldly claim we have an accurate representation of the Bible in front of us today. Yes, different authors had different flavors. Mark emphasized different points of Jesus than Matthew emphasized. One Gospel writer wrote with a Jewish focus while another had a Roman focus. The point is not in the minute differences. The point is that the entire New Testament is in harmony with the message that Jesus is the risen Son of God and Savior of the world.

Throughout the entire Bible, you cannot help but notice an amazing uniformity to its message. *Through roughly forty writers of Scripture, the Bible stays focused on the overarching plan of God to redeem mankind to himself.*

You Can Have Confidence

When you pick up a copy of the Bible today, you can have confidence that you are reading an accurate representation of what was originally written. In Matthew 5:17-18, Jesus taught that the Bible (specifically the Old Testament) was the Word of God. Since the New Testament is correct, the Old Testament is correct as well because the New Testament builds upon the Old. Jesus taught a very high view of Scripture and made it very clear that the Scriptures pointed directly to his coming to earth (Luke 24:44-46).

Some say this is crazy and that God's Word from two-thousand years ago could not be available to us today. From my perspective, I choose to believe that *the same God who holds our galaxies in place is the same God who can preserve his written Word throughout the centuries.* This is a smaller step of faith in my opinion than to accept anything to the contrary.

It was Voltaire, a French enlightenment writer and deist, who famously stated that within one hundred years of his time Christianity would cease to exist as humanity knew it. Yet just fifty years after his passing, the Geneva Bible Society moved into his house and began printing numerous copies of Scripture! God's Word cannot be stopped.

The Bible is the #1 bestseller of all time by far. While its message will always face attacks, *you and I can have confidence that we can discover the one true God through the God-given pages of Scripture.*

Start Reading Today

Every tool you have holds little value for your life until you put it to use. If you have not already, go out and pick up a good Bible and start reading today! I would recommend getting a wide margin *English Standard Bible* with cross-reference notes. This will allow you to add personal notes in the side sections and quickly see parallel verses that connect with the verses you are currently reading.

Christian movie actor Kirk Cameron offered these simple words of advice: "Put your nose into the Bible every day. It is your spiritual food. And then share it. Make a vow not to be a lukewarm Christian."

I have learned through a lot of trial and error that it is good to look at a map while I am on a journey. A map brings perspective. It brings clarity to what seems like an endless sojourn. In the same way, God's Word reveals how our time in this world is significant. If we trust its message and author, it will take us where we need to go.

Through the Bible, we are able to see what God is like, how we can serve him better, and how we can know him personally for ourselves. Reading the Bible will make all the difference in your life!

Action Points

1. Do you own a good copy of God's Word? If so, what kind?
2. How often do you currently read the Bible? Are you comfortable where you are?
3. Make a commitment to read at least one portion of Scripture a day.

—— **Day 6** ——
Jesus Is Who He Claimed to Be

"You must make your choice. Either this man was, and is, the Son of God, or else a madman or something worse. You can shut him up for a fool, you can spit at him and kill him as a demon or you can fall at his feet and call him Lord and God, but let us not come with any patronizing nonsense about his being a great human teacher. He has not left that open to us. He did not intend to."
—C.S. Lewis

John: "Do what I say!"
Max: "Why?"
John: "Because I said so."
Max: "Any other reasons?"

Have you ever heard a conversation go around and around like this? One person makes a bold statement, while the other is not so sure of their claims. The problem is that there exists a fundamental flaw in reasoning. The person speaking assumes they have the authority to make the claim they are asserting on others!

Let's look at another example:

Janice: "I believe the Bible."
Sondra: "Why?"
Janice: "Because it is God's Word."
Sondra: "According to whom?"
Janice: "The Bible."

Philosophers refer to this as "circular reasoning." When it comes to the Bible, okay, so yes we can believe the words we have today are accurate and true. But so what? Why should you and I have to listen to these words? Why should we make them the authority for our life? Why can't we just treat Scripture as any other great piece of literature? The answers to these questions all point back to Jesus.

Jesus Made Some Bold Claims

In the Bible, Jesus made some sweepingly bold claims. These are claims that can be verified and checked. I am talking about statements that would cause people to question the speaker's sanity if they were uttered today! In addition to claiming to be the only way to the Father in John 14:6, Jesus said he and his Father were one (John 10:30).

Jesus claimed to be God! This should lead us to ask, on what basis did he make these claims? It is only as we begin to answer this question that we come face to face with a clear reality: *No other person could do what Jesus did!* Mathematically, historically, and logically it is impossible.

Most people you talk to will accept that Jesus was a great person. But they have a much harder time accepting him as the God of the universe to whom they are called to submit their lives. This is why these next few sections are so important. They are designed to build a framework that gives you solid confidence in the God you serve.

With that being said, let's dive in and take a look at Scripture's bold claims about Jesus.

Jesus Arose from the Dead

Scripture claims Jesus bodily arose from the dead. That is a bold claim and one that distinguishes him from all competing gods! The apostle Paul makes it clear in 1 Corinthians 15:12-19 that the bedrock of the Christian faith is the resurrection of Jesus Christ. He goes as far as to say that if the resurrection of Jesus is a farce, the message of the gospel is meaningless.

Both the New Testament and the Old Testament point to the resurrection of Jesus. The gospel writers of Matthew, Mark, Luke, and John all record Jesus' resurrection.

I cannot stress this enough. If Jesus arose from the dead, he absolutely was who he claimed to be – the Son of God. If Jesus was the Son of God, we must believe what he said.

Your belief in Jesus Christ all hinges on the resurrection of Jesus Christ.

The Resurrection Stands Scrutiny

Because the resurrection is the key to belief in Christ, skeptics fight this tooth and nail. So let's deal with several key myths surrounding the resurrection of Christ.

Myth #1 – Jesus did not really die

Maybe Jesus did not really die on the cross. Perhaps he fell into a state of unconsciousness and walked out of the tomb on his own accord. However, this theory does not stand up to reasonable scrutiny. Just a casual glance at the level of brutality to Roman prisoners moves us to dismissing this as a viable option. Roman floggings and crucifixions were sickening beyond belief.

The idea that Jesus woke up under his own power, walked past a squadron of Roman guards stationed outside, and met with various people afterwards makes no logical sense.

Myth #2 – The Romans stole the body

According to various sources, Jesus was killed and placed in a borrowed tomb for three days. The tomb was guarded by Roman soldiers who were probably issued by Pilate himself. The Romans would have had no reason to steal the body, and the Roman guards most certainly would not have had any ulterior motives. Guards who did not fulfill their duties were often sentenced to death. This theory seems unrealistic at best.

Myth #3 – The Jewish leaders took the body

What about the Jewish leaders? Could they have possibly taken the body to ensure the disciples did not steal it? If any argument does not stack up, it is this one. There was little the Jewish leaders had to gain by stealing the body. Logically, they certainly would have been quick to reveal him when the disciples started speaking of Christ's resurrection.

The Jewish leaders were the very ones who came to Pilate and requested a guard to begin with. They were well aware of Christ's claims, and an empty tomb was certainly not what they were hoping to find! This argument does not hold any weight.

Myth #4 – The disciples stole the body

The disciples had very little incentive at this point to steal the body. First, there would be a high risk in doing so. Stealing a body underneath the noses of Roman guards was not exactly a common, pardonable offense.

Second, the Jewish leaders and Romans were against them! Any associate of Jesus was not viewed very favorably at that time. They would have subjected themselves to likely ridicule, possible persecution, and maybe even death.

Third, Scripture points out the disciples were in hiding and on the run. They clearly thought the jig was up. Jesus was dead. *If they were not willing to stand with Jesus while he was alive, it is almost certain they would not have risked their lives for his body when he was dead.*

The resurrection of Jesus Christ stands the test of outside scrutiny.

WHAT KIND OF GOD DO I SERVE?

The Resurrection Changes Everything

Grasping the reality of the resurrection is a game changer! There is something very powerful about the testimony of the disciples. Literally, one week they are all running from having anything to do with Jesus, and the next, eleven out of the twelve are willing to lay down their lives for what they believe to be true. Quite a change!

After his death and resurrection, Jesus showed himself alive by many proofs, as Acts 1:3 indicates. Through Jesus' appearance to his disciples, a group of timid men who ran when Jesus was captured were transformed. The disciples had little advantage to mentioning the name of Jesus after his death. Being associated with a man who was crucified made little sense. Yet nearly all of the disciples were eventually killed for their faith and all faced persecution.

Few people die for what they know to be a lie. The disciples confidently believed that Jesus had indeed risen from the dead. As a direct result of their witness the New Testament church was formed and is alive today!

The resurrection changes everything!

Jesus Fulfilled Dozens of Prophecies

Aside from the resurrection, another incredible testament to the validity of Jesus' words was his impeccable fulfillment of prophecy. Jesus fulfilled dozens of prophecies from the Old Testament – writings that had already been in circulation for hundreds of years. There are roughly sixty major messianic prophecies, while there are roughly 270 ramifications of prophecy that were fulfilled in Jesus Christ.

For instance, Micah 5:2 prophesied that the Messiah would be born in Bethlehem. Isaiah 7:4 foretold his virgin birth. The Old Testament predicted what family line he would come from, his name, the coming of John the Baptist, that he would be mocked and killed, and that he would ascend into Heaven. The list goes on and on.

In his book *Science Speaks*, mathematician Peter Stoner showed the overwhelming improbability of just a few of these prophecies being fulfilled by one man. Over six hundred students at Pasadena City College worked together to collaborate the data. In their calculations, they worked with just eight of the potential hundreds of prophecies.

They considered the Old Testament prophecies that Jesus would be born in Bethlehem, have a forerunner, ride into Jerusalem on a donkey, be betrayed by a friend resulting in death, have his coat sold for thirty pieces of silver, have the money given to the house of the Lord, make no defense at his trial, and have his hands and feet pierced.

In their calculations, they showed that the probability of just eight prophecies being fulfilled were 1 in 10 to the 17th power. For you non-math people like me, that is 1 in 100, 000, 000, 000, 000, 000! In other words, this would be like covering the entire state of Texas two feet deep in quarters, and having the task of picking one particular quarter while blindfolded! And this is just if eight of these prophecies were fulfilled, let alone if we attempted to calculate all several hundred.

The ways that Jesus fulfilled what was prophesied in the Old Testament is nothing short of miraculous!

Jesus Is Who He Claimed to Be

The very fact that Jesus arose from the dead and fulfilled so many prophecies supports the conclusion that he is who he claimed to be. And Jesus was not coy about who he was. He said in no uncertain terms that he was the Son of God.

WHAT KIND OF GOD DO I SERVE?

As British author C.S. Lewis famously stated about Jesus:

> You must make your choice. Either this man was, and is, the Son of God, or else a madman or something worse. You can shut him up for a fool, you can spit at him and kill him as a demon or you can fall at his feet and call him Lord and God, but let us not come with any patronizing nonsense about his being a great human teacher. He has not left that open to us. He did not intend to.

Admittedly we have covered some deep stuff on this day. You might be saying to yourself right now, "I picked up this book to be encouraged and motivated! Why on earth are we talking about topics like "Why we should believe the Bible" and "How Jesus arose from the dead"?

Let me assure you that this is intentional. I am a big believer in setting a framework before getting into the practical aspects of Christian living. In construction, you always set the frame in place before you hang the drywall. The drywall is important and necessary to complete the house, but without a proper framework everything will fall to ruin. If we do not get the fundamental truths of God's Word and Jesus Christ set in stone, all of the other information we add to the mix will rest upon a shaky foundation.

I have no doubt that over the next few years of your Christian journey Satan is going to throw arrows of doubt and unbelief your way. He will do all that he can to make you doubt Scripture and doubt Jesus. But it will be in those times of darkness and despair that you will be called to stand upon what you know to be true.

During times of heartache and confusion, you can take confidence knowing you serve a risen Savior. This reality does something for me! It enables me to face tough days with the solid confidence that Jesus Christ, the Son of God, has everything under control.

Action Points

1. Why do you believe Satan attacks the truth of Jesus and God's Word so aggressively?
2. Consider looking up resources on the resurrection and various prophecies fulfilled by Jesus. Turning to authors like Josh McDowell, Lee Strobel, and Norman Geisler is a great place to start.
3. How does Christ's resurrection give you confidence today?

————— **Day 7** —————

Jesus' Claim to Truth Clarifies Reality

"The person who has trusted Jesus Christ has not only become acquainted with truth; he or she has the Truth living inside!"
—Josh McDowell

Jesus' call in Scripture for us to "take up our cross and follow him" is an exclusive, not an inclusive appeal. It bears repeating, Jesus does not call us to accept him as A God, he calls us to accept him as THE God.

That last statement is where a good deal of people fall off the Christian bandwagon. "How exclusive, how judgmental, and how arrogant are you followers of Jesus to believe he is the *only* way to eternal life?!" Ever run into someone like this and not know what to say? I have, and answers to these questions are not always easy.

All Roads Do Not Lead to God

A more politically correct statement that many people have bought into today is: "All roads lead to God."

The illustration about a common elephant is often used to illustrate how all religions point to the same God. Picture you are in a room of several people with a blindfold over your eyes. Standing in the center of the room is a giant elephant. Since you are standing by the head, you describe the eyes and the trunk. Another person standing by the ears describes what he feels, your friend standing by the back leg describes what he feels (probably not very pleasant), and so forth. The point is that you all are touching the same elephant. You are just feeling different parts.

Skeptics of Christianity sometimes say this is like the plethora of religions around the world. All of the various gods we serve merely comprise one giant elephant. Each of us just happens to experience a slightly different side of him. Sounds convincing, right? What arrogant and deceived monsters these Christians must be to claim there is only one way to God!

Here is the problem. Believing all religions are just a part of one elephant and that "all roads lead to God" is anything but noble. In fact, *this* is actually the height of arrogance. For anyone to assert that all religions are just different parts of one god assumes *they* know what every religion in the world has to offer. By *their* own declaration, they are proclaiming that *they* understand the entire elephant. *They* know what Hindus, Muslims, Jews, and every other religion teaches and understand how they all tie together.

In all actuality, this seems to me to be a lot more arrogant and requires a good deal more faith than simply saying you believe there is only one God because you have encountered him.

Absolute Truth Makes Logical Sense

The idea that one way is correct and other ways are wrong makes perfect logical sense. It goes in accordance with the way that we live our lives day to day. Clearly, some choices we make in life are good ones, while others can be bad ones. *All choices are not good, and all choices are not bad.*

For instance, if I were to fill six containers, three containing 100% natural mountain water and the other three containing poisonous hydrogen cyanide, the all or nothing approach would get me into a lot of trouble. All contain liquid, but clearly all are not good for my body.

Sadly, we live in a world where morals are subjective instead of objective. Everything is relative! What you believe is right for you, and what I believe is right for me. The logic is, "Well, as long as you just believe, then you are okay." But again, this reasoning breaks down in every other area of life. If I am driving in a car across a state or province and I intend to go west, it will be impossible to ever reach my destination if I choose to go south – no matter how much I BELIEVE.

Everything cannot be relative. Some things must be absolute. As Paul Copan notes, here is how a true relativist must argue: "Nothing is objectively true, including my own relativistic position, so you're free to accept my view or reject it." A true relativist cannot state with certainty any matter and so their arguments are relatively weak (pardon the pun!).

Jesus Is Truth

Jesus is truth, and *truth is essentially that which is in complete harmony with reality and true regardless of time or culture.*

In the Bible, Jesus Christ claimed there was only one way to God the Father. He left no room for any middle ground. In John 14:6, Jesus not only claimed to be the *way*, he claimed to be the *truth* and the *life*. He claimed that no one can go to the Father, thus entering into Heaven, except through him.

In the trial leading up to his crucifixion, Jesus is questioned before Pilate and is asked this question in John 18:38: "What is Truth?" For Pilate, all truth was relative and left up to popular majority rule.

The problem Pilate had is the same one many people have today. Truth is not found in an argument. *True truth is found in a person, and that person is Jesus Christ!* Josh McDowell says it this way, "The person who has trusted Jesus Christ has not only become acquainted with truth; he or she has the Truth living inside!"

Truth Clarifies Our Choices

Because Jesus is truth, we have a starting block on which we evaluate every choice we make. When you have truth, there is no need to look for an alternative. It is meaningless to search out endless paths that are faulty and only lead to despair.

I remember sitting next to a gentleman on a plane from Denver to Dallas on one occasion. We struck up a conversation, and when he learned I was a pastor, we shifted into a discussion about God. He was quick to affirm that he was a follower of Jesus, and he went on to list the numerous attributes of Jesus he appreciated. However, from there he also went into a host of other religions, pointing out the helpful aspects of these as well.

I then asked him something to the effect of, "Sir, do you believe that everything good is found in Jesus Christ?" He paused and then affirmed that he thought he did. This led me to follow up and ask, "Can any other religion offer you anything positive that Jesus cannot offer?" He had to pause a little longer. Finally, he responded, "No, I do not believe so." My final question to him then was, "So if you already have what you believe to be the perfection of truth, why would you go and search for something else?" Cue a restroom break and the end of the conversation.

Please understand that my goal is not to be overly simplistic. I just want us to really think through what we believe. If Jesus is our Lord and Savior, why are we in need of anyone or anything else? Many people are quick to point out the differing values of dabbling in multiple religions. This one teaches me to love family; this one helps me mentally focus, or this one helps me morally. But this always leads me to question: What can this religion offer you that Jesus cannot? If the answer is nothing, then why would you pursue it? On the flip side, if you have found something out of harmony with what Jesus would offer, thus out of harmony with truth, is that something genuinely worth pursuing?

I know talking this way tends to cause skeptics to scream "close-mindedness!" But is it really? Is it actually close-mindedness to refuse other options when you have found complete and total satisfaction? Is it close-minded to refuse an inferior vacuum cleaner when you already have a top of the line model tucked away in your closet? Is it close-minded to turn down a Volkswagen Beetle (no offense if you have one!) if you already possess a Mercedes?

Starting with Jesus changes everything. It changes the relationships you choose to pursue, the lifestyle decisions you make, and how your mind chooses to operate. When you have Jesus, you have satisfaction. Nothing else can compare.

Remember, Jesus never comes into our lives to be A truth, he comes to be THE truth.

A Closing Thought About Knowing God

In this entire week, we have talked a lot about Jesus and what it means to know him. So let me leave you with some closing thoughts before we move on to our next section.

During my time as associate pastor at Eastlake Community Church, our motto that hung on our back wall was simply this: "Knowing God; Winning Others." Pretty simple, eh?

Sometimes, I fear at times we get hung up on terms. We throw around phrases like: "God is my strength, my all in all, or my rock."

All of these are biblical and well based. But the question that should continually bring us to our knees before God is simply this: "Do I know him?" Not "Do I know about him?" but "Do I know him?"

The question then becomes, how do we turn our knowledge about God into knowledge of God? In his book *Knowing God*, author and theologian J.I. Packer answered this question. He wrote, "The rule for doing this is simple but demanding. It is that we turn each Truth that we learn about God into matter for meditation before God, leading to prayer and praise to God." In other words, do not let your knowledge of God sit on a shelf. Use what you know about God to pursue and deepen your relationship with him all the more!

So where are you? Are you actually investing time in your relationship with him? Have you treated him as the most important person in your life? Do you spend regular time with him at the start or close of every new day? Or, has he become a back-burner item in your life? Only you can answer these probing questions.

In our next section, we are going to go in depth about how we can intensely enjoy our relationship with God. But before we get there, just take a few moments and pray to God. Be open and honest before him, and resolve in your heart that above all else, you want to know him!

Action Points

1. Discuss the differences that exist between absolute truth and relative truth.
2. How does starting with Jesus as truth change the way we view other religions?
3. Do you have someone in your life who struggles with accepting Jesus as the only way? How can you use the truth you have learned today to help them?

Week 2

I Serve Someone Who Created Me to Glorify and Enjoy Him

Day 8
Enjoying Life Comes Through Enjoying God

"He who knows what it is to enjoy God will dread his loss. He who has seen his face will fear to see his back."
—Richard Alleine

Everyone is on a quest for personal enjoyment. Think about it, why did you do what you did this morning? Why did you eat what you ate? Why did you watch what you watched? Why did you buy the item you bought? Ultimately, each of these answers comes back to your desire for personal enjoyment. You make decisions in life based upon what you believe will bring you happiness.

We all want enjoyment in life. But this quest should make all of us stop and ask ourselves this question: Is what I am pursuing right now bringing me the greatest source of enjoyment? Or, is there something greater?

In this section, I want to walk you through what I believe the Bible says is the answer to our great desire for enjoyment. To do this though, we have to start from the beginning and establish some fundamental realities about our relationship to God.

You Were Created by God

First, you and I must understand we are not self-starters in the truest sense of the word. God is the originator of your life and my life. He is sovereign above all creation. Whatever God pleases to do, he does (Psa. 135:6)! His nature is everlasting (Isa. 40:28). He transcends time and space. He has no beginning, and he will never have an ending. He is eternal (Rom. 16:26). In Colossians 1:16, we read that by him all things visible and invisible were created. The God we serve created everything in our world and in the heavens!

This reality is foundational to coping with problems we may face in this life. Biblical scholar B.B. Warfield made this observation: "A firm faith in the universal providence of God is the solution of all earthly troubles." When you really grasp that God is your Creator, your perspective in life changes.

Genesis 1:1 says, "In the beginning, God created the heavens and the earth." All things were made by him. In just six days he took a world that was dark and without shape and transformed it into a world of land, water, and sky. It is through him all vegetation was formed. Through his words galaxies came into existence. And by his sovereign and perfect will, all of the animals in our world were breathed into being. Psalm 19:1 states with good reason, "The heavens declare the glory of God."

But even more amazing than all of God's other creation is the fact that he created you and me. You were created in the very image and likeness of God (Gen. 1:26-27). He made you distinct from all other creatures of his creation. You did not evolve over time from a primate species. You were created by God!

Because we are created in the image of God, our lives are precious. Unlike all of the other creatures in God's creation, humans are commanded not to murder one another (Gen. 9:6). This is because each life is sacred. God created us male and female for a purpose. He created us body and soul. And while 2 Corinthians 5 indicates our earthly body will one day perish in the ground, our souls will remain.

You Were Created for God

In Jeremiah 1:5, God says these words to the prophet, "Before I formed you in the womb I knew you, and before you were born I consecrated you." Psalm 139:13 and 16 reiterate this point. To God, our lives are sacred from the moment we are conceived.

You may think you came into this world by accident but actually God created you on purpose. He created you, as Revelation 4:11 indicates, according to his will and for his pleasure.

Because we are created by God, we are his possession (Matt. 12:13-17). We belong to him! Elisabeth Elliot, wife of Christian martyr Jim Elliot, stated these profound words: "God is God. Because He is God, He is worthy of my trust and obedience. I will find rest nowhere but in His holy will, a will that is unspeakably beyond my largest notions of what He is up to." This means that even in the shakiest of times we can take confidence in the fact that we are God's!

Being created for God is far from bondage for a believer in Christ. It is actually through this realization that we experience the greatest liberty. No human can carry the load of living for themselves without turning into an egomaniac. This is a responsibility that can only be carried by God. He is the source of all fulfillment. Philip Yancey writes, "A God wise enough to create me and the world I live in is wise enough to watch out for me."

You were created by God and you were created for God.

You Were Created to Enjoy God

God's greatest desire for our lives is that we find our ultimate enjoyment in him. He is the one our hearts really desire. It is him we are really longing for in the midst of our pursuit of temporary earthly pleasures. Saint Augustine offered this simple and yet profound prayer to God when he said, "You have made us for yourself, O Lord, and our heart is restless until it rests in you."

I've just got to stop here and say that if your heart is habitually restless, there is a reason. It is more than eating the wrong diet, failing to properly work out, or the stress of financial worry. There is a God-shaped hole in your life that only God was meant to fill.

God wants you to receive your enjoyment from him. He has no interest in forcing you to obey a list of random commands. His will for our lives is always in our best interest. *Every law God gives his followers is for their provision and protection!* Obedience simply for obedience sake is drudgery. But obedience out of genuine enjoyment and satisfaction is what God desires.

Just as you have a natural desire to pursue enjoyment, Jesus had this same desire. Hebrews 12:2 points out Jesus' motivation for going to the cross was the joy that was set before him. This joy was fulfilling the will of his Father in Heaven by dying to redeem mankind. Jesus went through the greatest hardships any human being has had to experience. He took the weight of sin upon his shoulders. Yet because he saw the big picture and the joy that awaited, he pressed forward. Jesus had an eternal joy in mind that was greater than any earthly competition. It was this joy and hope that led him to forgive those who persecuted him.

Christians who lose sight of the joy of serving God say something about how unfulfilling they find God to be. Serving God is not always easy, but it should always be joyful for our ultimate joy awaits us!

If you want to enjoy your life more than you ever have before, start by enjoying the God you serve! As Benjamin Whichcote rightly notes, "We never better enjoy ourselves than when we most enjoy God."

When we enjoy God fully, we will long to spend time with him and will mourn when we have disappointed him. Richard Alleine says, "He who knows what it is to enjoy God will dread his loss. He who has seen his face will fear to see his back."

How much do you enjoy God?

Steps to Enjoyment

The roadmap to fully enjoying God is outlined in Scripture. Over the next several days, we are going to break down the steps to really enjoying God.

It does not come naturally. It requires intentional desire on your part to not settle for anything short of ultimate enjoyment. Here are the different elements we will discuss:

Goal	Motivation	Character	Process	Test	Result
Glorifying God	Love	Holiness	Sanctification	Fruit	Praise-filled Satisfaction

All of these areas are rooted firmly in Scripture. They are naturally interconnected. It is not as if they each come in their own separate package. Each one is intricately connected to the topics previous and the ones that follow. As we grow in each of these areas, it is my prayer that our passion and enjoyment of God will increase.

Do you really want to enjoy God to the fullest? Meditate on this question and then tomorrow let's see what God has to say about this in his Word.

Action Points

1. Can you honestly say you currently enjoy your relationship with God?
2. What do you believe hinders you from enjoying him more?
3. How does being created in God's image make a difference for how joyfully you should live your life?

Day 9
Glorifying God Becomes Our Goal

"The chief end of man is to glorify God and enjoy him forever."
—Westminster Catechism

The pathway to really enjoying life never begins with us. It always starts with God. He is our source of enjoyment, and failing to find our joy in him will leave us empty and unfulfilled.

Our first step to enjoying God is found in glorifying him.

Everyone Glorifies Someone (Two Types of Glory)

The *Merriam Webster Dictionary* defines glory as the beauty or splendor that brings praise to someone or something.

Everyone gives glory to someone. There are two chief types of glory in Scripture. First, there is a godly glory, and then there is a fleshly glory. One has an everlasting heavenly mindset while the other is earthly and finite (1 Cor. 15:40).

We willfully choose to give glory to one or the other.

Option A: Willfully Give Glory to the Flesh

Sadly, many often love the glory of men more than the glory of God (John 12:43). This fleshly glory is entirely self-centered and sinful. It is based on the lust of the flesh, lust of the eyes, and pride of life. It is this glory that blinds unbelievers from seeing the glory of Christ (2 Cor. 4:4). The more we have a heart that glorifies the flesh, the less we have a heart that glorifies God. *To not give God the glory he deserves means you have erected another god in his place.*

Everything humanity does apart from God is tainted by sin. Seeking our own glory is seeking everything that is self-centered and finitely focused. Romans 3:23 says we have all fallen short of the glory of God. Giving glory to our flesh will cause us to despair. It is a hopeless pursuit.

Option B: Willfully Give Glory to God

On the other hand, choosing to give glory to God is another story. God's essence is holy and loving, and his glory is the radiance of his essence. John Piper states that the glory of God is, "The beauty of His manifold perfections." God's perfections manifest themselves in different ways. Sometimes they are seen through a brilliant visible display. Other times they are seen in his perfect moral character. Both of these ways point to God's amazing sovereignty.

1 Corinthians 10:31 tells us that whatever we do, we are to do it to the glory of God. Our ultimate goal should always be to give glory to him. This is the measuring rod by which we will all be judged.

To glorify God means we find our enjoyment in him. *We always truly glorify what we most passionately enjoy.* We acknowledge, appreciate, and demonstrate through our actions that we esteem his manifold perfections.

We Become Like Who We Glorify

If we seek our own glory, we will operate in the flesh. If we speak on God's authority, we will operate in his Spirit (John 7:18). If we consistently long for the approval of man, we have a fleshly mindset. We will speak and act in ways that bring attention to us. But if we seek God's glory, we will look for ways to bring attention to him through our lives. The only reason we should do anything is to give glory to our Father in Heaven (Matt. 5:16).

Everyone glorifies someone. Either we glorify ourselves or we glorify God. There is no middle ground.

God Glorifies Himself

Isaiah 48:3-11 indicates that God does everything for his own name's sake. He accomplishes his purposes for his glory. Because God is perfectly holy and loving, his character is flawless. He is the highest form of enjoyment and everlasting happiness. Unlike us, he cannot find fulfillment in any other.

For God to seek happiness in another would be a pointless pursuit. John Piper states, "God is one Being in all the universe for whom seeking His own praise is the ultimately loving act. For Him, self-exaltation is the highest virtue." J.I. Packer says, "The only thing that God is bound to do is the very thing that he requires of us – to glorify himself."

But why is this the case? Follow me carefully here because these next few statements are very important. If God is the source of all perfection and the highest form of enjoyment, rejoicing in himself is entirely noble. For God not to enjoy himself would make him less than perfect in happiness. And thus, this would mean that all of our joy found in him would be incomplete. God has always existed, and he has never had a beginning. While our perfections are always tainted, his perfection is pure. God gives his glory to none other (Isaiah 42:8).

How does God glorify himself? Writer Frederick Grant points out, "God glorifies himself in revealing himself." When he reveals his glory for others to see, he glorifies himself. When he created this world so that others could enjoy it, he received glory and praise.

God wants to reveal himself more to you. For in doing so you will enjoy him more completely and give him greater glory. Make no mistake. It is not as though God needs us to add to his glory. As Jonathan Edwards observed, "God is infinitely happy in the enjoyment of himself." But it is out of this infinite happiness that he invites each of us to come and partake.

Because God is the source and end of all things, glorifying himself is a natural necessity. And for our sakes, we can thank him that he does!

Ways God Reveals His Glory

We were created to glorify God and put to death the works of the flesh. Isaiah 43:7 says God created you for his glory. The prophet Jeremiah states that God knew us before we were formed in the womb. And before we were formed, his intention for our lives was that we bring glory to him.

There are three ways God chooses to reveal his glory to us. He does it through his creation, character, and presence.

Creation – Isaiah 6:3 tells us the whole earth is filled with God's glory. King David stated in Psalm 19:1, "The heavens themselves declare the glory of God." God's glory is everywhere! 1 Corinthians 15:41 lets us know God's glory even differs from star to star. Romans 1:23 strongly warns us not to settle for glorying in God's creation. We must seek God himself!

Character – God reveals his glory through his character. We see that he is never changing today and forever (Heb. 13:8). His way is completely perfect (Psa. 18:30). His words are completely pure (Psa. 12:6). Everything that he does is for our best interest. His character is impeccable!

Presence – While God's glory is everywhere in one sense, the glory of his presence varies from place to place and person to person. Moses was someone whose face shone from seeing the presence of God, and yet his glory was less than Christ's (Heb. 3:3). When the sacred Ark of the Covenant was captured from the Israelites in 1 Samuel 4, God's presence was noticeably different. The people had disobeyed, and the glory of God left their nation.

It is easy as believers to settle for the first two types of glory. We speak highly of his creation and his character, all the while failing to experience his manifest presence. We grow slack in our obedience to God. Relationships with others are severed, and then we wonder why God does not reveal himself to us.

Don't get me wrong. I marvel at God's creation, and I long for his character in a big way. But God help us not to settle for this. Help us to long for his manifest presence in our lives!

Glorifying and Enjoying Are Connected

We have established that God naturally has to give glory to himself because he is the highest form of enjoyment. This leads us to then ask, but what about us? Why are we expected to give glory to God? Doesn't this start to make God out to be an ego-maniac?

To answer this, we should start by observing that God is in no way responsible to answer to us. He does not have to respond to our questions. His thoughts are much higher than our thoughts (Isa. 55:9). He is the potter and we are the clay. That being said, it makes logical sense why God would have us glorify him.

Glorifying God and enjoying him are intricately connected. The West-minster Catechism states, "The chief end of man is to glorify God and enjoy him forever." C.S. Lewis put it this way: "In commanding us to glorify him, God is inviting us to enjoy him." This connection is explicit. Glorifying God brings us enjoyment of him.

We can enjoy God because he is the perfection of enjoyment. This is why he glorifies himself. Because God glorifies himself, he gives us the most perfect source of enjoyment when we place our hope in him. As my friend Darnell Wilson says, "If God told us to glorify the second most glorious thing in the universe that would be the opposite of love." God knows that by us glorifying him we will experience the greatest joy possible!

God's Glory Can Never Be Thwarted

Ultimately, God will receive glory in every situation. The glory of God's presence in our lives can be rejected. The glory of God's creation can be marred. But *the glory of God's character can never be diminished!* In every situation God is working for our good and for his glory.

Augustus Strong states these reassuring yet sobering words: "God will get glory out of every human life. Man may glorify God voluntarily by love and obedience, but if he will not do this he will be compelled to glorify God by his rejection and punishment."

In all situations, God's character shines boldly, declaring the awesome majesty of his essence. While it may appear at times as though Satan has the upper hand, we can rest confident that our glorious God stands sovereign over all his creation.

Scripture says one day everyone will give glory to God (Phil. 2:11). Even the demons of Hell will acknowledge that Jesus is Lord. Those who live in rebellion will give glory to God through their destruction. For through their willful rejection of God, he displays his perfect justice.

Throughout Scripture God shows how he is still glorified regardless of the actions of people. Pharaoh of Egypt tried to keep Moses from going to the Promise Land. Yet God glorified himself through Pharaoh's rejection of him.

There is no situation in which God cannot be glorified. Nothing too great or small, evil or good can keep God from receiving glory. For through all situations, God is able and eager to demonstrate the manifold perfections of his character. In pain he loves to display his comfort. In hardship, he shows forth his mercy. Through poverty or the greatest sickness, God's glory can be found on display.

John 11:4 shows that God receives glory in suffering. However, his glory does not come through seeing the pain on our face and tears rolling down our cheeks. His glory is revealed as he displays his perfection in the midst of turmoil. In fact, Romans 8:18 tells us that the sufferings of this life cannot even be compared to the glory we will experience in the life to come.

The greatest suffering this world has seen came when Jesus died on the cross. Yet, it is in this same suffering that the apostle Paul said he gloried (Gal. 6:14). The story of Job in the Bible teaches us much of the character of God. He allowed Job to suffer pain at the hand of Satan, but Satan could do nothing without his permission.

When our glory is in Christ alone and we enjoy him completely, there is extraordinary assurance for our lives. Jude 24 lets us know God is able to keep us above stumbling and to present us before him in glory.

It is here that you and I are presented with a choice. We can give glory to God and be glorified in Heaven one day. Or we can be like Pharaoh in Exodus and let God display his glorious justice through our rejection of him (Ex. 14:17).

How We Willingly Glorify God

I hope that you want to give God glory out of willing service. To willingly give glory to God means we reflect the excellence of his character through our lives.

We reflect his character through the lifestyle we live and the praise that we offer. When we glorify God in our lives, his presence indwells us, his character transforms us, and we display the majesty of his creation for others to see.

Through glorifying God and putting our enjoyment in his ultimate perfection, we suddenly find purpose and meaning. As we glory more in God's manifold perfections, our enjoyment level and personal perfection increases.

One of the great truths of God's Word is that God does not need us to give him glory. God is self-sufficient. *Giving glory to God is not necessary for him, but it is necessary for us!* The exciting part is that as we give him glory, we experience everlasting enjoyment in this life as we prepare to glorify God forever in our life to come!

Action Points

1. Since glorifying God is the highest form of enjoyment, what are some ways you will intentionally give more glory to God?
2. How do you gain confidence knowing God's glory can never be thwarted?
3. How do you find glorifying God and enjoying him to be interconnected?

—— Day 10 ——
Love Becomes Our Motivation

"Love is the only fire that is hot enough to melt the iron obstinacy of a creature's will."
—Alexander MacLaren

Love must be our motivation for glorifying God. Trying to give glory to God without a heart of love is legalism. It leads to frustration and an attitude that resigns itself to never being able to please God.

Unfortunately, love gets used in so many ways that it begins to lose its meaning. We love our family. We love our pet. We love our car. But surely love has differing levels of priority. Love for our new snowmobile and love for our spouse should be very different!

WHAT KIND OF GOD DO I SERVE?

Love Defined

To love others means we want to have the highest possible relationship with them. It was Saint Augustine who said, "Love is the alignment of the will with the desire to be one with someone or something." In other words, love compels us to get rid of distractions or hindrances in our life that would keep us from loving our object of affection.

When we love someone, it is our passionate desire to have the greatest relationship with them that is humanly possible. This means we confront any thing or person that stands in the way of our love for our object of affection. True love calls us to deal with problems and not ignore them.

For most, love is conditional. We love someone until they have offended us by their words. We love until they have cheated us in business. We love until...fill in the blank. But true love has no boundaries. Sometimes love calls us to make tough choices or choices that may make others angry and resent us. Still, we press on with the intention of having the greatest and most fulfilling relationship possible.

When we love someone, we will do whatever it takes on our end to have the highest relationship with them possible.

Love in the Bible

Love is the essence of God's expressed character, and is at the heart of every command he breathes in Scripture. 1 John 4:8 says God is love. Both the Old Testament and New Testament affirm that loving God first and others second is our highest priority (Matt. 22:37-38).

Repeatedly the Old Testament testifies to the great unwavering love of God. It was his steadfast love that would pursue and extend to great men and women like King David, Queen Esther, and the prophet Hosea. He demonstrated his love to the nation of Israel through repeatedly pursuing them, even when they turned their backs on him to serve false gods.

In the New Testament, God's love continues. It was his love for humanity that sent Jesus to lay down his life on the cross for our sin. While many in Greek and Roman culture were teaching only *erotic* or sensual love, our God calls for true unconditional *agape* love. It is a love that is focused on others.

To the world, God's love demonstrated in the Bible is appalling. What kind of God would send his Son to be hung on a cross? However, through reading the hundreds of references to God's love, it starts to become clear that God calls his followers to love at a level this sin-filled world will never understand.

From beginning to end, God's love is written on every page of Scripture.

The Essence of Loving God

A heart that loves God will obey and serve him completely (Deut. 11:13). It is through reading his Word that we enjoy him more deeply and our care for others becomes greater.

One of my spiritual heroes is the 18th century founder of Methodism, John Wesley. His teaching on love is very insightful and profound. My college professor, Dr. Philip Brown, adapted Wesley's definition of love for God and published a great workbook entitled *Loving God*.

Here is his revised definition: "To love God is to self-sacrificially commit oneself to delight in Him, to rejoice in serving Him, to desire continually to please Him, to seek our happiness in Him, and to thirst day and night for a fuller enjoyment of Him."

Self-Sacrificial Commitment – Love always starts with the basis of self-sacrifice. In Matthew 10:37-39, Jesus told his followers that loving him comes above all else. It comes above love for family and it involves taking up a cross that symbolizes a total death to self.

Delight in Him – Psalm 37:4 calls us to delight ourselves in the Lord. The word delight means to find exquisite pleasure in. When we delight in God, we naturally want more of him. We enjoy him more than our favorite food and cannot wait to experience all he has for us.

Rejoice in Serving Him – A true servant who loves God does not serve him out of bondage but out of love. Repeatedly, the apostle Paul referred to himself as a "bondservant" or willing slave of Jesus Christ. He did not have to serve Jesus but willingly chose to. Psalm 100:2 tells us we are to serve the Lord with gladness. It should be our greatest pleasure!

Desire Continually to Please Him – An unwilling servant will cut corners. Whatever is fastest is best. On the flip side, loving servants of God will go out of their way to please him (2 Cor. 5:9). They do more than what is asked. They do not look at commands in Scripture as "necessary evils." Rather, they are hungry to learn more of God, so they can please him more!

Seek Our Happiness in Him – Our enjoyment quest will never be satisfied until our happiness rests in God. Psalm 36:9 says our fountain of life is in God. He is the source of all true happiness.

Thirst Day and Night for a Fuller Enjoyment of Him – Our quest for enjoyment is never-ending. In Psalm 63:1, David says his soul thirsts for God. Finding our enjoyment in God is like discovering a fridge full of water on a hot summer day. You find yourself constantly going back for more.

Loving God Is a Pleasure

Love for God means we are willing to selflessly lay down all our prideful ambitions. Your marriage goes from being about making you and your spouse happy to making God happy. Your career is no longer yours. Everything is God's, and he has the right to tell you to pursue or give up the path you are on.

When we love God, it becomes our delight and desire to do his will and to please him. When we wake up in the morning, the question is not, "How can I make myself happy?" It is, "How can I bring the most glory to God?"

The more we love God, the more we will seek our happiness in him and grow to thirst for him. True love for God is not merely mechanical. It is a joyful pleasure that everything in our being longs to do! Just as a young person tries to please their date, so we wake up with the intense desire to please God through everything we do.

It is through loving God that we know how to love others. In fact, we can never properly love others beyond our love for God.

The Essence of Loving Others

Loving others is contingent on our love for God. If we don't get the first step right, all of our love for others will be disordered. We will love others according to our flawed understanding instead of God's perfect standard.

However, we will find that when we build our love for others upon our love for God, we set ourselves in position to love others the way God intends.

1 Corinthians 13, rightly labeled "The Love Chapter," gives us a detailed picture of how love is to be shown to others. The apostle Paul states that love is patient, kind, does not boast, is not arrogant or rude, does not insist on its own way, and does not rejoice in wrongdoing.

He then goes on to list five steps of love that build upon one another. Each of these are very important.

First, love bears all things – To bear all things means we cover and protect others. This does not mean we conceal sin, but we work to cover over their potential faults rather than exploiting them. Every day we have opportunities to expose the faults of others, don't we? A coworker makes a mistake, and we have the choice to go out of our way to make sure the boss knows. Our spouse comes home a little later than promised, so we have the option of holding their failure over them during the entire evening.

True love means we do not exploit the faults of others. Loving others means we give them the same benefit of a doubt that we wish others would give us.

Second, love believes all things – When we love someone, we seek to believe the best about them. We are not naïve with our head in the sand, but we look for reasons to speak well of them to others.

We look at a person and see the good things about them before we see the bad. They are innocent before proven guilty. We assume their motives are pure. Rather than being irritated that our neighbor's dog is loose in our yard, we choose to believe it got out by accident.

Third, love hopes all things – Even when we have no reason to believe in others, we still hold out hope. Our hope is rooted in the faithfulness of God. We know that even though there is no reason to believe in this person any longer, God still longs to work his redemptive plan in their life. We hope and pray when others have given up in despair.

Fourth, love endures all things – True love can endure any test. It does not lose patience. Love outwaits others. Even when they continue to resent you, speak evil, and say harsh statements against you, your love endures. Love has no ego. It speaks up for the abused and afflicted, and never mistreats another because of personal ambition or revenge.

Often, the route to winning someone over in love is to simply outwait them. Many times people with few friends wear out their welcome with people very quickly. By being someone who can endure their harsh words or negative spirit, you can quickly grow closer to them than any other person has been able to in the past.

Fifth, love never ends – Love has no time limit. Our love for others should be everlasting. Even though people may grow distant from us, our love stays the same. And when love bears, believes, hopes, and endures, love cannot fail! It is a sure recipe for success.

Love Is Up to You

Just because you can teach and speak about love does not mean you know how to love. There are many who can speak articulately about the nature of love, yet they cannot carry on a meaningful conversation with their child or speak to their friends about God. Their love is right in theory but does not play out into practice.

I really like this quote from Scottish minister, Alexander MacLaren. He said, "Love is the only fire that is hot enough to melt the iron obstinacy of a creature's will." Powerful! True love will cause us to do what we never dreamed before was possible. At times, love will be tough. But the rewards are not even comparable to the cost!

True love is the only pure motivation to glorify God and enjoy him forever.

Action Points

1. How has your understanding of loving God and loving others deepened through this reading today?
2. What is your motivation for giving glory to God? Is it really love or is something else in that place right now?
3. "Love outwaits others." Who is someone in your life right now that needs you to outwait them in love?

Day 11
Holiness Becomes Our Character

*"The only way we can be holy is to be connected
to the source of holiness."*
—Allan Brown

In a relational sense, holiness is the grand purifier of love for others. Becoming holy enables us to love God and love others fully.

Holiness is a character switch. It is not accepting the normal standard. Holiness is not removing ourselves from people and living in a monastery. True holiness calls us to engage and love at a level our world cannot understand.

Holiness defined means a separation from all that is common and ordinary.

God Is Holy

All holiness starts with God. He alone is the perfect embodiment of holiness. God's holiness is the connecting link to all of his attributes. I like the way the *Dictionary of Bible Themes* puts it. This states that God's holiness is, "The moral excellence of God that unifies his attributes and is expressed through his actions, setting him apart from all others."

The Hebrew Old Testament uses the root word for holiness (*kodesh*) over 830 times. The frequent usage of this word strongly implies that God believes it is important. Throughout Scripture God emphasizes holiness. From the beginning of creation, God begins the process of teaching humanity that he requires they live their lives void of sin and filthiness. He calls us to be set apart unto God. He teaches us that he is separate and distinct from all others.

Twice in the Bible, Isaiah 6:3 and Revelation 4:8, the words "holy, holy, holy" are used to refer to God. This is not done by accident. In ancient writing, repetition was used for emphasis, much as underlining is today. Holiness is the only characteristic of God that is used three times in succession. Never is there "love, love, love" or "mercy, mercy, mercy" in reference to God, but there is *"holy, holy, holy."* The biblical writers wanted us to know that God's holiness was, and is, a big deal!

Luke 1:49 tells us God's very name is holy. He is above and separated from all that is contrary to his character. Twentieth century systematic theologian Louis Berkhof correctly noted, "God's holiness is first of all that divine perfection by which He is absolutely distinct from all His creatures, and exalted above them in infinite majesty." His perfect holiness sets him apart from any rival god. No one can compare to him!

God's essential character is holiness. Author John Oswalt states, "God defines his holiness in terms of his character." By looking at the character of God, we see his holiness on display. *All of God's attributes flow out of his holy character.* The foundational building block for beginning to understand God's character starts with an understanding of his holiness.

God Makes Others Holy

Throughout the Hebrew Old Testament, God taught his people the importance of holiness. He taught it to Abraham and Jacob. Ezekiel 20 shows us that the children of Israel were used to serving pagan gods in Egypt. But in the book of Exodus, God pours out ten plagues on the Egyptians as a demonstration of his holiness and separation from all other gods.

In Leviticus God repeatedly teaches the Israelites tangible examples of holiness. All of the dietary laws and "clean" versus "unclean" food types you see in the Old Testament were for the purpose of teaching the Israelites the importance of holiness (Mark 7:19). In Leviticus 10:10, God showed the Israelites they were to distinguish between the holy and the common. God taught holiness to great biblical heroes like King David by showing him there is a standard of right and wrong. The idea that God expects people to be holy is firmly grounded in the Old Testament!

The Greek New Testament uses the word holiness (*hagios*) several hundred times as well. In Romans 12:1, the apostle Paul appeals to believers that they present themselves holy to God. Then in 2 Corinthians 7:1, Paul calls on believers to cleanse themselves from defilement so that holiness could be brought to completion in their lives.

Scripture and church history show us that not only is God holy, but he calls others to be holy as well.

God Desires to Make You Holy

God's calling of holiness extends from the words of Scripture to our lives today. In Leviticus 20:7-8, God teaches us that one of the primary marks of holiness in our lives is obedience to his Word.

Throughout the Bible, we can see that God desires to make us holy. Ephesians 1:4 says that before the foundation of the world, God chose us to be holy and blameless before him in love. 2 Timothy 1:9 tells us we are set apart for a holy calling.

The moment we surrender our lives to God his holiness is imparted to us. We are holy not of our own doing or clever works. Rather, we are holy because we have the presence of a holy God dwelling inside of us!

The Bible makes it clear. God expects us to be holy. In Leviticus 11:45, Moses pens these words of God, "You shall therefore be holy, for I am holy." In 1 Peter 1:16, the apostle Peter echoes this quote and affirms we are called of God to be holy as he is holy. We are called to be set apart from all that would defile and distract us.

This begs the question, how can we become holy? As Old Testament scholar Allan Brown notes, "*The only way we can be holy is to be connected to the source of holiness*" – God. This is important to remember! While God's holiness is *independent* and he needs no other, our holiness is completely *dependent* on our connection with him. God's holiness is completely infinite while ours is finite and limited.

Do not ever become arrogant for one moment. Remember that all of your holiness only comes from having the presence of a holy God infilling your life! Author A.W. Tozer said, "Holiness, as taught in the Scriptures, is not based upon knowledge on our part. Rather, it is based upon the resurrected Christ indwelling us and changing us into His likeness." His desire is to make us holy. But in order to receive his holiness into our lives we must accept his gracious offer to be in union with him.

Rest assured, if God commands you to be holy, he will give you the grace and power to accomplish what he has asked. World famous evangelist Billy Graham stated, "The will of God will never take us where the grace of God cannot sustain us." *God never calls us to live what he will not empower us to become!*

When we are connected to the source of holiness, God's Holy Spirit lives inside of us. Just as God is set apart from all that is common and ordinary, so his people are called to be set apart from anything that would defile them.

The Goal of Holiness Is Becoming Like Jesus

To be holy is to live and act like Jesus. The moment we surrender our lives to Christ, we are asking his holy presence to come and indwell us.

This journey to become like Jesus is indeed a journey. Philippians 1:6-11 talks about the ongoing work God does in our lives to conform us to his Son's image. Holiness does not mean there is no room for change. Jesus was holy and yet he grew in stature and favor with God while he was on earth (Luke 2:52).

The goal of holiness is to become like Jesus Christ. Our consuming passion is to walk in all of the spiritual light God gives to us (1 John 1:7). We are willing and eager to remove anything from our lives that would hinder this pursuit. When God shines his searchlight on our soul and reveals a dark area we need to improve or change, our desire is to readily obey him.

This entire life is a process of conforming our lives to the holy image of Jesus Christ. 1 John 3:2 gives us the awesome hope that one day we will see the one to whose image we are being conformed. I look forward to that day – big time!

A Thought from My Heart

Out of all of the chapters I have written in this book, this is the one I approached with the greatest deal of fear and trepidation. I grow concerned sometimes in our modern Christian world that we have lost much of the awe of God's holiness. We have bought into the lie that daily habitual sin is the norm for believers. Consequently, we think that strongholds of sinful habits in our lives are acceptable.

We have bought into the lie that says believers are not intended to really be holy. Sure, holiness is a great goal to shoot for, but it is realistically unattainable. Sadly, I believe this says something about our perception of God's power. I believe by denying God's ability to empower people to be holy, we actually attack his sovereignty. We settle for a big view of sin but a small view of God.

Everything in my heart and everything I know from Scripture cries out against this thinking! God did not create us to be filled with 60% of him and 40% of self. He calls us to surrender our whole beings to him. He wants to fill us entirely with his holy presence.

Yes, I am reminded daily of my complete and total inability without God. My heart resonates with the prophet Isaiah when he entered the presence of God and remarked, "Woe is me! For I am lost; for I am a man of unclean lips (Isa. 6:5)." I am nothing without God! That being said, I take great hope that the same God who enables others to be holy and calls me to be holy will be faithful.

In the following chapter, I am going to lay out the steps to holiness. However, before reading these steps, it is critical to do an internal survey. Ask yourself, "Do I have a desire to be holy like Jesus?" It sounds like a softball answer. Of course I want to be like Jesus! But let's think about it. To make a commitment to be like Jesus means you live your life as he did. You give when you feel you can give no longer. You weep over what breaks the heart of God. You offer grace and forgiveness to those who offer you none in return.

Holiness is the essence of who God is; it is the model for what we are meant to be, and it is the paradigm in which the church of Jesus Christ is expected to live. With God's help, and only through his strength, you can have the heart of Jesus when he said in John 5:30, "I seek not my own will but the will of him who sent me."

Holiness is serious business. In fact, Hebrews 12:14 tells us that without holiness, no man will ever see the Lord. Holiness is anything but a drab and dull doctrine. It is not a list of rules to be painfully obeyed. C.S. Lewis once stated, "How little people know who think that holiness is dull. When one meets the real thing, it is irresistible! If even 10 percent of the world's population had it, would not the whole world be converted and happy before a year's end?" He is absolutely correct.

The degree to which you will be holy is the degree to which you are set apart to God as his possession. You are called to be holy as God is holy. How will you respond to this incredible invitation?

Action Points

1. How has your understanding of holiness changed as you read this chapter?
2. Do you believe you can be holy?
3. How does holiness cause you to better glorify and enjoy God?

——— Day 12 ———
Sanctification Becomes Our Refiner

"Sanctification is the process whereby the Spirit of God takes the Word of God and changes us to become like the Son of God."

God's refinement process for making us holy is sanctification. To be sanctified is to be made holy. They are intricately connected.

It has been said, "Sanctification is the process whereby the Spirit of God takes the Word of God and changes us to become like the Son of God." The *Merriam Webster Dictionary* defines sanctification as "The act of God's grace by which the affections of men are purified, or alienated from sin and the world, and exalted to a supreme love to God."

Sanctification begins day one of our salvation experience. From the moment we ask Jesus Christ to come into our lives, he comes inside and begins a process of conforming us to his image.

The key word in that last sentence is process. There are no microwaveable Christians. *Sanctification does not mean an end to growth. It is actually a commitment to growth.* As my friend Darnell Wilson puts it, "Sanctification means you have stopped seeing Christ as a ticket and have started seeing him as a treasure."

God wants to do an incredible work in your life! Biblical commentator Adam Clarke says, "Many talk much, and indeed well, of what Christ has done for us: but how little is spoken of what he is to do in us! and yet all that he has done for us is in reference to what he is to do in us."

Sanctification Is Refinement

The sanctification process can be compared to refinement. The purpose of refining a metal is so that we can separate what is bad from what is good. Likewise, sanctification refines those areas of our lives that are fleshly and self-focused.

Because we are born with a desire to sin, we naturally accumulate sinful habits of pride and selfishness. These are reinforced in our lives the longer we fail to deal with them.

The good news is that there is no junk in our lives that is too big for God to deal with! He wants to purify our hearts and set us free from anything that would hinder us from becoming like Christ. He wants to sanctify us.

Growth Phases of Sanctification

Just as refining a metal takes a series of steps, so refining a person takes a series of steps as well. Through the refinement process of sanctification God the Father, God the Son, and God the Holy Spirit work to make us holy.

When you read the Bible, you will notice there are differing phases of sanctification. As believers grow and mature, they are called to a new level of surrender and conformity to Jesus Christ.

Sanctification should be a natural on-going process in the life of a believer. The more we want to glorify and enjoy God out of a heart of love, the more we will want to be sanctified holy and transformed into the image of Christ.

Initial Sanctification

When we first give our lives to Jesus, God completes in our lives an initial level of sanctification. We are passed from death to life. We are sanctified to God as his possession.

1 Corinthians 1:2 and 6:11 both point to the fact that new believers in Jesus Christ are sanctified holy. Acts 26:18 says we are sanctified when we place our faith in Jesus Christ. Hebrews 10:10 reinforces this reality. Salvation and initial sanctification happen simultaneously. The moment we give our lives to Jesus Christ, Scripture refers to us as "saints." A saint is someone who is set apart holy to God for his purpose. To be a saint is to be a disciple of Jesus Christ.

When you openly give your heart to Jesus Christ with no reserves, you are asking him to sanctify you holy as he is holy. You are entering into relationship with him where he is the teacher and you are the student. Through giving your heart to God, you are asking him to refine you. You are saying, "Jesus, I have a lot of rough edges in my life, but my heart's desire is to look like you. Please shave off my rough edges and transform my character so that when people see me they see you."

Initial sanctification is the gateway to all future sanctification.

Total Sanctification

Subsequent to the initial sanctification that takes place at our moment of salvation, there is additional work God wants to do. This involves completely dying out to self and allowing our lives to be more greatly purified and empowered to love God and others as never before.

The Bible uses different terms for this, but the idea is still the same. 1 Thessalonians 5:22 labels it as complete or entire sanctification. Ephesians 5:18-21 calls it being filled with the Spirit. Romans 12:1-2 refers to it as presenting our bodies as a living sacrifice to God. In each of these examples, the apostle Paul is addressing believers who were already initially sanctified. Still, something was missing in their lives. God wanted them to go deeper in their level of surrender and commitment.

To be filled with God's Spirit and sanctified entirely does not mean you become perfect. It does not lift you above the possibility and temptation to sin. It does not suddenly move you from being a second class to a first class Christian. Rather, it is just another simple yet bold step of obedience to become more holy like Jesus Christ.

Through being filled with God's Spirit, we give more control to God, receive greater victory over willful sin, become more purified in motives and intentions, and gain a fresh new power to minister to others. For believers, this happens in many different ways. For some it comes naturally and close to their initial sanctification experience. Others need more time to allow God to speak to them about areas that need to be totally surrendered. The point of total sanctification is not how it happens. The point is getting to a place where everything is on the table before Jesus Christ. Whatever he says, we will obey! Hey, this might be new to you. If it is, hang on till day 17 when we look deeper into what the Bible says about this.

Initial sanctification is a *denial* of self, total sanctification is a *death* to self. It is not just giving God access to your life, it is giving him entry to any area of your life he chooses to enter.

Final Sanctification

Ultimately, we will never be completely conformed in word and deed to the image of Christ in this life. We will always have personality flaws, odd idiosyncrasies, and possibly unrecognized sinful areas that will only be ironed out in the life to come when Christ returns for those who serve him.

However, 1 John 3:2 tells us we will one day be like Christ for we shall see him as he really is. When we see Jesus Christ in all of his beauty and splendor, life will take on meaning as never before. The attractions of this sinful world will fade completely.

This reality caused songwriter Helen Lemmel to pen these famous words: "Turn your eyes upon Jesus, look full in His wonderful face. And the things of earth will grow strangely dim in the light of His glory and grace."

I don't know about you, but I look forward to this day with great anticipation!

Sanctification Always Involves Progression

Ultimately, sanctification always calls for progression. Because it is a purifier of our holy character and expressions of love to others, sanctification naturally calls for growth. Just as our love for God and others should always be increasing, so should our refinement of this love increase at a similar pace.

God uses this process to get to the heart of our issues. Sanctification gets to the heart of our addiction to a habit we have never broken. It confronts a man or woman who struggles with anger and resentment. It battles against strongholds we have allowed Satan to establish in our lives. It transforms a timid believer into one who boldly stands with Christ.

All three of these sanctification phases naturally build upon one another. Each step of the way, our God helps us to become more holy like him. It is a continual quest to become more like Christ. And along each step of the way, God is progressively drawing us to himself.

God Wants to Sanctify You!

The moment we begin our journey of sanctification, we hold our lives up to the standard God set in his Word. We allow God's Holy Spirit the freedom to convict us of areas in our lives that are wrong.

As author and pastor Mark Batterson writes, "It is much easier to act like a Christian than to react like one." We all know how to play the part. But personal sanctification helps us react in ways we never would have done on our own.

Sanctification is like hot water that is poured over a tea bag. The hot water does not make the tea. Rather, it reveals the contents of what the tea bag holds inside. When God begins to refine us through sanctification, hot water is applied to our life. He begins to reveal to us thoughts and actions that are not Christlike. This is where you and I are faced with a choice. We can resent this pressure and draw back, or we can allow God to refine us and go to new heights spiritually.

For me, becoming sanctified wholly meant I had to give up a serious anger problem. It meant I had to give up my self-rights. Gradually, as I have grown in my relationship with Jesus, God has progressively sanctified me in fresh new areas. Some of these have included my desire for personal fame, needing to be accepted by others, and feelings of worry about the future.

For you, it might be different. Maybe you are afraid to witness to others. You justify your fear with "not wanting to be pushy," but really you are not surrendered to God's Holy Spirit. Perhaps you have feelings of bitterness over a situation that has gone south, and you refuse to forgive. Or, there are areas of your life where you still want to remain in control. You want the benefits of serving God, but you do not want the responsibility that comes with these benefits.

I do not know what your situation is. However, I can promise you, based on the authority of God's Word, that personal growth in sanctification and holiness will radically change your life in ways you cannot begin to imagine. Oh, the pains of life might still remain or even grow worse. But your responses will become more and more like the perfect example of holiness – Jesus Christ!

Action Points

1. How has your understanding of sanctification deepened from reading this section?
2. What are a few key ways God has had to refine you since you became a disciple of Jesus?
3. In what way do you feel sanctification causes us to better glorify and enjoy God?

Day 13
Fruit Is Our Litmus Test

To bear fruit is to display the character of Jesus in our
lives in such a way that ourselves and others
see noticeable growth and change.

Followers of Jesus demonstrate one type of fruit while followers of Satan produce another type of fruit. The fruit we display is the litmus test that gauges our level of surrender to Jesus Christ.

Glorifying God Yields Fruit

Fruit is an outward representation of the true contents contained in the vine. Godly fruit is an open display of the character, actions, and attitude of our one true vine – Jesus Christ. *To bear fruit is to display the character of Jesus in our lives in such a way that ourselves and others see noticeable growth and change.*

John 15:16 says God chose us so that we would bear fruit. The moment we come alive in Christ and start bearing the fruits of the Spirit, we become different. Matthew 3:8-10 shows us that bearing fruit must follow our repentance of sin. There is a natural connection. When you bear fruit, you do not stay the same. You go through a ripening process and become sweeter for others to taste!

Jesus had a lot to say about sweet fruit. In Matthew 7:18-19, he points out that healthy trees naturally bear fruit, and every tree that does not bear fruit will be thrown into the fire. That's a strong statement! He also taught us that trees are known by their fruit (Matt. 12:33). If you have a corrupt tree and a corrupt life, you will produce corrupt fruit. But if you have a tree that has Christ as your root, you will produce sweet fruit.

A life that glorifies God will bear fruit. There are no ifs, ands, or buts about it. Jesus said in John 15:8, "By this my Father is glorified, that you bear much fruit and so prove to be my disciples." You cannot claim to be Jesus' disciple on one hand while displaying the works of the devil on the other.

Fruit Always Grows

Jesus taught us in Matthew 13:23 that we all bear fruit in varied amounts. *The quantity of fruit you bear is not as important as the quality.* Romans 7:4 tells us we must die to our old law in order to bear fruit. Until you allow God to put to death the wicked fruit in your life, you will never bear the fruit of righteousness.

If you eat any fruit at all, you can observe quickly what fruit does when it is not connected to the vine. If fruit is not growing, it soon becomes rotten and of little use. Similarly, if we try to produce fruit without being connected to Jesus, we will decay spiritually and grow ugly.

Jesus says strongly in John 15 that bearing fruit requires us to abide in him. To abide in Christ means we continue to grow and produce his actions that are in harmony with his holy character. Jesus goes as far as to say that those who do not bear fruit will be pruned away. Abiding in Christ is an ongoing process. It is not a one-time experience where we "get a little bit of Jesus in our lives."

The apostle Paul showed bearing fruit comes naturally from increasing our knowledge of God (Col. 1:10). As our knowledge of him, and application of this knowledge increases, so does our fruit.

James 3:17 says when we seek God, the wisdom he offers is full of good fruits. God cares that we bear fruit. If we do not grow our fruit, we may have it taken away from us. We should take to heart the lesson given to the Jewish nation. Jesus said that the Kingdom of God was taken away from them because of their failure to produce fruit (Mat. 21:43).

There is no Miracle Growth with fruit. Jesus said we are to bear fruit with patience (Luke 8:15). This means we do not get ahead of God. Many times, we like to believe we can outgrow God. We say, "Okay God, I've learned this lesson already. Can't you give me something else?!" But God's timing is always best, and he knows precisely how long we need in whatever situation we are going through – even if it seems unbearable at the time.

Healthy fruit always grows.

Fruit Comes in Different Forms

Fruit looks different with different people. Galatians 5:22-23 says this, "But the fruit of the Spirit is love, joy, peace, patience, kindness, goodness, faithfulness, gentleness, self-control; against such things there is no law."

This is what fruit looks like. If you are a new believer, maybe fruit is displayed through having greater patience with your spouse. Perhaps it is shown through apologizing to a coworker when you would have normally run them over with your words. Or, it could be breaking free of an addiction that has held you in chains for many years. Fruit is displayed differently, but it is unquestionably recognizable. We notice it, and others notice it around us. No good tree bears bad fruit, and no bad tree produces good fruit (Luke 6:43).

Fruit always comes through walking in all of the light God gives us. By light, I mean that which God reveals to us and that which we have the ability to obey. Ephesians 5:8-9 tells us that because we are now children of light, we are supposed to bear the fruit of light which is good, right, and true.

While good fruit comes in different forms, it is always recognizable (Matt. 7:16). *If you profess to have Christ in your life but do not display his lifestyle and behavior, your fruits betray you.*

Great Fruit Comes from Heavy Pruning

When we give our hearts to Jesus Christ, we die to our old selves. This is the start of our sanctification and pruning process. For a farmer, pruning is essential to the growth of fruit. A branch not trimmed correctly will not produce the maximum amount of fruit.

In our lives, Jesus likens us to the branches of a vine. He says that every branch in him not bearing fruit will be pruned, so that it can bear more fruit (John 15:2). This pruning process can often be painful. It involves God trimming the very core of who we are and cutting away those things that are detestable to him. It may be that God prunes us through taking away some of our security. Maybe you rely too heavily on your job, so God allows it to be taken away from you.

I believe God's primary way of pruning our lives is through bringing us into contact with other people. He uses them to speak to us, work on us, and shape us. Pruning is not fun, but it is very rewarding! Accepting the pruning process requires discipline. But discipline, while often painful, always yields fruit (Heb. 12:11).

Jesus' death on the cross appeared to be the crushing end of many people's hopes and dreams. Yet in John 12:24, Jesus said these profound words, "Unless a grain of wheat falls into the earth and dies, it remains alone; but if it dies, it bears much fruit." This was to say that his death was necessary so that many lives could be touched. Through his death, life came to our human race.

Ultimately, our lives are pruned of sin and deadness so that they can be filled with the fruit of righteousness (Phil. 1:11). We are pruned so that we can better display God's character to those around us through our lives.

Fruit Is for Our Benefit

The more we give to others, the more fruit we reap for eternity (Phil. 4:17). I honestly believe that no human being has ever really had to sacrifice in the truest sense of the word, because sacrifice means we have given something up. But in reality, the more we give the more we receive. God always gives us more than we can ever give to others!

Bearing good fruit does a profound work inside of us. Romans 6:22 says fruit leads to our sanctification and eternal life. Gaining fruit and our sanctification process fit hand and glove. *Just as sanctification produces greater fruit, so the fruit we gain increases our level of sanctification.*

You will never really enjoy life until you are bearing the fruit of the one who gave you life in the first place. Everyone bears fruit. What type of fruit are you bearing?

Action Points

1. What good fruits are evident in your life today?
2. Has God ever had to prune you? How has that time made you stronger as his servant?
3. Why is bearing fruit so important to glorifying and enjoying God?

— Day 14 —
Praise-Filled Satisfaction Is the Result

"God is most glorified in us when we are most satisfied in him."
—John Piper

When we glorify and enjoy God to the fullest, we experience lasting satisfaction and peace. When our supreme desire is to delight ourselves in God, he gives us the desires of our heart.

We can have a peace that no matter what the situation, we know God is sovereignly in control!

To be satisfied only comes through giving glory to God, displaying a heart of love, having a character of holiness, and bearing the fruit of the Spirit. Anything short of this is a facade.

True Satisfaction Always...

...Starts with God – When we look back from where God has brought us, we can have satisfaction in the present and hope for the future. The Psalmist cried out in Psalm 16:11, "In your presence there is fullness of joy." We serve a God who is always good, wise, faithful and sovereign. He is always faithful and never makes a mistake.

...Grows Continually – Temporary satisfactions always become stagnant. This is why a person whose heart is set on the flesh becomes easily dissatisfied. Their marriage partner becomes boring to them, so they move on to someone else. They lose fulfillment doing the same routine job, so they quit with no way to support their family.

Satisfaction with God is a different story. It must always grow. 2 Peter 3:18 calls us to grow in the grace and knowledge of Jesus Christ. Each day is a new adventure, and as we grow spiritually, the waters of our hearts are turned and our satisfaction keeps from becoming stagnated. We can never learn enough about God. There is always a deeper level of satisfaction to attain!

...Rests comfortably through uncertainty – The greatest test of our satisfaction in Christ is when really good times or really bad times come our way. In the really good times, it is easy to become satisfied in God's provision instead of God himself. In hard times, it is easier for us to respond in our own strength rather than falling to our knees and receiving Christ's strength.

When we are satisfied in Christ, we are able to face the fiercest storms and remain calm. The great problem with many Christians is that they do not rest completely in Jesus, so when hard times come, they resort to figuring life out through their own means.

Satisfied followers of Christ will thrive through any situation. Their view of God is not determined by circumstances.

True Satisfaction Is Never Anxious About ...

...What we shall eat or drink (Matt. 6:25) – When we serve him, God will always provide us with the proper amount of food and drink that we need to accomplish his will.

...What we shall wear (Matt. 6:31) – Many of us are so incredibly blessed in this area. I look in my closet, my dresser, and shoe rack and realize I have so much more than I need.

...What we shall say (Mark 13:11) – Disciples of Christ do not constantly obsess about getting the right words into a conversation. Yes we use tact. Still, we must remember it is not our words but God's Spirit that produces a life change in a person's heart.

...What will happen tomorrow (Matt. 6:34) – It's easy to be so future-focused that we lose our present value. But if you want to be holy like Jesus, this has to change. You do not need to worry about what will happen tomorrow, for God already knows.

...Anything! (Phil. 4:6) – The bottom line is we are not to be anxious about anything. Our satisfaction in God should be so high that life's circumstances cannot knock us spiritually. Problems may arise, but our satisfaction in God should be so high that we refuse to cave in to temptation.

True Satisfaction Always Ends in Praise

C.S. Lewis stated, "I think we delight to praise what we enjoy because praise not only expresses but completes the enjoyment."

Think about this for a minute. What do you do when you eat a food or watch a movie you enjoy? What is your natural reaction? Don't you naturally just want to tell someone else about it? I know when I've experienced something good, I automatically tell my wife. (Fortunately for her, she *gets the privilege* of hearing a lot about hockey!) It is a natural expression of satisfaction.

So here is a question for you: Do you naturally express praise to God for what he has done in your life? Do you speak highly of him to others? When was the last time you talked about him to your family or friends? Your answers to these questions reveal something about you.

How you praise God reflects your level of satisfaction in him.

Do You Have True Satisfaction?

I want you to meditate on these thought-provoking words from a 1733 sermon by Jonathan Edwards. He said:

> God is the highest good of the reasonable creature, and the enjoyment of him is the only happiness with which our souls can be satisfied. To go to heaven fully to enjoy God, is infinitely better than the most pleasant accommodations here. Fathers and mothers, husbands, wives, children, or the company of earthly friends, are but shadows. But the enjoyment of God is the

substance. These are but scattered beams, but God is the sun. These are but streams, but God is the fountain. These are but drops, but God is the ocean."

I fear too many times we are satisfied with that which is trivial. We are constantly looking for temporary forms of satisfaction. We watch endless TV programs, engage in mindless entertainment, and spend hours of our time feasting upon things that bring no eternal satisfaction.

In his book *A Hunger for God*, John Piper says, "If you don't feel strong desires for the manifestation of the glory of God, it is not because you have drunk deeply and are satisfied. It is because you have nibbled so long at the table of the world. Your soul is stuffed with small things, and there is no room for the great." Wow! That is a convicting and powerful thought.

Satan wants us to settle for temporary forms of satisfaction. But the God we serve has something very different in mind. He wants us to find our total enjoyment in him. When we do this, we experience lasting satisfaction in this life and anticipation for the life to come. This is a good place to be.

If you want to enjoy God to the fullest, you must come to the place where you find all of your satisfaction in him.

Action Points

1. In light of what you have read, would you describe yourself as restless or satisfied in God?
2. Why does praise bring us satisfaction?
3. How does praise naturally complete the process of glorifying and enjoying God?

Week 3

I Serve Someone Who Wants to Give Me Total Freedom

Day 15
God's Ultimate Rival Is Sin

*"A man by his sin may waste himself, which is to waste that
which on earth is most like God. This is man's greatest
tragedy and God's heaviest grief."*
—A.W. Tozer

God created you to glorify and enjoy him forever. *The easiest
way to break your satisfying relationship with God is to sin.* Sin is the
antithesis of all that God is. It is so disgusting in the eyes of God that
he cannot be tempted by it (James 1:13). To him, sin is repulsive
and the furthest step from enjoyment.

*When we sin, it is a stab to the very heart of God, and the number one
way we create barriers in our relationship with him.* It says to God that we
view our relationship with him as second place. The great writer
A.W. Tozer said, "A man by his sin may waste himself, which is to
waste that which on earth is most like God. This is man's greatest
tragedy and God's heaviest grief." There is no such thing as "private
sin." Every sin we commit is an attack against our maker.

What Is Sin?

There are two chief ways to define sin, one from a broad
perspective and the other from a more narrow perspective.

Broad Definition – In its broadest sense, to sin is to "miss the
mark." Picture an archery range. Just as a shooter can miss his or
her target, so sin in a person's life is missing God's intended goal. It
is any violation of any law put forth by God (1 John 3:4). This
includes both what we know and what we do not know.

Narrow Definition – From a narrower point of view, to sin is to
intentionally violate the known will of God for our lives. We know

what God has said about this act or decision, and we still choose to go against what he has commanded.

We know that all sin is horrible in God's eyes. But the sin God chooses to hold us accountable for is that which we have done in willful rebellion against him. In day 16 we will discuss this more in detail, but this gives us a good starting point.

Who Has Sinned?

Everyone has sinned and fallen short of the glory of God (Rom. 3:23). You were born with a desire to commit sin. There are no exceptions to this rule. You did not somehow get the "good" gene and rise above the capacity to sin.

Before you will ever develop a hatred against sin, you must first grasp the depth of your own sin. It was your sin and my sin that put Jesus on the cross (1 Pet. 2:24). Looking at the span of history as a whole, Jesus Christ came down to earth because we needed a Savior. Because of our sin, we deserve death (Rom. 6:23). Anything less than this is a tremendous gift from God.

Where Did Sin Originate?

Sin originated with Satan and came into this world as a result of one man's choice. Romans 5:12 says sin and death entered into the world because of Adam, the first man ever created. Adam's wife Eve was the one who was tempted directly by Satan and was deceived. But it was Adam who knowingly sinned against God and brought a curse upon the human race (1 Tim. 2:14). Through his decision, the human race was brought under the curse of sin.

As a result of this fall, Psalm 51:5 tells us that sin, or inherited depravity, is passed on to every person at the moment of conception. We are born into sin. From the very minute we are born, there is a part of our nature that wants to go our own way and do our own thing (Isa. 53:6). This does not mean we are held guilty and responsible for the individual sin that Adam committed (Ezek. 18:20), but the results of his sin have a marring effect upon our lives.

The apostle Paul describes our spiritual condition without God as being someone who is dead (Eph. 2:1-3). Apart from God's marvelous grace, your natural default mode will always be to sin and to serve Satan, the father of sin.

What Does Sin Do?

Sin is serious because it separates us from God. It is a roadblock to being holy. It makes it impossible to fully love God and love others, and it brings shame rather than glory to the name of God. Romans 6:16 teaches we are either a slave to righteousness which leads to life or a slave to sin which leads to death. Sin always leads to spiritual death (James 1:15).

To willfully sin against God is to place yourself in opposition against him. It is the highest form of pride imaginable. Scripture says God opposes those who are proud (James 4:6). He rages in battle against those who contest his reign. God has no room in his kingdom for those who are rivals against him and servants of sin.

Sin always separates us from God.

How Much Do You Hate Sin?

There is no love for God without a profound hatred for evil. The more I talk with people who are broken, and the more I hear the horrible impact sin has upon their lives, the more I hate it. I absolutely detest it with everything in me. I hate how sin destroys marriages. I hate how sin wastes time in people's lives as it deceives them for years on end. I hate sin when I see the minds it corrupts and think of the billions of people it has sent to hell.

WHAT KIND OF GOD DO I SERVE?

Often, I've found Christians are quick to talk about their love for God, but they are slow to talk about their hatred for evil. But I have found the Christians I love and respect the most are those who have learned to hate evil. Psalm 97:10 throws this challenge to us, "O you who love the Lord, hate evil!"

The test of your hatred for sin is your readiness to exterminate it from your life. Do you really hate sin? Do you hate it enough that you will clear out those gray areas of your life? Areas that only God knows about?

Imagine your child walking into your house one day. As they come to give you a hug, you see something in their hair ... a louse! What would you do? Would you smile and not say a word? My guess is you would not. You would not reason, "Oh that's just a part of who they are!" You would not say, "Well, no one but me will ever know!" You would go into action mode. Your kid's hair would be washed and a thorough examination of your house would be in order. Why? Because you realize this problem cannot afford to be ignored without significant repercussions.

I am challenging you to take this same type of action in your soul. Hate sin with everything in you! My plea to you today is to let your love for God be the intense motivator to rid your life of any willful sin against God. Ask him to reveal to you new areas that you need to surrender to him. And through his power and strength, he WILL give you the power to live above habitual, willful sin!

Action Points

1. Describe the change in your life now that you are a servant of God and not a slave to sin.
2. How does having an intense hatred of sin lead towards having a greater love for God?
3. Is there any sin in your life that you find more appealing than your love for God? If so, make a decision today to deal with it.

Day 16

Sin Leads Us Down a Path

"We have been playing with our definition of sin to excuse people who can't seem to get out of it."
—Jim Plank

As we stated in the last chapter, sin comes in two different forms. There are both willful and unintentional sins. In the Old Testament, the sacrificial system was different for each of these two types of sin. For example, Leviticus 6:2-5 gives us an illustration of willful sin while Numbers 15:27-31 gives us a case of unintentional sin.

All sin required a sacrifice. But the only way there could be a sacrifice for sin was for the guilty party to admit their wrong. There had to be genuine repentance. There was and is no form of sacrifice for ongoing deliberate sin against God.

In one sense, all sin is equal in that it always mars our relationship with God. But in terms of consequence, there are levels of severity to which sin is punished. For instance, the sin of murder has higher ramifications than does the sin of gluttony. You will probably not spend the rest of your life in prison for eating too many candy bars!

Four Stages of Sin

All sin, great and small, is like a cancer that spreads throughout our bodies. Just as cancer has varying stages of severity, so sin has differing stages as well.

Stage 4 – Sins of High-Handedness

The maximum form of sin against God is what the Bible terms a high-handed sin. Sins of high-handedness are not only willful

WHAT KIND OF GOD DO I SERVE?

sins. They are willful sins directly committed with the intention of blaspheming God. The number one goal in committing this sin is to bring God pain and diminish his glory.

In Numbers 15:30, God told the Israelites that a person who sins high-handedly reviles the Lord. All who did so were to be cut off from God's people. Their sin was so poisonous and toxic that God did not even want them being around his children.

If you are deliberately committing sins of high-handedness against God, every second that you remain alive is a miraculous gift.

Stage 3 – Sins of Passion

Just below sins of high-handedness are sins of passion. These are sins that after we know what is right, we still willfully choose to do what is wrong.

Our enjoyment of the flesh is so great that it exceeds our enjoyment of God. It is extremely important for us to confront sins of passion. *Sins of passion which we refuse to confront will often become our besetting sin.* Refusing to confront sins of passion leaves the gate wide open for Satan to control our lives. He deceives us into believing our sins are normal, and this is how it will always be. We will *never* be able to get victory, so we might as well just accept that "We are not perfect, just forgiven."

In the Bible, King David showed that the remedy for willfully sinning against God is to earnestly seek his mercy. Directly after committing a sin of murder and adultery, he offered these simple and humbling words in Psalm 51:1, "Have mercy on me, O God, according to your steadfast love; according to your abundant mercy blot out my transgressions."

If you desire to be free from sins of passion, you must get radical in asking God to cleanse you and believe he will give you the strength to overcome any temptation.

Paul even goes so far as to say that violating our conscience is a sin against God (Rom. 14:23).

Stage 2 – Sins of Omission

Sin is not necessarily a willful act. Sometimes, it is willful inaction. James 4:17 says that he who knows what to do and does not do it, for them it is sin.

Sometimes people like to think, "Hey, if God only holds me accountable for what I know, why should I choose to learn more of his will? I might as well be ignorant, so I can continue to sin as much as I want!" But this type of thinking reveals their true inner corruption. They do not truly love God and seek their enjoyment from him. They still have the misconception that sin is more satisfying than God. So in this sense, their sin is not ignorant. It is willful.

While sins of omission appear passive in nature, they are aggressive in behavior.

Stage 1 – Sins of Ignorance

Sometimes, sin is committed unknowingly. Numbers 15:27-31 teaches us there are sins a believer can commit that are unknown to them but are short of the perfect will of God.

I John 1:7 assures us that if we are walking in all the light, we are cleansed from sins of ignorance. We do not have to walk around in fear, dreading that we might have unknowingly sinned against God in some way. This should give us great peace and comfort in light of eternity.

However, while sins of ignorance may be covered in Christ's atoning work, their results can cause major devastation in our lives. Sin, known or unknown, always brings pain and suffering.

The greatest way to discovering what may be sins of ignorance in your life is to be sensitive to hear God's Holy Spirit in the small things. When he speaks to us about apologizing, we obey immediately without debate. When we are uncertain about pursuing a questionable opportunity in our life, we do not "try it till we get burned." We stop and wait for God. The quicker we respond to God's voice, the faster he reveals sins of ignorance in our life.

The second way we identify sins of ignorance in our lives is by asking other honest believers if there are areas in our lives that we need to improve. Find someone whom you have allowed to speak boldly to you and is in a place to confront you over your attitudes and actions.

One of the great problems with sins of ignorance is they can lead to problems for future generations. Big sins are easier to identify. But little borderline sins such as gossip and personal slander are tougher. We excuse our actions as "having a good time." Eventually, if we continue down this path, our careless attitudes will lead to great problems, and we are left to question why our children grow up to resent our faith.

Three Steps to Sin

Sin is inevitably a part of our world. The question is not if we will encounter sin. The question is how we will respond. James 1:14-15 gives us a threefold process of temptation that we all encounter. It says, "But each person is tempted when he is lured and enticed by his own desire. Then desire when it has conceived gives birth to sin, and sin when it is fully grown brings forth death."

Step 1 – Desire

First, there is a desire. *Having a desire to sin is not sin.* Acting upon that desire is. Every sinful action starts with meditating on a desire. A thief walks into a store because he has meditated on a desire to take what is not rightfully his. A husband walks into a strip club because he lost fulfillment in his marriage and began desiring something else.

The greatest way to resist these desires is to call on God and refuse yourself the permission to meditate on them. As the old saying goes, "We can't help the birds that fly in the air, but we can keep them from building a nest in our hair." Temptations fly over our heads all the time. It is our responsibly to ensure they do not enter in and corrupt our souls.

Every evil desire presented to you by Satan gives you an awesome opportunity to declare your loyalty and allegiance to Jesus Christ. Through making a choice to focus your mind on those things that are pure, you will be able to control your desires.

Step 2 – Decision

It is hard to define, but there is a moment when our desire to sin transitions over into mental assent. We go from saying, "This is wrong," to saying, "Well maybe it isn't that bad."

I remember the story of a certain young married preacher who was on the road and was spending the night at a family's home. The grind of trying to minister was taking its toll on his life. It just so happened that at this home there was an attractive young woman who was very sensual in her behavior. After everyone else in the house went to bed, this preacher turned on the study light in his room to make some last minute preparations to his upcoming messages.

Several minutes later, there came a knock on his door. It was this woman. Dressed inappropriately, she asked him if she could come in to receive some "counsel." His defenses came up immediately, and he rejected her offer, trying to go back to his studies. A few minutes later, he heard another knock, and she again tried to seduce him, but he refused and stopped answering the door. She returned a couple more times. However, with each instance he felt his resistance level dwindling. Finally, he made up his mind that the next time she knocked on his door, he would let her in – but fortunately for him, that final knock never came.

Question: Did this man sin? In one sense, he did not commit a blatant wickedness that anyone else could see. He had been faithful to resist. But in the eyes of God, he knew and later admitted that while he had not committed adultery in action, he had committed sin in his heart. The moment he said in his heart he would act upon these tempting desires, he opened his heart to Satan's control. His desire had turned into a decision.

Sin against God is a heart condition. Yes, actions mean a lot and bring serious consequences. But while man looks on the outward, God looks on the heart. The moment our hearts have turned to rebellion against God is the moment sin begins to invade and take control of our lives and eventually our actions.

Step 3 – Death

Sin always leads to death. Yes, sin can be pleasurable, and this is an important point to make. You can really, thoroughly enjoy sinning for a period of time! Sin can bring you a lot of fun, and it is for this reason that many choose to continue on in sin. However, as Hebrews 11:25 points out, sin's pleasures are always fleeting. They do not last, and sin always brings death.

Continuing to sin passionately in your life will lead to separation from God. Just as a marriage relationship can be destroyed through evil choices, so our relationship with God can be broken by sin. God always holds up his end of the bargain. He is always faithful. We, on the other hand, have the choice to stay in relationship with him or walk away from our relationship and choose spiritual death.

There Is an Alternative!

God's Word calls us to a different kind of death. It calls us to be dead to sin. Romans 8:13 says that while we will die if we live according to the flesh; if we live according to the Spirit we will live! Galatians 5:19-21 lists the more overt sins of the flesh. Verses 24-25 go on to say that they who are Christ's have crucified the flesh with the affections and lusts. We are to be dead to sin!

If we live by the Spirit, we will continually put to death any deeds of the body that are contrary to the Spirit. Romans 6:2 says that as born again believers we are to be dead to sin. Romans 6:11 says we are to reckon ourselves dead to sin and alive unto God through Jesus Christ our Lord. Romans 6:19 says as servants of Jesus, we must yield all of our members as servants to righteousness unto holiness. Romans 13:14 says make no provision for the flesh to gratify its sinful desires.

The Bible commands us in 2 Timothy 2:22 to flee youthful lusts. This is not impossible! *Everything God calls us to do he will give us the strength to accomplish.* Philippians 4:13 tells us it is possible to be all that God desires of us through his power working in us. This is because we operate through HIS strength and not our own. 1 Corinthians 10:13 encourages us by saying no man experiences temptations that are different from other people. We will not be tempted beyond our ability to resist!

God and Sin Are Incompatible

God does not possess and indwell vessels that are filthy. For instance, the Old Testament speaks of pagan idolatry in the temple of God. As a result, God's presence left the building. God refuses to share the same stage and be rivaled by sin.

1 Corinthians 6:19-20 says that our bodies are temples of the Holy Spirit. God will not indwell a temple that is corrupted with

sin and filth. The only temple he indwells is one that is holy and set apart to him alone.

I fear too often we excuse our sins as "bad habits." As Pastor Jim Plank states, "We have been playing with our definition of sin to excuse people who can't seem to get out of it." Rather than persisting to hit the mark God has set, we move the target to fit our own agenda.

From a biblical perspective, we have a clear decision to make. Either we can accept Jesus' work of transformation into our lives, or we choose to allow the devil to have control. I love these words from biblical scholar Dennis Kinlaw. He says, "When a person loses control of himself and rests totally in the hands of God, he then finds himself."

Jesus says that we cannot serve two masters (Matt. 6:24). We either choose to serve him, the originator of life, or Satan, the originator of death. The choice is up to us!

Action Points

1. Do you understand the difference between unintentional and intentional sin? How would you explain it to someone else?
2. Think about the four levels of sin listed in this chapter. Which one do you believe you struggle with the most?
3. How should the realization that "all sin leads to death" change our tolerance of it in our lives?

Day 17
Freedom Only Comes Through Jesus

"Any battle for victory, power, and deliverance – from ourselves and from sin – which is not based constantly upon the gazing and the beholding of the Lord Jesus, with the heart and life lifted up to Him, is doomed to failure."
—Alan Redpath

God offers no Band-Aid solutions for dealing with sin. He only cares about getting to the heart of a matter. Before we ever had any intention of receiving help for our sin problem, God loved us and had mercy on us (Eph. 2:4-5). He has a plan that has and will deal with the sin nature in your life if you will let him.

I have already shared the basic plan of salvation God offers to everyone. But salvation takes on new meaning and new appreciation when we realize all God has done for us. Without understanding how far Christ came for us, we will never be inclined to draw very close to him!

Because God the Father knew the state of our world, he decided to send his Son Jesus as the Savior. Jesus had this method of salvation planned before the world ever began (Rev. 13:8). There has been and always will be only one plan of salvation.

This plan involved five parts that were centered around the life and ministry of Jesus.

1 – Jesus Descended To Earth

The first part was Jesus Christ, the Creator of the world, descending to earth. Imagine that! *He came down to temporarily dwell among us so that we could go up to live eternally with him!* Yes, this was the will of God the Father, but Jesus agreed willingly and in unity. This was not an "if I have to" decision!

Jesus did not come down to fit our purpose. He came down to give us purpose. The incarnation of Christ was completely necessary. He had to come down and identify with us. For in order for Christ to pay for the sins of man, he had to be both fully God and fully man – the God-man. This meant he emptied himself of his divine privileges and took on the form of a servant (Phil. 2:7). He still remained to be God but set aside those privileges to suffer the pain of humanity.

In John 10:30, Jesus said, "I and My Father are one." He absolutely claimed and demonstrated he was God by his ability to forgive sin, raise the dead, and offer eternal life. At the same time, Scriptures like Matthew 4:2 show that Jesus grew hungry, tired, and thirsty; all characteristics of man.

The reason he needed to function as the God-man was to amend the alienation that had taken place between God and man. Operating fully in each role, he united both sides together so that we have the opportunity to have direct communication with God.

Through coming in the flesh, Jesus offered man the opportunity to be in holy union with God the Father. Our communion with God can be restored! As James Torrance states, "The prime purpose of the incarnation, in the love of God, is to lift us up into a life of communion, of participation in the very triune life of God."

Jesus descended to earth for you.

2 – Jesus Lived a Model Life

We were born with the nature of sin. Jesus was not born with this nature and thus never sinned (1 Pet. 2:22). Throughout his life, Jesus progressed in wisdom and knowledge like any other man (Luke 2:52). His two natures continued to exist distinctly but in harmony with one another.

During his time on earth Jesus embodied what it meant to be holy and to love his Father and others in a perfect way. At times he displayed anger, tears, pain, and joy. But in each of these instances, he beautifully displayed total godly perfection. He came not to be served, but to serve (Matt. 20:28).

As the God-man, he functions and fulfills the Old Testament roles as our prophet, priest, and king. As a prophet, Jesus declares his Father's will to us. As priest, he offered himself as a sacrifice and stands as the mediator between God and us. And as our king, he stands triumphant above all and gives us the assurance he will reign supreme for all ages!

Jesus lived a model life and he calls you and me to follow his example.

3 – Jesus Died on the Cross

Jesus was righteous in every way, and yet he chose to die for the unrighteous. Just think about that for a minute. He could have destroyed this world and built another that robotically loved him. Instead, he gave men and women the choice to reject him and demonstrated the ultimate loving act through his death on the cross. In this death, there are several important notes to remember.

Jesus Died Voluntarily

Jesus' death on the cross was a voluntary act. He could have called ten thousand angels to bring him deliverance, yet he chose the cross (Matt. 26:53). Jesus died because mankind was lost. He died because he had great love and mercy for others. He died because he was the only one who could legitimately accomplish this work. He died because he loved you!

Jesus Died to Break Sin's Power

Jesus died for those who were ungodly (Rom. 5:6-8). This demonstration of inconceivable love was for all people – including you (2 Cor. 5:14)! He died for your transgressions (Isa. 53:5) so that you could have the opportunity to experience eternal life (John 3:16). He took the curse that was upon sinful humanity and placed it upon himself (Gal. 3:13) – thus carrying the greatest burden anyone has chosen to carry. Just think about this.

Picture in your mind the greatest sin you have ever committed. Think how much pain that caused you. Now just think that Jesus Christ carried the weight of that guilt AND the guilt of every person who has lived and ever will live. When I think about this for just a minute, my appreciation for Christ's work on the cross goes through the roof. What incredible love compelled him to go through this so that we could have life!

Christ had to shed his blood. According to God's law, there could be no forgiveness of sins without blood being spilt (Heb. 9:22). The blood that was spilt had to be from a perfect sacrifice. Because humanity is conceived in sin, no mere man or woman could atone for our sin. Only Jesus in his deity could perform what was necessary. Through the precious blood of Jesus, we are redeemed (1 Pet 1:18-19)!

He came with the purpose to wash our sins with his own blood (Rev. 1:5) and to destroy the works of the devil in our lives (1 John 3:8). He came to break us free from the chains and bondage of sin and to break sin's power over us. If this doesn't cause you to rejoice, I don't know what will!

Jesus Died for All

1 Timothy 4:10 helps us understand that Christ's atoning work on the cross was *sufficient* for all humanity, but was *efficient* only for believers. Jesus offers his gift of salvation to all, but he doesn't force anyone to accept his gift. As 1 John 2:2 says, Jesus is the propitiation, or appeasement, for the sins of the *whole* world.

God desires that all men be saved (1 Tim. 2:3-4). He never desires that anyone should perish and spend eternity in hell (2 Pet. 3:9). Titus 2:11 reiterates this point by saying, "For the grace of God has appeared, bringing salvation for all people." Galatians 2:20 shows us that Jesus gave himself personally for you!

4 – Jesus Resurrected from the Dead

The resurrection is the hinge point of our hope. If Christ did not die, and the resurrection never took place, our faith is in vain (1 Cor. 15:14). The resurrection is the foundation for all that Christians believe. And as we have already addressed earlier, the resurrection is historically verifiable.

Jesus did not just come back to life; he was resurrected. There is a difference. Jesus was the first to be resurrected from the dead (1 Cor. 15:20-23). Yes, a man named Lazarus was brought back to life, but he would later die. Jesus Christ arose from the dead in his eternal resurrected body and will never die again (1 Cor. 15:41-44).

After his death, Jesus remained on earth for forty days and showed that he was alive by what Acts 1:3 calls "infallible proofs." It is the hope of the resurrection that empowered the disciples to stand for Christ 2,000 years ago, and it is this same hope that gives hope to believers today!

5 – Jesus Ascended into Glory

After his closing commission, Jesus blessed his disciples and then ascended into Heaven from Bethany (Luke 24:50). Now he sits in a seat of authority at the right hand of God the Father (Mark 16:19).

When Jesus died on the cross, the disciples ran in fear. However, when Jesus ascended into Heaven, the disciples went into action! Jesus pointed out to them that it was to their advantage that he go away so that the comforter could come to them (John 16:7). This was the Holy Spirit. Think about that! Jesus was with them in the flesh and in person, yet he said it would be even better for them when he left!

Jesus' closing words for his disciples before he left were given on a mountain in Galilee where he gave them the Great Commission (Matt. 28:19-20). Here they are: "Go therefore and make disciples of all nations, baptizing them in the name of the Father and of the Son and of the Holy Spirit, teaching them to observe all that I have commanded you. And behold, I am with you always, to the end of the age."

If you really believe Jesus arose from the dead, this passage should cause you to evaluate your priorities every single day. Are you doing what you are doing with the purpose of reaching others, or are you living to gratify your flesh?

Jesus Came to Give You Victory over Sin!

When I think about all Christ has done for me, my motivation and longing to sin suddenly becomes very small. Why on earth would you and I want to do anything to displease the one who has done so much for us?

Everything in me cries, "God, show me any area of my life that is not pleasing in your sight. Reveal to me those deep areas of pride and self-centeredness and remove them from my life!"

Every victory we intend to win is completely contingent on our level of connection with Jesus. British evangelist Alan Redpath rightly stated, "Any battle for victory, power, and deliverance – from ourselves and from sin – which is not based constantly upon the gazing and the beholding of the Lord Jesus, with the heart and life lifted up to Him, is doomed to failure."

God's gift of salvation is not the gift of an object but a person. It is an invitation to a personal relationship with Jesus. John 17:3 says we have spiritual life through having this personal relationship with him. He is God's plan for dealing with sin in our life!

In case you missed it in skimming over this section, Jesus died on the cross to give you victory over sin! He did not die with the intent that you would serve him one day and sin like the devil the next. Through his power, you can see sin's hold broken in your life.

Through the power of Jesus Christ you can experience victory over sin!

How High Is the Level of Your Gratitude to Jesus?

The more I meditate on all Jesus Christ has done for me the more I am just overwhelmed by his great love and compassion. My gratitude goes through the roof!

I believe one of the reasons we begin to grow cold in our service to Jesus is we fail to reflect upon all he has done for us. Before you go about your day, I challenge you to stop and take some time to reflect on the great lengths Jesus took to give you freedom. Think about how we, because of him, can have a relationship with God.

We are free to serve our God because of the incredible sacrifice made by Jesus Christ!

Action Points

1. What aspect of Jesus' life and ministry sticks out to you the most?
2. Think and mediate on the significance of Jesus Christ becoming the "God-man." Why was this necessary?
3. How does the fact that Jesus voluntarily died for us make his death that much more meaningful?

Day 18
The Holy Spirit Wants Full Control

"It is part of our human problem that we would like to be full of the Spirit and yet go on and do as we please!"
—A.W. Tozer

Jesus left so that the comforter could come, but here is a newsflash: *God the Father did not send you the Holy Spirit to be a joint shareowner of your life. He gave him to you so that he could take control.* The Holy Spirit does not come to add a little spice to your heart. He comes to fill it.

Every believer who accepts Christ will come face to face with the Holy Spirit. The moment you surrender your life to Jesus, the Holy Spirit comes in and possesses your heart. When he enters in, he will confront you with some very deep problems in your life. These problems trace their way back six thousand years to the beginning of the human race. The Holy Spirit wants to get to the heart of your depravity.

By nature, you and I are control freaks. We like to think we can run our lives the way we choose. We control our finances; we control our lifestyles, and we control our destinies. *The reason we are control freaks by nature is because we are sinful by nature.*

Psalm 51:5 says you and I were born into sin. Rebellion and selfish control come naturally. It is in our DNA. It was our sin that separated us from God, but it was our sin nature that gave us the bent to sin in the first place. Thankfully, God the Father sent the Holy Spirit to change this. He sent him to take control.

As you go through this reading today, you will notice it includes a slightly longer portion of text. The reason is because this topic is critically important to all believers. It marks the difference between serving "half-heartedly" and serving "all-out" for God. With that being said, let's kick this off by talking about death (happy way to start, I know!).

Control Calls for Absolute Death

We were born INTO sin, but we were not born TO sin. God has no interest in you continually sinning against him! 1 John 3:8 says, "Whoever makes a practice of sinning is of the devil." Willful, habitual sin against God must not be the norm for a believer! And as Richard Foster says, "Will power will never succeed in dealing with the deeply ingrained habits of sin." We need God to do HIS work.

Romans 6 is a classic passage that gives us a picture of the freedom God wants to offer us. In verses 1-2, Paul asks this question: "What shall we say then? Are we to continue in sin that grace may abound?" He then goes on to answer his own question, "By no means! How can we who died to sin still live in it?"

The phrase, "By no means" was the strongest linguistic way possible for Paul to say NO WAY or IMPOSSIBLE! Verse 7 says those who have died to self are set free from sin. Verse 12 says we must not let sin remain in our bodies. And verse 22 tells us to transition from being a slave to sin to being a slave to righteousness.

Colossians 3:1-10 challenges believers to "put to death" earthly wickedness and put on the new self. This is not a self controlled by the flesh but one controlled by the Spirit. It's saying we develop a whole new pattern of practices. Our habitual sins and wicked habits can be broken!

You are NOT intended to sin!

Control Calls for Total Surrender

This quote from author Dennis Kinlaw grabbed my attention when I first read it. He correctly writes, "We have largely preached the gospel of Christ as a way to find freedom from the consequences of our sin, rather than freedom from the sin that causes those consequences." Let that sink in.

We want God to take care of our poor financial status, but we do not want him to deal with our sin of laziness. We want God to restore our relationship with a family member, but we do not want him to deal with our actions that have brought this division. We want God to improve our health as long as we do not need to change our sinful eating habits.

In Romans 12 verses 9 and following, Paul lays out the picture of God's intentions for a Christian. We are called to genuine love that outdoes others in showing honor. We are called to rejoice, live in harmony with others, and bless those who persecute us. We are called to repay evil with good.

Sounds great doesn't it? But how on earth do we live this way? Here is the secret: *The key to being a Romans 12:9-21 Christian is to first become a Romans 12:1-2 Christian.* Let's get the picture. As in 1 Thessalonians, Paul is again speaking to believers. This time he calls on them to present themselves as a living sacrifice. He is asking them to present their spiritual bodies as a burnt offering before God.

The Jewish believers knew exactly what Paul meant. They understood the sacrificial system in the Old Testament. Paul was asking believers to yield themselves wholly to God. By presenting themselves as a burnt offering, nothing was to be left of self!

When you first gave your life to Christ, this was just the beginning. In a moment of time, you passed from death to life. But for most believers, after that commitment, there still remains an unholy selfish mindset. Sinful habits remain that, for one reason or another, just cannot seem to be broken. Ministry to others lacks power and effectiveness. The joy, love, and glory of God we speak so eloquently about does not shine through our lives to others.

The underlying problem goes back to this overarching issue of control. There are a couple areas in life we want to hold back from God. Perhaps it is bitterness over a parent we hate. Maybe God has asked that we terminate a physical relationship we want to continue. Perhaps we feel prompted to step out in faith on a new endeavor but refuse to go because it seems "unreasonable." Maybe we have an introverted personality and feel God might be asking us to witness in a way we feel is impossible.

Every situation is different for every believer. Rest assured though that *the battleground for control of your life always takes place on the side of the largest mountain you refuse to surrender.* You can either let God take control of this mountain or you can persist to hold it back.

Sadly, so often we go on, day after day, pleading with God to speak to our lives while refusing to obey his voice. We begin to realize that every advancement we try to make spiritually is hindered by one or two areas of unsurrender. As a result we grow stagnant, cynical, and excuse our sinful behavior as natural. After all, "It's just the way I am!"

We want the benefits of serving God, but we are not ready to give every part of our lives to him. We want to give him the title to our spiritual home, but we do not want him to search through the closets of our soul.

Giving control of your life to the Holy Spirit requires that you surrender completely to him.

Control Calls for Complete Cleansing

When we surrender, we are then in a right position to ask God to cleanse us. In Psalm 51, King David is in anguish over his sins of adultery and murder. He is thoroughly miserable and he cries out to God in verse 7 saying, "Purge me with hyssop, and I shall be clean; wash me, and I shall be whiter than snow."

Hyssop was a small plant that was used by the Israelites as a means of cleansing. It was this same hyssop the Israelites used when God told them to mark the doorways of their houses when the plague of death was upon the Egyptians (Ex. 12:22).

David goes on in verses 10-11 of Psalm 51 to say, "Create in me a clean heart, O God, and renew a right spirit within me. Cast me not away from your presence, and take not your Holy Spirit from me." David desperately wanted the Holy Spirit's anointing upon his life. But he knew the only way this would happen was if he were cleansed of his iniquity.

In 2 Cor. 6:11-7:1, Christians are told they need to cleanse themselves from all filthiness and bring holiness to completion. This completion does not mean we suddenly become perfect, and there is no room for growth. Rather it means we allow God to take a giant broom to our lives and sweep out those corners that are dusty and distasteful. We acknowledge our shortcomings before God, but do so in confidence that we are doing all he expects of us. In so many ways, this is a place of tremendous liberation!

If you desperately want the Holy Spirit's anointing upon your life, you must seek the cleansing that only he can give.

Control Calls for Entire Sanctification

God's work of sanctification is never complete in this life. However, the Holy Spirit does want to get us to a place of complete or entire sanctification. This does not mean all future sanctification is done in our lives, and we have no room for improvement. (I wish that were true!) *Entire sanctification means every area of the revealed will of God in your life is brought under the lordship and control of the Holy Spirit.* There is nothing you will hold back from him. Your cards are on the table.

Let's look at an example in Scripture. Take the believers Paul addresses in 1 Thessalonians. Here were some great people. They loved God and wanted to serve him. Paul even referred to them as model Christians and that they were examples to other believers (1 Thess. 1:7). They probably memorized every Sunday school verse in church! Yet in spite of this high moral lifestyle, there was still something that was lacking inside of them. Their love for others needed to be increased (1 Thess. 3:10-13).

In 1 Thessalonians 5:23-24 Paul tells the believers, "Now may the God of peace himself sanctify you completely, and may your whole spirit and soul and body be kept blameless at the coming of our Lord Jesus Christ." These people were already Christians, yet God wanted to do a greater work in their lives. The Holy Spirit was in their lives, but he was not completely running the whole show.

Control Calls for Comprehensive Infilling

God's purpose of cleansing us of our self is to fill us with himself. It is kind of like remodeling a house. All of the rotted out sofas, rusty drain pipes, and moldy bedrooms must be cleaned out before you want to move inside. Just as you would not want to live in filth, so our holy God does not infill filth! He only fills that which has been set apart to him.

The book of Ephesians is a beautiful letter which the apostle Paul wrote to believers. In Ephesians 3:14-20 and Ephesians 5:18 he uses some different language and calls these Christians to be "filled with the Spirit."

This body of believers in Ephesus had already received the indwelling of the Holy Spirit when they were saved. They were displaying the fruits of the Spirit. Because they were believers, they each had some level of spiritual gifts. They had a lot of the Spirit, but they were not *filled* with the Spirit. There was a greater work that God wanted to do in their lives. And there is a greater work God wants to do in your life!

In order to be filled with the Spirit you must consider yourself dead to sin and alive to Jesus (Rom. 6:11). You must make a total surrender to him (Rom. 12:1-2). You must allow God to completely cleanse you (2 Cor. 6:11-7:1). You must have a heart that says, "Yes, Lord, I want you to sanctify and refine me in any area of my life (1 Thess. 5:23)!"

Always remember this, the degree to which we are filled with the Holy Spirit is the degree to which we have given control to him.

Control Calls for Humble Christlikeness

In the Gospels, Jesus set the standard for being filled with the Spirit. It was through the Holy Spirit that Jesus went where he did and spoke what he spoke. Wherever the Spirit wanted him to go, he went. It was the Spirit that guided Jesus to go into the wilderness for forty days to be tempted of Satan (Matt. 4:1). Whatever the Father spoke to him through the Spirit, he obeyed. He did not come to do his own will but the will of the one who had sent him.

It is out of this model life that Jesus urges us in Luke 9:23 to take up our cross daily. We are called to continually put our selfish natures to death. It is a continuous day-by-day death (1 Cor. 15:31).

You can just imagine the mental picture that went through people's minds when Jesus told them to take up a cross. Many of his audience had no doubt witnessed crucifixions and heard the shouts of pain from those who were crucified. The cross was not a fine piece of jewelry they hung around their necks. It was not a picture they hung up in their children's bedroom. Everyone knew the cross symbolized certain, gruesome death!

Yet death to self and fullness of the Holy Spirit is what Jesus Christ requires.

Every Great Believer Has Faced This Decision

In the early chapters of Luke's book of Acts, we can see prime examples of new believers who were filled with the Spirit and empty of self. As the book goes on we see men like the apostle Peter, who adamantly denied Jesus three times, risk death for Christ's sake.

The apostle Paul persecuted numerous believers. Yet, when Christ revealed himself to him, Paul made the decision to let go of all he had known to follow Jesus. He then went on to pen much of the New Testament. What was the difference? What happened that made the change? The difference was their total surrender to God and the fullness of the Holy Spirit.

Every person who has ever done anything great with God has first had to come to a place of total surrender. I know that is a bold statement, but I believe it to be fundamentally true.

Look up spiritual giants like Hudson Taylor, John Bunyan, Amy Carmichael, Oswald Chambers, D.L. Moody, Andrew Murray, Billy Graham, and so forth. Each of these men and women give different accounts, but the underlying theme is death to self and fullness of the Holy Spirit.

The Day I Gave Up Control

I remember the day I fully surrendered my life entirely to God. I was twelve years of age. Before this point, I had always been someone who had a terrible problem with anger. For the most part, I was a good kid who loved God. Still, I found there were key points in my life when I found myself absolutely incapable of responding to life's situations the way Jesus wanted me to respond. I remember things like hitting my brother with hockey sticks when we'd play, throwing my mom up against our kitchen cupboards, and fighting with my best friend every time we met. (I was a joy as a kid.)

However, when I totally surrendered my life to Christ, the Holy Spirit came in and did a remarkable transformation. My angry nature was transformed into one of love for God and others. Since that day, there have been several instances where that love has been tested big time! And time after time, although I have been far from perfect, I have marveled at the strength and power I have witnessed God pour into my life in moments I know I would have failed on my own.

Without question, I would not be where I am today without this death to self. I would be skeptical, small minded, and completely caught up in myself and what others thought of me. My heart cannot rejoice and thank God enough for the freedom he has offered through this amazing gift!

Enough about me though. Let's talk about you. I honestly believe God wants to do great things through your life (I promise this is not just a cliché)! That being said, *God sovereignly chooses to do his greatest work through those who are completely surrendered to his perfect will.* We have to choose if we want him in control! Author A.W. Tozer said, "It is part of our human problem that we would like to be full of the Spirit and yet go on and do as we please!"

Making a full surrender to God does not lift you above the possibility to sin, but it does empower you with all of the grace that you need to live above it! *Filling up with God does not keep us from having to apologize and admit we are wrong. It makes us ten times quicker to do so!*

When we give up control of our lives to the Holy Spirit, he does not leave us just to drag ourselves along. He walks with us each step of the way. He empowers us and will take us to new levels that we have never known!

If you want to be dead to sin and filled with God's Spirit, I invite you to pray this simple prayer with me:

Dear Holy Spirit, I want to be dead to sin and alive unto you. I give you any area I have not surrendered and I want you to know in advance I will do whatever it is you ask me to do. When you say speak, I will talk. When you say move, I will go. When you say stop, I will be still. I do not just give you ownership of my life, I give you control. Use me how you will. Break me as you wish. Take from me what was never mine. I leave myself completely at your disposal. With your strength, I will apologize when I am wrong. I will back up when I have gone too far. And I will walk in all of the light and knowledge you give me. I believe your word and surrender all of my life to you. Empty me of self, fill me with you, and sanctify me to the image of Jesus Christ. Amen!

Action Points

1. What thought challenged you the most as you read through this section?
2. What area of control do you sense has been the most difficult for you?
3. Has there been a time in your life when you have made a complete surrender to the Holy Spirit? If not, I urge you to do so today.

Grace Is Our Lifeline from the Father

*"Grace is what all need, what none can merit,
and what God alone can give."*
—George Barlow

Grace. It's something we're familiar with but never fully appreciate. We talk and sing songs about it but seldom take time to stop and reflect on its meaning.

Writing on grace is ridiculously challenging. How do you write about something that is so awesome and seemingly so crazy? In many ways, I feel as though I am a free rider in the school of grace. I feel as though I have given so little, and yet have experienced and received so much.

Everything good you or I will ever do is always a result of the grace of God. Grace gives us a whole new perspective in life. It should cause us to become very humble. It should keep us from becoming arrogant and thinking we have accomplished anything in our own power.

Because grace is so amazing, it is sometimes difficult to comprehend. Part of our problem in understanding God's grace is we picture it as an item we can attain. But as George Barlow writes, "Grace is what all need, what none can merit, and what God alone can give."

There is nothing you or I can do to earn the grace of God. In Andy Stanley's book, *The Grace of God*, he writes, "To say that someone deserves grace is a contradiction in terms." How true! We, because of our sin against God, deserve Hell. But this is where grace steps into play.

What Is Grace?

In a simplistic sense, grace is getting what we do not deserve. But it is more than that. Author Philip Brown states, "God's grace is the outreaching of his love and mercy to undeserving people, producing in them the desire and power to do his will."

That second part is critical. God's grace not only is offered to undeserving people, but it also gives us the strength and ability to do God's will! Scripture is clear that we are saved by grace (Eph. 2:4-5). It is only because of the grace of God that we are what we are (1 Cor. 15:10). And Philippians 2:13 says strongly that it is God working in us that enables us to live for him and to do his good pleasure.

Grace is amazing and so much more than a "hand-me-down" token from God.

In the Beginning ... Grace!

God's grace is evident on every page of Scripture. It starts with God's very desire to create mankind. It was his grace that brought us into existence.

It was his grace that redeemed Adam and Eve after they sinned in the garden. It was his grace that saved humanity through the faithfulness of his servant Noah. It was his grace that was extended to Abraham and through this one man all of the nations of the earth would be blessed. His grace extended to David, a murderer and adulterer. His grace reached out to the children of Israel in the book of Hosea when they rejected him.

Jump into the New Testament, and you see his grace extended to people like Zacchaeus, a wicked tax collector. He extends it to disciples like Peter who denied him in a storm of cursing. His grace reached out to a man named Saul who had previously been an active persecutor of those preaching in the name of Jesus.

Sometimes it is easy to get a twisted view of God's grace when we only look at a small portion of Scripture. We read verses that show God commanding Israel to wipe out an entire city and ask ourselves, "Where was God's grace?" We question how a loving Father could ever send his Son to die on a cross.

However, the more I study each account in Scripture, the more I am in awe and realize God's standard of grace is a whole lot higher than mine. It reaches much farther than mine could ever reach!

Every law God ever gives in Scripture is birthed out of the unfailing grace of God. As Pastor Andy Stanley writes in his book *The Grace of God*, "The law of God is actually an expression of the grace of God."

God is more interested in giving us a relationship than a rule book. It is the grace of God that precedes every rule he gives us. If we are not careful, it is easy to read the Bible as a list of rules that are binding on our freedom. We feel as though God's law limits our liberty when really just the opposite is true. It is because of God's grace that he gives us his law.

Grace always comes before any action we take.

Grace Is Determined by God

There are differing levels of grace that God chooses to give to people. Some get more; some get less. In Matthew 11:21-24, Jesus rebukes the villages of Chorazin and Bethsaida because they had rejected the grace given to them. He said these words in verse 21, "Woe to you, Chorazin! Woe to you, Bethsaida! For if the mighty works done in you had been done in Tyre and Sidon, they would have repented long ago in sackcloth and ashes."

Jesus knew that Tyre and Sidon would have accepted him had they heard his message like those in Chorazin and Bethsaida. Yet he chose to sovereignly give each set of towns a differing level of grace.

Why? We're not entirely certain, but we do know that the amount of grace God gave in each instance was enough.

In Titus 2:11-12, Paul tells us that the grace of God is offered to all. Theologians call this prevenient grace. This is the grace that enables men and women to have a desire to serve God. Grace is not reserved for a select few. Everyone receives God's grace, but God determines the amount each person receives.

God's grace is never equal, but it is always sufficient.

Grace Draws Us

God's grace extends to every person long before they even think of surrendering their lives to him. It is God's grace that enables us to respond to salvation. Romans 2:4 says it is God's kindness that leads us to repentance. Theologian James Torrance writes, "Repentance is our response to grace, not a condition of grace." John 6:44 says, "No one can come to me unless the Father who sent me draws him." God does this through offering every man and woman a sufficient amount of grace and the desire to be his follower.

Without God the Father's drawing in our lives, we would have no desire to serve God. While the grace of God draws all men, there are no promises for how long it will continue to draw. God alone is the judge. This is why "I'll do it later" thinking is horrendous. The idea that you or I can come to God whenever we want to is foolish, and it is arrogant. God does not owe you the privilege of multiple chances to accept him.

Because of this realization, we should view salvation in a whole different perspective. We take no credit for our salvation experience. It was not our faith that did the work of saving us. As theologian John Stott points out, "Faith's only function is to receive what grace freely offers." To take credit for your salvation is as ridiculous a concept as taking credit for a Christmas gift you were given!

WHAT KIND OF GOD DO I SERVE?

Without God's grace in our lives, we would be Romans 3:10-18 persons. We would stumble along with no fear of God and no peace in our lives. Yet, because of God's drawing in every person's life, each person has the opportunity to accept his amazing grace.

Grace Empowers Us

Grace does not end the moment you give your heart to Christ. It sticks with you. It is God's grace that gave you the strength to get out of bed this morning. It is God's grace that keeps you alive today. And it is God's grace that gives you hope for tomorrow.

Through Jesus Christ, grace and truth are offered to us (John 1:17). Through God's grace, we are given the strength and the power to live above sin. As Philippians 2:13 says, "It is God who works in you, both to will and to work for his good pleasure."

It is through God's grace that we have the ability to love when we find it convenient to hate. It is God's grace that enables you to smile instead of curse. And it is God's grace that empowers you to live in obedience to Christ.

Just think of all the gracious blessings God gives to us. He gives us the means to commune with him in prayer. He offers us a written copy of his Word. He offers us to partake in remembrance of him through communion. He graciously calls us to be baptized into his death and raised in the likeness of his image. Through his grace, he gives us the opportunity to serve others. We are offered so many "means of grace"!

Grace is not given because we have done. It is given so we can become! Saint Augustine said, "For grace is given not because we have done good works, but in order that we may be able to do them."

God's grace not only reaches to those who do not deserve. It empowers and enables us with the ability to serve! God's grace and

God's power are intricately connected. *You cannot experience God's power apart from God's grace.* This whole idea of freedom from sin and surrender to the Holy Spirit's control is a cruel joke if grace is a myth. Living like Jesus is an impossibility apart from grace.

Grace Can Be Rejected

While God's grace draws and sustains us, it is possible to resist. We can frustrate the grace of God as the apostle Paul warns in Galatians 2:21. Paul goes on to advise in Hebrews 12:15 that we must not fail to obtain the grace of God through our sinfulness. Our sin never thwarts the sovereign plan of God, but it can reject his outpouring of grace on our lives.

Sadly, grace is easy to take advantage of. Grace is treated by many as a "Get Out of Jail Free Card." It becomes a ticket to take advantage of God's amazing generosity and serves as a license to sin. After all, if God gives grace to people who don't deserve it, why shouldn't I sin all the more, so God can give me more grace?! The apostle Paul strongly addresses this in Romans 6:1-2. He is emphatic that we must not abuse the grace of God. We do not sin more to test how much grace we can receive from God.

We all need a constant infilling of God's grace. Humility plays a role in receiving more grace. James 4:6 says, "God opposes the proud, but gives grace to the humble." The more we stay surrendered to God and resist the devil, the closer he will grow, and the more his grace will fill us.

The reassuring reality for our lives is that God's grace is always greater than sin. Yes, there is still a struggle. Yes, we must walk step-by-step and put to death the deeds of the flesh. Still, grace is greater because it always contains the presence of Jesus. It sustains us, and as Max Lucado writes, "Sustaining grace promises not the absence of struggle but the presence of God."

Grace Will See Us Home

I love these words from perhaps the most familiar hymn in all of history, "Amazing Grace." The author, John Newton, pens these powerful words, "Tis grace that brought me safe thus far and grace will lead me home."

It is because of God's grace that we have the anticipation of seeing Jesus face-to-face. Philippians 1:6 gives hope to those who are actively in a relationship with Christ. He says that God who began a work in us at salvation will complete it at the coming of Jesus Christ. Author Lewis Smedes said, "Grace is the gift of feeling sure that our future, even our dying, is going to turn out more splendidly than we dare imagine."

Meditate on these words about Jesus from Max Lucado. He writes:

> He himself is the treasure. Grace is precious because he is. Grace changes lives because he does. Grace secures us because he will. The gift is the Giver. To discover grace is to discover God's utter devotion to you, his stubborn resolve to give you a cleansing, healing, purging love that lifts the wounded back to their feet.

Grace is our lifeline from God the Father. It is what saves us, sustains us, and gives us hope for the future!

Action Points

1. Why is the "second part" of grace so important for us to remember?
2. How should the fact that God's grace can be rejected sober us today?
3. How does grace empower us on our Christian journey?

Day 20
God Is Freely Giving in His Triune Nature

*"It is possible to give without loving, but it is impossible
to love without giving."*
—Richard Braunstein

God has always been a giver. Giving you total freedom from sin is not an action that is out of the ordinary. It is in complete harmony with his character.

No doubt you have come across people in your life who were takers. Every interaction you have with them, they constantly beg you for something. Eventually you make it a point to avoid them. No one enjoys being around a greedy taker.

When it comes to God and all he offers us, sometimes it is easy for us to approach his offer with skepticism. We think he must be looking to take something from us. But God's generosity and the grace he offers to us is not held back with invisible strings.

He freely offers it to us because that is who he is.

God Is Triune

God's generosity flows out of his holy and loving nature. Let me explain what I mean. One of the factors that distinguishes our God from all others is what we call God's Trinitarian nature. God is one being and three persons. No, this does not mean three gods. Rather, these three distinct persons function as one to make up the Godhead – God the Father, Son, and Holy Spirit.

Scripture is clear these three names do not refer to the same person. For instance, Jesus says in Matthew 28:19, "Go therefore and make disciples of all nations, baptizing them in the name of the Father and of the Son and of the Holy Spirit." Take a look at Matthew 3:13-17 and see how when Jesus is baptized, the Father speaks from Heaven and the Holy Spirit descends in the form of a dove. In 2 Corinthians 13:14, the apostle Paul spoke of three persons individually.

God the Father is the head of the trinity. Often the Bible will make references to God when it is speaking directly of God the Father (E.g. John 3:16). This can appear confusing at first, but it makes sense when we look at the surrounding verses.

God the Son is Jesus Christ. When we say Jesus is God's Son, this does not mean he is inferior. Jesus Christ came in the flesh and dwelt among us (John 1:14). Everything was made by Jesus Christ, and he is the one who serves as the mediator between us and God the Father (1 Tim. 2:5). Jesus spoke often of his Father during his life and even through his suffering on the cross (John 17). There is no question that Jesus definitely claimed to be God (Matt. 4:7).

God the Holy Spirit is the convicter and comforter of humanity. When Jesus ascended into Heaven, he promised to send a comforter, which is the Holy Spirit, or Holy Ghost (John 14:26). As comforter, the Holy Spirit operates completely as God. In Acts 5, Peter catches Ananias and Sapphira lying to the Holy Spirit. And in verse 4 he tells them they have lied not unto men but unto God. Scripture repeatedly refers to the Holy Spirit as God.

Both the Old Testament and the New Testament strongly point out there is only one God (Deut. 6:4; 1 Cor. 8:6). Inside of this oneness, there exists these three distinct persons who function to make up the Godhead.

It is this triune nature of God that helps us understand his incredible generosity.

God's Nature Makes Him Giving

In order to love, there must be both a "lover" and a "loved." In order to give, there must be both a giver and a recipient.

The God of the Bible is distinct from every other god because he is the only one whose very nature is one of selfless, giving love. Unlike other gods, our God did not need us in order to be considered loving. His threefold nature shares in a natural loving state. *While other gods are takers, our God is a giver.*

Because God the Father, Son, and Holy Spirit are in a perfect triune relationship with one another, giving is an intricate part of who they are. They mutually give to one another and share the same motivation and passion because they are one.

It is out of this loving relationship that God invites us to participate. He is naturally giving because this has been how he has always existed throughout eternity.

God's Giving Nature Causes Him to Communicate

Another distinction between the God of the Bible and other types of gods is that God the Father and the other two members of the trinity are dialogical. This means that they talk to each other and communicate on a personal level. As Dennis Kinlaw points out, "It is the nature of love to communicate. Ultimately love, if it can speak, cannot remain quiet."

Take a young couple who have recently fallen in love. After getting through those awkward stages, there is a natural desire for them to express that they love one another. Some of you reading can remember those days very well. It might not have been comfortable at first, but it felt so right! Your love could not go unspoken.

The God we serve is someone who communicates within himself and communicates with his children. Author John Zizioulas states, "Death for a person means ceasing to love and to be loved, ceasing to be unique and unrepeatable." The moment you decide to withdraw from people and pull back from giving or receiving love, there is an inward part of you that dies.

This point bears some more thought. Maybe you have been a giver your whole life. You have given and given to others but seemingly have received nothing in return. Unfortunately, something has snapped within you. Maybe you got burned one too many times and you have decided to block people out and become inwardly focused. Let me just say that this is a dangerous place to be. And if you do not deal with this bitterness, it will eventually lead to your destruction.

God, the great love giver, calls for you to give love to others. He calls for you to become connected to him, and out of this connection offer love to others.

God Gives So You Can Give

There is nothing God gives to you that he does not intend for you to share with someone else. One of the reasons for this goes back to our study on enjoyment. We cannot fully appreciate and enjoy a gift until we have expressed its pleasure to others.

In this section, we have talked a lot about all God wants to do for YOU. He wants to set you free from sin, fill you with his Spirit, and help you to grow into the likeness of Christ, so that one day you can stand blameless before God the Father.

But God's transforming work in your life will never be complete until you begin to share your transformation with others. Richard Braunstein rightly stated, "It is possible to give without loving, but it is impossible to love without giving." Love calls for us to give.

Give to others as God, the awesome three-in-one, gives to you!

Action Points

1. How does God's nature make him giving?
2. Why is it sometimes hard for us to serve a God who is a perfect giver?
3. How giving are you as a person? Do you naturally hoard what God has given you, or are you quick to pour into the lives of others?

Day 21
You Can Settle or Press On

"We often become more interested in the blessings of Christ than Jesus Christ himself."
—Dietrich Bonhoeffer

I believe in decision points. There is a time and a place when we decide to accept or reject God's gracious gift of salvation. There is a time and a place when we decide to totally surrender everything in our life to Christ or hold everything back. These might happen together, or they might happen separately.

You decide how deep you want to grow spiritually. Most Christians settle for little of God. They have just enough of him to call it a relationship, but they could tell you very little of the God they serve. Their motivation to spend time with him is not as great as their desire to fill themselves with the things of this world. As a result, they wander along through life and remain content to "get by" as a Christian rather than thrive in the power of the God they serve.

All throughout history, men and women have had to make the decision of whether or not to completely surrender their lives to God. Abraham loved God, but his willingness to sacrifice his son Isaac took him to a different level. However, God was testing Abraham's love; he did not require Abraham to sacrifice his son.

One of my favorite stories is the one of Abraham's grandson Jacob. Here was a man who was used to controlling his life. He was a manipulator and called the shots. But God, through a night of intense struggle, broke Jacob down physically and spiritually. As a result, Jacob's name was changed to Israel, and he became the father of a great nation.

Moses was a murderer and afraid to speak in public. Yet through an encounter with God, he was given the strength and boldness to lead the entire nation of Israel out of Egypt. He had a decision to make, and he made the right call.

I believe that every great advancement of the kingdom has always started with a decision point. It is a line in the sand moment.

Stagnation Leads to Stink

Satan hates decision points. His strategy after we have made this decision is to keep us immobilized. Think about a stationary bike. We can pedal all we want, but we never go anywhere. This is exactly what the devil wants for your life. He wants to keep you from growing. He wants you to run through life as a hamster that runs mindlessly in a hamster wheel.

If Satan cannot get you to forsake God, he will do all he can to make you neglect him. Satan does not want you to grow. The differences between a stagnant Christian and a vibrant one are subtle, but radical.

A sign we have settled spiritually is when we begin to make statements like, "I guess this is the way it will always be." Our talk of God resorts to what he did for us years ago as opposed to what he is doing for us today. We lose confidence in his cleansing power and are skeptical when others testify to his goodness and transformation. Dietrich Bonhoeffer noted that we are prone to being more interested in the blessings of Christ than Jesus Christ himself.

Little growth happens in our lives if we aren't intentional. If we are in a place of ministry, this is strongly apparent because few people want to follow us, and our works often fizzle out. The Bible studies we lead are lifeless, and lives are not changed.

We may still enjoy talking about God, but our attitudes reflect anything but his character. We are quick to criticize and are easily offended. Our conversation of Scripture begins to revolve around meaningless jargon that adds little value to the Kingdom. We are quick to point out the faults of others because we want to cover up the hypocrisy in our own hearts. Gossip becomes our friend because it serves as a means to discredit others while making us feel better about our own spiritual filthiness.

Take this statement to the bank: *Wherever there is spiritual stagnation, there is always stink.* We may speak the same words as before, but they lose their power. We may act very similarly, but all people see in us is self. As a result, others begin to see through our self-constructed façade.

How to Break Out of Stagnation

The way you break out of spiritual stagnation is by retracing the route that got you there in the first place. You make a complete re-surrender of your life to God and plead for his forgiveness. He will then confront you with your greatest demons of struggle.

At the root of all spiritual stagnation is pride. We are too proud of our own abilities to acknowledge our need for God. We selfishly enjoy sleeping in just a few minutes longer each day more than spending time with God. Sports camps and parties take the place of church and spending time with fellow believers. We stop studying God's Word as a means of producing life change and look at is as a means of proving our point.

The first step to breaking out of spiritual stagnation is to humble yourself before God. Stop making excuses. Admit what everyone else around you already knows, or are beginning to "smell."

How Do I Know I Am Where Jesus Wants Me to Be?

My hope is that you have a desire to be all that Jesus wants you to be. The question many people have though is, how do I know? How do I know I am doing exactly what Jesus wants? "Is it even possible to know?"

One of the lies Satan tries to get us to buy into is that discomfort is never from God. He makes us think spiritual warfare is a joke. So, when we are confronted with areas of our lives that make us uncomfortable, we rebuke Satan and run from this discomfort. We resort to going out to watch a movie. Maybe we pick up a new exercise routine. We try to eat healthier or get a better job. All of these are okay, but they will not solve an attitude or character of self-centeredness.

Ask yourself some of these questions. Was there a time and a place that I gave my life to Jesus Christ? Have I surrendered everything and asked to be filled with the Holy Spirit? Am I living above willful, habitual sin? Am I walking in all of the knowledge God has revealed to me?

If the answer to all of these questions is yes, but you still feel discomfort, do two things. First, rest comfortably knowing you are doing all God wants of you. Second, pursue God passionately. Ask him to reveal areas of your life that are unsurrendered to his will, and he will be faithful to show you!

In our pursuit of God we must show great patience. One of the reasons many Christians fail to be filled with the Holy Spirit is they get in a rush, but God uses the process of time to reveal our deepest insecurities and points of self-centered control.

When you are doing all that God wants you to do, there will be a peace and humble confidence that will sweep over your soul. Maybe this happens dramatically at an altar with many tears. Maybe it happens silently in the quiet of your home. Either way, God's Spirit will give you confidence and peace when you are living as he wants you to live.

Keep Pressing On!

As you have read the last several sections, I am well aware the devil may be playing mind games with you in your head. If you are grounded in Christ and living as he desires, Satan will use these chapters to beat you up and tempt you to doubt your relationship with God.

If you are stagnant, Satan will offer you excuses. He will cause you to underestimate the power that he holds over your life. He will cause you to fear what giving everything to God will cost you. He will tell you that you have tried this before and it will not work.

My prayer as you read is for you to go back to the basics of what it means to really serve God. Make glorifying and enjoying him your top priority. Refresh yourself with his overwhelming love for you, and let this be your motivator to know him deeper. Ask him to make you holy and perfect in desire and motivation before him. Call on him to sanctify your heart and reveal to you areas of your life that may not be surrendered to his control.

Being totally surrendered to God is an ongoing process. It is something we have to do daily. Mark it down, at least a couple of times each year we will be faced with major obstacles that will call into question our total commitment to this relationship. There may also be long periods of discouragement and unrest.

During these times, I challenge you to not be fearful. Keep pressing on towards God and rest comfortably in the knowledge that he has all things under control!

Action Points

1. Why is it that it is so easy to become stagnant as believers?
2. What area of your life is stagnant and in need of growth?
3. Take a few moments to pray and ask God to give you the strength to keep pressing on, regardless of the temptation to give up.

Week 4

I Serve Someone Who Reveals Himself to Me Through His Word

Day 22
Why the Bible?

"Isn't it amazing that almost everyone has an opinion to offer about the Bible, and yet so few have studied it?"
—R.C. Sproul

God's Word is our primary way of discovering his character and our chief weapon against Satan. Since this is the case, we had better know how to allow its power to work in our lives.

The Bible Is True

As we already established in the first section, the Bible is completely reliable and trustworthy. It is our foundation for understanding God and reality.

The Bible is both infallible and inerrant. Before we move on, it is important to know what these two words mean. Biblical scholar Daniel Wallace offers a helpful perspective. He states, "My definition of infallibility is the Bible is true in what it teaches. My definition of inerrancy is that the Bible is true in what it touches." There are no doctrinal inconsistencies in Scripture.

In 1978 a group of over 200 biblical scholars came together in Chicago to form what would be termed, "The Chicago Statement of Biblical Inerrancy." The critical takeaway was that the Bible is true in all of its teaching, and any modern line of thinking that contradicts the Bible is in error.

If you have any doubt in the Bible's truthfulness, you will waver in how you apply it to your life. Your witness will be weakened. You will go down a slippery slope that calls into question every other teaching of the Bible – especially in areas where temptation fights you the most. *Doubting the Bible's truthfulness always leads to denying our God's faithfulness.*

There have been multiple times when I have come across what I view to be a contradiction in the Word of God. But every time, after further study and prayer, I have come away more convinced than ever of the Bible's unity in message.

The Bible Tells a Story of Redemption

The Bible was not randomly thrown together with no unity in message. On the contrary, its message is bold and clear! The Bible tells the story of man's relationship with God, broken by sin, but restored through Jesus Christ.

If you were to summarize the entire Bible into one word, you could use the word "redemption." From Genesis to Revelation, we can see God's hand working to redeem sinful humanity to himself. There is one key common denominator between the first chapter of Genesis and the last chapter of the Revelation – Satan is absent! God the Father's plan in perfect redemption is a world that is absent of Satan.

God the Father's goal in redemption is to mold us into the character of his Son Jesus. As John Oswalt points out, "The goal of redemption is transformed character, and unless that goal is achieved mere deliverance from a sense of condemnation is misshapen at best and abortive at worst."

God redeems you so that he can transform you.

The Bible Is a Roadmap

Reading God's Word is like looking at a giant roadmap. It points us to where we need to go next. Psalm 119:105 declares, "Your word is a lamp to my feet and a light to my path." In the same chapter in verse 11, the psalmist states, "I have stored up your word in my heart, that I might not sin against you."

Knowing God's Word guards us against sin and magnifies our love for God. It demonstrates how to prosper in this life and how to prepare for the life to come. As John Barth once remarked, "The Bible is not man's word about God, but God's Word about man."

Our walk with God is like a journey. If you want to reach your destination, you must study closely the road map he has given to you.

The Bible Is Alive

Physical road maps are dull and boring (in my humble opinion). But the road map of God's Word is alive and fresh! Hebrews 4:11 says, "For the word of God is living and active, sharper than any two-edged sword, piercing to the division of soul and of spirit, of joints and of marrow, and discerning the thoughts and intentions of the heart."

Just that thought should radically form the way we share Jesus with others! We must not share with our own strength, our own power, and our own words. We must speak through the power of God's written Word!

Hebrews 10:11-18 teaches us the Holy Spirit is speaking every time we read Scripture. The quickest way for a believer to begin to discern the voice of God in prayer is to read his words in Scripture. Through reading the words of Scripture the Bible comes alive and is penetrating.

No amount of teaching or Christian resources can substitute for the reading of God's Word.

The Bible Changes Lives

The goal of reading and studying the Bible is life change. We must not read it to better defend our positions or merely become more knowledgeable about ancient civilizations. We must read it with the purpose of allowing God to transform our character and actions.

God's Word always points to Jesus Christ, the incarnate Word. He alone is able to change lives.

Do You Study the Bible?

The greatest and only weapon a child of God has in their artillery bag is the Word of God. Theologian R.C. Sproul once marveled: "Isn't it amazing that almost everyone has an opinion to offer about the Bible, and yet so few have studied it?"

Maybe you say you believe God's Word. That's fair enough, but how often do you read it? Have you ever read it through from cover to cover? When was the last time you read God's Word and made a lifestyle change because of it?

You are on a journey to discover who God is and what your place is in this world. Fortunately, God has written out for you all that you need to know!

It is up to you. Do you only want to speak about the God of the Bible? Or, do you want to put the gloves on, crack open its pages, and study the Bible for yourself?

Action Points

1. How have you noticed the story of redemption throughout your reading of Scripture?
2. In what ways has the Bible changed you since you have begun reading it?
3. Do you have a strategy for reading the Bible on a daily basis? If not, I encourage you to start one today.

Day 23
How Do I Study the Bible?

"Where one man reads the Bible, a hundred read you and me."
D.L. Moody

The pathway to discovering who God is starts with our study of his written Word. In *Living By the Book*, the late Howard Hendricks listed three reasons for why he believes every Christian should study the Bible.

The first is that Bible study is essential to growth (1 Pet. 2:2). You cannot grow if you are not studying the Bible.

Secondly, it is essential for spiritual maturity (Heb. 5:11-14). You will always remain an infant spiritually if you remain an infant in your understanding of God's Word. Spiritual maturity and our understanding of God's Word go hand in hand.

Third, studying the Bible is necessary for spiritual effectiveness (2 Tim. 3:16-17). Do you really want to be effective in touching others? Do you really want to lead your family in the ways of God? Do you really want to make a radical difference in this world? If so, studying God's Word is essential. Mark it down, *reading God's Word God's way always produces God's results!*

The more we study the Bible, the more we expand and grow as Christians.

How Do I Study the Bible?

There are multiple ways to study the Bible. For starters, you have to believe it has the power to change your life more than anything else you will ever read. If you do not believe this, you will be passive in your approach to studying it.

If you really believe God's Word has the power to change your life, you are ready to study it with a teachable perspective. Here are three steps to studying the Bible:

Step 1 – Start with Observation

Let's say you are planning to read a chapter of Scripture today. As you read, be prayerful and meditate on key phrases that stick out to you. Maybe you need to read the same passage multiple times. Perhaps you read a verse and God convicts your heart about an issue in your life. It's at that moment where you just stop and take a few minutes to repent before him. At other times, you may be in awe of his wonder, and it is then good to set some time aside and breathe prayers of thanksgiving to God for his faithfulness.

The key to observation is not to get caught up in outside distractions. This is a time where you and God's Holy Spirit meet one on one in a divine encounter. It is an opportunity for you to soak in God's goodness and meditate on his truth.

Step 2 – Move to Interpretation

After observation, then it is appropriate to move to interpretation. This will help to clarify and shine greater light on your early observations. Let's say there is a verse you do not quite understand. What do you do? Here are a couple of suggestions.

Research the Verse – Take one individual verse and study it. Begin looking at its structure and wording. Is a key word used elsewhere with a different meaning? Does the structure of the verse lend itself to one particular interpretation?

Read the Chapter – What is the main message of the chapter you are reading? How does this verse tie into the surrounding verses? Is the writer using figurative or literal language? Is it historical or poetic? Context is always king! *In order to interpret a verse correctly, we must look at it in light of the surrounding verses.*

Review the Book – Look at the entire book of the Bible you are reading as a whole. Get a feel for the author's tone and means of communication. Maybe look at other books this author has written in the Bible and see if what he says elsewhere helps to shed light on this particular passage you are reading. What was the culture of that day? What time period was this author writing?

Remember the Bible – Ask yourself how this verse ties into the overarching message of the Bible's theme of redemption. This is why it is so important to read through the entire Bible on a regular basis. *Looking at Scripture broadly gives greater clarity when we study it narrowly.*

Visit an Outside Resource – When you have exhausted your limited understanding of the Bible, bring in outside resources and look at others who have greater experience in this field of study. If you are serious about studying God's Word, it is important that you develop a tool chest of biblical study helps. There are thousands of fantastic resources available. Ask an experienced Christian to help you choose which ones are best.

These five steps will be a great aid in helping you better interpret more challenging passages of the Bible.

Step 3 – End With Application

Knowledge without application is of little value. It is the easiest thing in the world to read the Bible, find a verse that speaks to you, underline it, and shut the cover. In order to apply God's Word to your life, several deliberate actions have to occur.

It begins with what I have alluded to several times before. You must believe what you are reading! Do you really believe that the God who took the Israelites through the Red Sea, delivered Daniel from the mouths of lions, and arose from the dead has your situations under control? *If you do not believe what God has said, you will not trust what he can do.*

Next, immediately put into action the truth you have learned. *The longer you wait to apply truth to your life, the less likely you will be to act.* The devil loves to bombard us with thoughts of negativity. If you are not quick to act, he will soon cause you to forget what you have read.

Finally, let your application touch someone else. Tell them what you have read and learned. This will bring instant accountability and make you more cognizant to apply this truth to your life in the future.

Goal of Reading the Bible

If there was one statement my hermeneutics teacher Meredith Maser taught me, it was this: *The goal of reading the Bible is life change.* The goal is not to see how I can be blessed today. The Bible is to be read with the purpose of discovering who God is and how I can show him to those around me.

If Satan cannot keep you from reading Scripture, he will do his best to create a disconnect between what you study and how you live. He wants to turn you into a hypocrite. Satan wants you to speak about God's Word in such a way that awes people but shames God.

The goal of reading God's Word is life change. If God's Word is not transforming your life, this is not a God problem. It is a YOU problem!

Maybe you have heard it said, "Sometimes the only Bible people will ever read is you." The great evangelist D.L. Moody stated, "Where one man reads the Bible, a hundred read you and me." This convicts me! I am not just studying the Bible for myself. I am studying it so that I can point others to Jesus!

In everything you observe, interpret, and apply from Scripture, ask God to use it to transform your character. Ask him to make you holy as he is holy.

Action Points

1. Observe a particular passage of Scripture that you may be reading.
2. Take some time to interpret its meaning.
3. Now spend a few moments allowing God to apply its truth to your life.

—•••••— Day 24 —•••••—
Three Levels of Biblical Priority

"In essential beliefs we have unity. In non-essential beliefs we have liberties. In all our beliefs we show charity."

Every word of Scripture is important. But not every word is primary. Jesus' discussion with Nicodemus in John 3 and the genealogy of Adam in 1 Chronicles 1 are both important. But there is a difference in their level of priority to a growing believer. Genealogies are important for establishing context, but the message of the gospel is primary to someone who is searching after God.

Unfortunately, many believers look at the entire Bible as equal in priority. This results in the forming of sub-biblical cultures. One group decides to emphasize lifestyle principles; others focus on spiritual gifts, and another group may emphasize the importance of the sacraments. All of these are important, but they are not all equal in their priority.

We must ask ourselves, are we really emphasizing the main message of the Bible in our teaching? Or, are we focusing on just a piece of the greater picture?

As I look at the Bible through my limited understanding, I see three levels of priority. There is no exact boundary for each of these levels, and some of them overlap the ones previous and the ones following. But I believe they can be very helpful in understanding what we should emphasize as highest in priority.

Priority Level 1 – Primary Beliefs

Primary beliefs are those non-negotiable realities about God and others which we must accept when they are revealed to us.

In order to accept Jesus Christ as Lord, all that is necessary is repentance of sins, belief in who Jesus is, and a commitment to do his will. That is it – plain and simple. In order to grow and develop while we walk with God, we must embrace what the Bible clearly calls us to do. Failure to do so will lead to a disconnect in our relationship with him.

Scripture emphasizes our need to love God and others. Also, these are primary beliefs: The Great Commission is a must obey. Salvation is by Jesus Christ through faith alone. There is a literal Heaven and a Hell. Scripture is God's Word to us. This list could continue, but the basic marking of all of these beliefs in this category is that they are black and white in Scripture.

Every belief in this category is an essential belief. In order to remain in fellowship with Christ, you must accept what the Bible says in these areas of primary beliefs. This does not mean that you must fully understand all of them before you give your life to Christ. But as God reveals these truths to your life, acceptance of them is absolutely critical.

All of these beliefs are absolutely essential for a believer.

Priority Level 2 – Principled Interpretations

Principled interpretations are those areas that are not explicitly outlined in Scripture but can be pieced together through understanding God's Word as a whole.

These can be tricky. Understanding these principles is not always easy. It requires some work to piece together different passages of Scripture.

By principled interpretation, we begin to get the answers to questions like: Should I drink a Molson Canadian beer? How should I dress? What types of music does God want me to enjoy? Is going to a UFC fight glorifying to God? We also find better answers to theological questions like: Why did Christ have to die? What did his death accomplish? Is God really Trinitarian? And so forth.

Using principled interpretation is one of the signs of maturing believers in Christ. They stop using terminology like, "Well, I believe this is just something right for me," and instead dig into God's Word for themselves.

While good Christian men and women might debate topics in this category, God wants you to look into these matters and discover God's will for yourself. Often, the people most affected by your decisions in these areas are those who look up to you most. You might be able to do some things in good conscience, but your failure through neglect to observe what the Bible says will hinder your Christian reputation.

Principled interpretations may not be as explicit as primary beliefs, but they are still critically important.

Priority Level 3 – Personal Convictions

Personal convictions are those areas that are not binding on all people, but are given to believers based upon their sensitivity to the Holy Spirit.

There are some areas where Scripture may not explicitly forbid you to partake, but the Holy Spirit convicts you and tells you they are wrong. For instance, a former alcoholic may have been given a principled conviction by God to never step foot in a bar room again; whereas, a Christian who has no desire for alcohol may be at liberty to enter into that same bar and witness to those in attendance. God knows what one believer can stand and what another cannot.

For me, I make it a practice not to watch recreational media on my Sabbath day, Sunday. The reason for this is because media is a natural part of my life throughout the week. It often distracts me from focusing solely on God. While others can no doubt watch entertainment on the Sabbath with no problem, I conscientiously make it a goal not to do so myself.

Every believer should have a set of personal convictions. In order to establish a personal conviction, you must develop a self-awareness and connection with the Holy Spirit. Understand what areas in your life may be weak. Listen to God's voice in these areas. Rest assured, *failing to obey a personal conviction from God will always lead to allowing sin a stronghold in our lives.*

Problem and Solution

Problem – Here is the problem that I see many churches have today. When new believers give their hearts to Christ, churches often do one of two things: They only teach primary beliefs, or they try to hand all three levels to new believers in one shot! They try to microwave new believers to a place they have taken years to get to themselves. Both of these extremes are bad. The first leads to immature Christians who know salvation is important but see little of its outworking in their lives. The second leads to discouragement and a sense of being overwhelmed. It is like handing a baby a steak when it can only handle milk.

Solution – When we study the Bible and help others study the Bible, we must be thoughtful in our approach. Start by reading through the Bible for yourself. Focus on the words of Jesus. Get the big stuff right! Then, with God's grace and timing, ask him to continue to chip away any rough edges that would hinder your ability to love him and love others purposefully. Develop principles and personal convictions that will shape you.

Unity, Liberty, and Charity

I close with three thoughts that are common but true. The first is this: *In essential beliefs we have unity* (Eph. 4:4-6). We have ONE Lord, Savior, and faith.

In non-essential beliefs we have liberties (Rom. 14:1, 12, 22). Understand there are other Christians who are more advanced spiritually. Likewise, many are babes in Christ, and the reason they disagree with you is simply because they are not as far along spiritually. Be courteous and generous in your behavior.

In all our beliefs we show charity (1 Cor. 13:2). No matter what a person believes, God commands us to treat them with dignity and respect as his creation. Love does not mean we agree. But it means we are the bigger person and confident in who we are in Christ Jesus.

When we practice these three simple principles, God begins to enlarge us as people. We begin to see past the idiosyncrasies and potential oddities of others and instead see them as fellow brothers or sisters in Christ.

I leave you with this thought today: In your study of God's Word, make it your goal to apply the Bible with the correct method and the right motive. When you do this, Scripture will come alive to you in a fresh new way!

Action Points

1. Why are the three areas of biblical priority so important for believers to understand?
2. Write down some primary beliefs, principled interpretations, and personal convictions for your life. Search the Bible and allow this list to evolve over time.
3. In what ways do you find showing liberty, unity, and charity to others makes a difference?

— Day 25 —
The Old Testament Anticipates Jesus

"The covenant not only showed the people that they were not like God, but also that there was something in them which did not want to be like God."
—John Oswalt

The Bible is a library that tells the story of God's plan of redemption for mankind. The Old Testament is part one of this story.

Let me just say up front that this section might be a little heavy! But stick with me and hang tight because God has some great truths he wants us to experience. Are you game? Great! Let's dive in.

Understand the Structure

As a foundation, let's understand the structure. The Old Testament is comprised of thirty-nine different books by a variety of authors. It is divided up into five different sections: Pentateuch, Historical Books, Poetic Books, Major Prophets, and Minor Prophets.

The structure of our English Bibles today does not place these books in chronological order. Rather, they are grouped according to similarity in literature style. Verse structure and chapter breakdown were also a later addition by English editors.

Almost all of the Old Testament was written in Hebrew with a few select portions from books like Ezra, Jeremiah, and Daniel written in Aramaic. The Old Testament was later translated into the Greek language of the New Testament. This was called the Septuagint, and it can be helpful today in cross-referencing similar words and passages found in both the Old and New Testament writings.

It should be noted there are other sections of literature, such as the Apocrypha, that have not been included in Old Testament writings. The reason for this is their content is not inspired (God-breathed), and in some places is written from a fleshly point of view that paints a different picture of God than the inspired writings of Scripture.

Two Covenants for Redemption

In the Bible there are two covenants. Both of them point to Jesus Christ as Savior of the world. These covenants are termed the Old and New Testaments. The word "testament" in this sense literally means a "covenant."

The Old Testament was essentially a contract between God and his people, Israel. The law of the Old Testament did not save anyone. Rather, it revealed the sin of humanity. John Oswalt makes this observation. He notes, "The covenant not only showed the people that they were not like God, but also that there was something in them which did not want to be like God."

The first covenant points to Jesus' redemption while the second speaks of the fulfillment of his redemption. Saint Augustine said, "The New Testament is veiled in the Old Testament, and the Old Testament is unveiled in the New Testament."

How to Interpret the Old Testament

In the Old Testament, specifically the first five books, there are three types of laws given. There are moral, ceremonial, and cultural laws. Ceremonial and cultural instructions were given to a specific group of people at a specific time in history. Moral laws are those that are universally applicable to people of all times and places.

My professor, Allan Brown, simplified it to what he termed the UP/SA Principle: Universal Principle or Specific Application.

Universal principles are commands of God that do not change across time or culture. Specific applications were commands that were meant for a specific group of people at a specific point in history.

You are not expected to keep all of the dietary laws in the Old Testament. Those were specific applications. On the flip side, you are expected to keep all of the moral laws that teach us how to better love God and love others. These are universal principles that can be applied to all people.

If you do not have this filter in place, it will be difficult to rightly interpret the laws in the Old Testament.

An Illustration of the Law

Take this example. In Canada, you have two different branches of government. There is both federal and provincial. The federal law includes every citizen in Canada, whereas the provincial law only applies to those who are currently living in that particular section of the country. The provinces of Canada are subordinate to the federal governing authority.

Likewise, the provincial law is similar in nature to the Mosaic Old Testament covenantal law. It is not equally binding upon all people. There are parts of it that were only intended for a select group of people. However, because it was divinely inspired, it reflects the very nature of God and must be used to better understand God's requirements and God's character.

For you or me to say that the Old Testament is irrelevant to the believer today is to call into question the very character of God. It suggests that his nature changes from generation to generation. This could not be farther from the truth. We do not serve a God who changes. He is consistent and dependable, and everything recorded in Scripture can teach us something about God's plan of redemption for our lives.

Every Old Testament Book Speaks Redemption

Again, every book of the Bible trumpets redemption. Reading Scripture with this thinking should change our perspective. Everywhere we turn, we can ask ourselves this question: How does this passage tie in with the big picture of redemption?

Pentateuch is the word commonly used to group together the first five books of the Bible, Genesis through Deuteronomy. The word Pentateuch is a Greek word meaning "a five-fold book." All five of these books were written around 1400 BC. In Genesis, God establishes a perfect world without sin. Mankind is created in the image of God. But through Adam's disobedience, redemption is now made necessary. The world is a mess. As you might be able to relate, one of the problems in dealing with a mess is it is hard to know where to start! Thankfully, this is where God instills his old covenant as the beginning of a process of redemption. Through his covenant with Israel, God began to teach men and women how to have his holy character.

The *Historical Books*, which include writings from Joshua through Esther, continue building on this theme of redemption. We see God's redeeming work in men who had sinned like King David, who committed adultery. Women like Ruth, a Moabite outcast, is extended favor and redemption. Rahab was a prostitute, yet God redeemed her and showed her amazing favor. The Historical Books teach us that redemption is not just a concept; it is something God wants to do in the life of every single person!

The *Poetic Books* run from Job through Song of Solomon. Once again, God's redemption is on display for all to see. Through the examples of men like Job, David, and Solomon, the heart and soul of redemption is exposed. It is as though these books are a behind-the-scenes look at the deep questions every human being faces. Job wrestles with the incredibly profound concept of God's goodness;

Psalms is packed full of prayers to God for redemption; while Proverbs, Ecclesiastes, and Song of Solomon give us practical truths about God and people that can be applied directly to our lives and problems.

The *Major Prophets* include the writings of prophets from Isaiah through Daniel. A prophet, by definition, is someone who accurately communicates God's message for the future. These great men prophesied of the coming redemption of Christ. It was the prophet Isaiah who spoke clearly about the coming of Jesus Christ. Throughout the Major Prophets, God reminds his people that he is sovereignly in control despite any opposition he receives. Daniel teaches us that God raises up rulers and brings them low as he chooses. No emperor can stand against God and prevail. No one comes to power by surprise. And amazingly, God uses evil rulers to turn his people back to him.

The *Minor Prophets* include the books of Hosea through Malachi. The Minor Prophets teach us God is way more interested in redeeming men and women than they are in pursuing him. Hosea demonstrates God's love that reaches down to us even when we reject him. Jonah demonstrates God's compassion to see all men and women come to repentance. These books also teach that God is jealous for his people, and they beautifully show God the Father's love that compelled him to send his Son to die on a cross for our sins!

Don't Throw Out the Old

The Old Testament is still very much relevant to us today. The apostle Paul was very clear when he said, "Don't throw out the Old Testament!" Okay, so maybe he didn't say it in those exact words, but take a look at a few of these passages.

Not one passage in the New Testament calls for believers to throw out the law. Jesus said he came to *fulfill* the law and not to destroy it (Matt. 5:17). In fact, the Old Testament was actually written for New Testament Christians. In Romans 15:4, Paul tells the believers that the things that were written earlier were intended for the *present day* believers' instruction. It was not written for Old Testament believers alone. In 1 Cor. 10:11, Paul states that the Old Testament was written as an example for New Testament believers, and that it was written to instruct them.

Romans 3:31 is perhaps the clearest verse used by the apostle Paul to emphasize that the law was not strictly given for Old Testament believers alone. Paul asks the question, "Do we then nullify the law through faith?" He answers his own question by using the strongest form of negation in Greek and stating, "May it never be!" Paul lived according to the law and taught that the law is important (Acts 24:14 and Acts 28:23).

In Matthew 5:19 Jesus says that the one who breaks even the "least" of the commandments will be considered "least" in the kingdom of Heaven. The law was of utmost importance to Jesus.

The Old Points to the New

Everything in the Old Testament points to the New Testament. Jeremiah 31:31 foretold of the coming new covenant God would establish. The Old Testament and New Testament are intricately connected. *The Old Testament prophecies point to Jesus; the New Testament shows his fulfillment of these prophecies.*

Without the Old Testament, the New Testament makes little sense. It is through the Old Testament that we see the need for a deliverer and Messiah. As we have already discussed earlier, there are several hundred prophecies that were fulfilled by Jesus when he came to earth. Dozens of these are so obvious that it is just astonishing.

The Old Testament shows Jesus would be born of a virgin. His birthplace would be Bethlehem. He would come from the line of Abraham and the seed of David. He would have to flee to Egypt, and there would be a massacre of babies in the Messiah's birthplace. He would be called the Son of God. He would be falsely accused, betrayed, and silent before his accusers. His hands and feet would be bruised. But he would pray for his enemies and be the sacrifice for sin. His side would be pierced. He would be buried with the rich and resurrect from the dead. He would ascend to Heaven and sit on the right hand of God the Father.

One of the greatest faith-building exercises you can do is go through the list of Old Testament prophecies and find the verses that fulfill them in the New Testament. It begins to give you a whole new level of appreciation for God's faithfulness!

Through reading the Old Testament, we increase in thankfulness and value Christ's work on the cross more. *Without properly understanding the Old Testament, we will not rightly appreciate Christ's sacrifice for our redemption.*

Action Points

1. How has your level of appreciation grown for the Old Testament through this reading?
2. Pick a specific passage of Scripture in the Old Testament. Now ask yourself: How does this apply to the overall theme of redemption?
3. Why is it so important to read the Old Testament to get a proper understanding of the God we serve?

— Day 26 —
The New Testament Reveals Jesus

"Christ is enfolded in the Old Testament but unfolded in the New."

The New Testament fulfills what the Old Testament foretells. It is the grand crowning mark of God's inspired Word to us.

The New Testament picks up from where the Old Testament leaves off. To read only the Old Testament is like watching a movie without seeing the resolution and conclusion. There is a hollow emptiness and sense of un-fulfillment. You think, "Great story line. Horrible ending." (You can tell I have seen one or two of these films in my lifetime!)

However, the Bible is a whole different story, and when we read the New Testament in light of the Old Testament, we begin to see the Bible as it was meant to be seen.

Picking Up from the Old Testament

There was a four-hundred-year time gap between the Old Testament book of Malachi and the opening book of Matthew. The Jewish nation was enslaved by the Roman Empire, and many were in prayer for the promised Messiah that was prophesied in the Old Testament. Sadly, they wanted God to answer on their terms. Never a good idea!

Some have wondered why it took so long for Jesus to come into the world. I am not sure that I have the perfect answer. My professor, Bill Ury, speculated that perhaps one reason is because it took this long for humanity to realize they were in need of a Savior. Men and women always have the tendency to believe they can accomplish everything on their own. "I don't need anyone else. I'm a self-starter!"

When Christ came to earth, he was anticipated but not recognized. Everyone had a different perception of what they thought their deliverer and Messiah would be like. Even some of his own family initially rejected him.

When we read the New Testament, Christ clearly takes center stage for all to see. As has often been pointed out, "Christ is *enfolded* in the Old Testament but *unfolded* in the New."

Jesus Is the Fulfillment of the Law

While the Old Testament is filled with physical illustrations of the law, the New Testament gives us the perfect fulfillment of this law. Jesus Christ is the fulfillment that all the Old Testament writers longed for!

Romans 10:4 says, "Christ is the end of the law." The Greek word translated "end" is the word *teleos* and it does not refer to end in the sense of finality. Rather, it refers to the word "goal." Christ is the goal of the law, not the end of it, and everything in the law illustrates truth about Christ. As Jesus said in John 5:39, "The Scriptures testify about me." Everything we read in the Old and New Testaments points to Jesus in some form or fashion.

When Christ came, he did not come to destroy the Old Testament but to fulfill it. This new covenant that Christ brought did away with the ceremonial laws given by God under the old covenant. We are no longer required to eat certain foods while abstaining from others. That part of the law is over. But the part of the Old Testament law that remains is the universal principles God still wants us to remember today.

It is true Jesus came to give us freedom and liberty. But as author Greg Bahnsen points out: "The freedom produced by the Spirit never leads us away from fulfilling God's law." *God's freedom always empowers us to do God's law.*

The New Testament helps us correctly interpret the Old Testament. Take 1 Corinthians 9:8-11. Paul quotes from Deuteronomy 25:4, "You shall not muzzle an ox when it is treading out the grain." On the surface, this passage seems to be talking about being kind to animals. As Paul points out though, there is a deeper meaning at play. The main message God is trying to get across to his people is that laborers are worthy of their hire. In this passage in 1 Corinthians, we learn that ministers should receive compensation for their work. They should not be expected to work for free. (And everyone in ministry reading this book said a hearty "Amen!")

2 Corinthians 3 gives us a contrast between the two covenants. While the old covenant was one of the letter, the new was one of the Spirit. The old killed while the new gave life. The old was a ministry of death while the new was a ministry of life. The old condemned while the new brought about righteousness. The old was written with ink while the new was written with the Holy Spirit. The old was written on stone while the new was written on the hearts of men. The old covenant came with glory, but the new covenant came with the greatest glory. The old covenant's glory began to fade while the new would continue to shine. The old had a veiled glory while the new has an unveiled and everlasting glory. The old covenant was destined to be completed while the new one was intended to live forever.

Jesus modeled a perfect sinless life. He set the standard for how we are to live. Through passages like the Sermon on the Mount, he set the bar high for his followers. He tells us we are to love our neighbors as ourselves. While the Old Testament commands us not to commit adultery, Jesus tells us not to even look at a woman with lust. The old covenant said murder was wrong, but Jesus adds that hating a brother is considered murder.

Through his life, we are given the perfect representation of a holy life. No action he committed was wrong. He always demonstrated the perfect will of his Father in Heaven.

If you are a new student of God's Word, I encourage you to pick up a red-letter edition Bible (most Bibles are this way). Start reading the words of Jesus in each of the four Gospels. Meditate on the actual words of Jesus. And then expand your reading to all of Scripture and understand each passage in light of the life of Christ. Start getting into Christ's words and pursuing the character he calls you to have.

Jesus was the perfect demonstration of what it means to give glory to God. Every motivation for his actions was born out of love. His character was completely holy, and he demonstrated the fruits of being who he claimed to be – the Son of God.

Our number one pursuit in reading the New Testament should be to become like its author. As you read, ask yourself, how can I become more like Jesus?

Every New Testament Book Speaks Redemption

The *Gospels* are the first four books of the New Testament. They include Matthew, Mark, Luke, and John. Each of these different accounts gives a fresh look at Jesus Christ's time on earth and his work of redemption. According to Jewish custom, two or three witnesses were necessary to confirm or deny someone's testimony. By having several accounts of his life on earth, Jesus' existence, and thus his claim to be the Son of God, was verified. Matthew proclaims Jesus as King. Mark paints Jesus as a servant. Luke shows Jesus was human just like us, and John displays for us Jesus' divinity. These four books give Jesus' birth, time on earth, death on the cross, and ascension into Heaven. The story contained in their pages is the hope for all the world.

The *Acts of the Apostles* was written by the Gospel writer Luke. The opening chapters tell of Christ's ascension into Heaven and that through Christ's departure, the Holy Spirit came and poured out his blessing on the apostles. Men and women who had run in fear suddenly became bold and proclaimed the gospel. It gives us a model for how the church of Jesus Christ should be lived out in our community. The redeeming message of Christ is not for a select few individuals. It is for the world!

The *Pauline Epistles* are those books penned by the apostle Paul. They include the following: Romans, 1 & 2 Corinthians, Galatians, Ephesians, Philippians, Colossians, 1 & 2 Thessalonians, 1 & 2 Timothy, Titus, and Philemon. Paul is direct in these writings and helps us to understand the incredible profoundness of Christ's redemptive work in our lives. Paul was a highly educated man who spent years in preparation before ever penning these books. He writes to admonish believers and calls them to press on and become mature believers. He does not sugar coat anything.

The *General Epistles* are those books of the New Testament that include the following: Hebrews, James, 1 & 2 Peter, 1, 2, & 3 John, and Jude. These books further build upon the nature of living as Christ. They teach us the importance of being mature followers of Christ. They call us to a higher standard of Christian living. It is not enough to say we are followers of Jesus. We must demonstrate it through our actions!

The *Revelation* prophecies are of the second return of Christ when he comes back to earth. It is here that God's full redemptive work will be complete. The beginning chapter of Genesis and the closing chapter of The Revelation have something in common – Satan is absent! Fellowship with God is restored. God's big plan of redemption involves a whole lot more than enabling people to live better lives on earth. It includes eternity with him!

The New Testament Points to Our Eternal Hope

While the Old Testament pointed to the New, the New Testament points to the glorious future hope of every believer.

Every time we read the New Testament, we should be asking ourselves this question: How can what I am reading make me more like Jesus Christ? We are called to be wholly set apart to God as his possession, and we are called to walk in a manner that is worthy of this calling (Eph. 4:1).

Peter was clear in his writings that the New Testament is the inspired Word of God (2 Peter 1:19-21; 3:1-2; 3:16). Through the New Testament, we can rightly understand the Old Testament. But more than that, we are given a manual to live as Jesus wants us to live!

We can glorify as Jesus calls us to glorify. We can love as Jesus calls us to love. We can be holy as Jesus is holy. We can be completely satisfied and joyful as Jesus is satisfied and joyful.

The New Testament gives us the hope that we will see the one in whose image we are being perfected!

Action Points

1. Why is it so important to read the Old and New Testaments as a package?
2. Which book of the New Testament do you connect with the most?
3. Consider the confidence believers can have through realizing the New Testament points to our future hope of eternity with God.

Day 27
Practice Produces Change

"Practice is the hardest part of learning, and training is the essence of transformation."
—Ann Voskamp

Up until this point in this section, I have talked a lot about methods. Now I want to put these methods into practice. We can have all of the knowledge that we want in the world, but if our knowledge does not transform our thought processes and behaviors, it is of little value.

When it comes to studying the Bible, nothing can or ever will substitute studying it for ourselves. Some things in life only come through practice. *Practice shapes me into the person I am seeking to become.* Philanthropist Richard Carlson put it this way, "You are what you practice most."

Studying the Bible requires a lot of time and effort. It requires practice and training, but through this process, our lives will never be the same. My wife's favorite author, Ann Voskamp, stated, "Practice is the hardest part of learning, and training is the essence of transformation."

Practice is important! This being said, let's get in some practice time right now. I want to walk you through the process of how I discover something for myself from a text. This method is built upon what we have already discussed in the previous chapters.

Observe the Passage

Are you ready? Good! Let's take one of my favorite passages of Scripture, Psalm 37:1-9, in the English Standard Version. It says the following:

Fret not yourself because of evildoers; be not envious of wrongdoers! For they will soon fade like the grass and wither like the green herb. Trust in the LORD, and do good; dwell in the land and befriend faithfulness. Delight yourself in the LORD, and he will give you the desires of your heart. Commit your way to the LORD; trust in him, and he will act. He will bring forth your righteousness as the light, and your justice as the noonday. Be still before the LORD and wait patiently for him; fret not yourself over the one who prospers in his way, over the man who carries out evil devices! Refrain from anger, and forsake wrath! Fret not yourself; it tends only to evil. For the evildoers shall be cut off, but those who wait for the LORD shall inherit the land.

Just through simple observation, this passage is meaningful. It is reassuring and probably one we should memorize and put on a 5x8 card in our wallet or purse. It has a feel good message, if you will.

To make this exercise meaningful, read this passage again. Stop speed reading for a minute, and let your mind gear down and focus. (If you are like me, this is the last thing you feel like doing!) Meditate on the words from this chapter. If you are feeling ambitious, read it in a different translation. Let it soak into you.

Even as I read this, my praise for God increases. I say, "Thank you, Lord, for you are stronger than any other. Help me to trust and commit my way to you. Help me to wait on you."

I encourage you to write down a few quick observations you have before going on to the next step.

Interpret the Meaning

Moving on, let's dig a little deeper and see if there is any more truth we can glean from these verses that we did not receive in a simple reading. Ask yourself, "What is beneath the surface?"

Look at the Verses

First let's look at the verses. Does anything pop out to you? As I read these verses, several words pop out at me. I want to know, what words like fret, trust, delight, commit, and be still really mean. So I turn to the original language in which this writing was penned, Hebrew, to get a better understanding. Through using a good Bible program like *Accordance, BibleWorks,* or *Logos,* this is not as complicated as it may sound. If you do not want to get that technical, find a good Bible dictionary or lexicon to help you.

(NOTE: Now might be a good time to reinforce the fact that good tools make Bible study much simpler! You invest money in insurance, car payments, and your job on a regular basis. Invest money in your study of God's Word as well.)

After looking at these words, I am going to jot down some thoughts beside them that look kind of like this:

- *Fret* – Means to kindle oneself or burn with anxiety. That is interesting. So God does not want me to get my stomach tied up in knots over people who have done me wrong.

- *Trust* – *The Merriam Webster Dictionary* defines trust as "belief that someone or something is reliable, good, honest, effective." Hmm, is that really my picture of God right now? Sure I "trust" him, but do I really believe I can depend upon him?

- *Delight* – Means "to take exquisite pleasure in and to enjoy oneself in." Okay, I think I love God, but I am not sure if I really *delight* in him. It feels some days that I spend time with God because I have to rather than enjoying to be in his presence.

- *Commit* – The Hebrew word for commit literally means "to roll." This is cool imagery! So God literally wants me to roll my future into his hands and release it to him. God, please keep me from keeping my plans to myself!

- *Be Still* – The *Merriam Webster Dictionary* defines still as "lacking motion or activity." The last thing I feel like doing when I am anxious is to quit my activity. I want to increase it! I want to fix things through "doing more." But God is telling me to do just the opposite.

Understand the Context

Now that we have looked at the verses, let's broaden our thinking. Through looking at this passage, the other writings of David in Psalms, and the story of his life in books like 1 and 2 Samuel, Kings and Chronicles, we can understand where he is coming from to a greater degree.

Without question, David is going through a tough time with some people in his life. However, this is nothing new for David. In fact, just through doing a quick run through of the life of David, we can see he was a man who was familiar with enemies. His brothers looked down on him. Men like King Saul tried to kill him. The Philistines sought his death. His own son wanted his throne. I'd say if anyone had a reason to be anxious, it was David!

We are not positive what event is causing David so much anguish. Whatever the case though, understanding a little background from this writer adds some weight to his words.

Realize the Big Picture

From knowing what we know of the Old Testament and the New Testament, we can understand how this passage fits into the big picture of Christ's plan of redemption. We realize that fretting makes no sense because Christ has already overcome sin. We can trust God because his character is impeccable, and he gave his life for us on the cross. We can delight in him because he is the source of all enjoyment. We can commit our way to him because his divine foreknowledge sees all things – past, present, and future. And we can be still and rest in him, knowing that while we wait, he will move!

We could go much deeper and talk a lot more about what it really means to delight in God and so forth, but I hope you get the picture. Just through a little digging, the passage comes more alive in our minds.

Apply the Truth

God applies truths to us in different ways depending on our circumstances. Let me share how God applied this truth to me.

It was July of 2010, and I was doing an internship program at a church called Parkway House of Prayer in Roanoke, Virginia. The last two weeks of my internship were approaching when I felt God prompting me to commit this time to fasting and prayer.

I remember being out on a prayer walk one night when God specifically brought to mind the words of this passage. That was my observational stage. I thought, "Wow, what a reassuring passage," and I thanked God for it. Towards the end of my internship, I even preached from this chapter. Yet I did not realize how God would use this passage in my life in more ways than just preaching it to others (funny how he likes to do that).

As my fast drew to a close and my internship came to an end, my world began to really change. I remember praying distinctly for five key prayer requests during those two weeks. My thinking was, "I pray, God will fix these problems, and life will be better!" Only one problem – life suddenly got a lot worse. All five of my prayers were not answered in the way I had prayed. In fact, they all got a lot worse, and it turned out to be a really dark time in my life.

The last thing I felt like doing was trusting, waiting, and being still before God. I certainly did not feel like delighting in him. Still, it was through that situation God taught me a deeper side of him than I had ever experienced before.

My trust in him was strengthened. I learned to commit my way to him. Delighting in God became more than something I just talked about. And being still before God became a new reality in my life.

In some ways, I think we all like to keep God's Word at an observational phase in our life. We love inspirational passages. If we're feeling extra spiritual, we even enjoy studying and interpreting them. But we'll take a pass on the whole application part. *We want just enough of God's Word to make us feel better, but we have little interest in allowing it to transform how we think and behave.*

God help us. Help me.

Dig Deep for YOU

The more you study the Bible for yourself, the more you will enjoy it, and the more your life will be changed. Because the Bible is inspired of God, its message is always fresh and relevant to our lives. I cannot tell you how many times God has taken the words I read and directly applied them to my life.

For instance, this last week God convicted me on some of my humor. I was reading Ephesians 5:4, and it says, "Let there be no filthiness nor foolish talk nor crude joking, which are out of place, but instead let there be thanksgiving." In that moment, I had a choice. I could shrug and say, "I'm only trying to have fun," or I could listen to the promptings of the Holy Spirit and clean up some of my humor.

Question: What are you reading today? Whatever it is, my challenge is for you to break beneath the surface. Dig deep. Let it change you. I can tell you from experience that it is extremely rewarding!

Action Points

1. What do you think holds you back from studying the Bible more than you do?
2. What part of today's reading did you find to be the most helpful?
3. Do you find yourself applying God's Word to your life, or does it feel as though your readings do little to change your actions?

———•••••— Day 28 ——•••••—
Start Yourself and Tell Someone Else

"Start where you are, use what you have, do what you can."
—Arthur Ashe

The surest way to keep from digging into God's Word is to never start! Biblical resources are at an all time high, yet our culture is anything but biblical. I am convinced that the key to overcoming this battle in our individual lives is to just START!

Start reading the Bible today. Don't wait and put it off until tomorrow. Do not worry about always coming away with the correct interpretation. Just set up a resolution in your life that you are going to spend time in God's Word each day.

This might happen through an hour of study in the morning. It may be fifteen minutes before you go to bed, or it may be listening to God's Word being read as you drive to work. Whatever it is, make the decision that each day you are going to read God's Word – no matter what!

That being said, here are some principles that I believe can aid you as you begin your journey.

First Things First

Chances are, what you do first at the start of your day shows your level of priority. Do you flip on the TV to catch the morning news cycle? Do you turn on the coffee pot and plug in the toaster to get something to eat? Or do you spend several minutes in front of a mirror getting ready for the day?

Each one of these says something about what you prioritize. You get a bite to eat because food is a priority. You fix your hair because looking nice is a priority. And you take in some news or entertainment information because that is a priority.

However, if you are going to become a mature follower of Jesus Christ, you need to begin the process of prioritizing what is most important in your life. And there is no better way to do this than by spending some time alone with God at the start of your day.

Spending time with Jesus at the start of your day gives you nourishment to live like Jesus the rest of the day. Yes, you might be a night owl or work exotic hours, so the start of your day is not always the best. But I still maintain that getting started with God is important. Maybe it is only five minutes, and you spend more time later. The point is that it's like physical food. You can eat after the day is done. The problem with that strategy is you will suffer in hunger the whole day! I believe a better alternative is to eat spiritually at the start of the day and use that food to energize your words and actions.

Have a Plan

It has been said, "The difference between a dream and a goal is a plan." When it comes to reading God's Word, you must have some sort of plan in place. Otherwise, you will wind up reading whatever looks good to you that morning (often Psalms), and you will not get the full truth of God's Word into your life.

I believe a good goal for every believer should be to read the Bible through at least once a year. Maybe some days you read an extended portion of Scripture and other days just a few verses.

Another important goal is to memorize Scripture. This has been one of the most rewarding experiences of my life. Pick a book like James and determine to commit it to memory. Sound crazy? It is doable! The way Jesus fought off Satan was through quoting Scripture from memory. Follow his example. I use a Bible app to help me. You might like flashcards. Use whatever suits you best.

Everyone has a list of excuses for why they cannot memorize. But these mostly boil down to spiritual laziness. We do not sincerely believe God's Word has the power to change lives. Chances are, if I gave you $100 for every verse you memorized, you might be a little more likely to memorize! The motivation would outweigh the difficulty. Likewise, the greater appreciation you develop for God's Word the more convicted you will be to commit large portions of it to memory.

Talk to God and develop a plan that will maximize your spiritual growth.

Read Prayerfully

Your reading of Scripture should harmonize with your prayers to God. As you read, have a prayerful spirit. Be asking God to give you the tenderness to apply what you are reading.

If we have made up our minds to study God's Word, Satan likes to take us to extremes. On one hand, he will urge us into studying the Bible like a textbook. Before long, if we are not careful, we enjoy studying about God more than spending time *with* him. We scorn Christians who make statements like, "God spoke to me." We look at every issue as black and white. Communicating with God becomes of little importance to us.

On the flip side, the alternative is to become very free spirited. We view every issue we face as demonic oppression. We did not get the closest parking spot at the grocery store because Satan was fighting against us. We become very sporadic in our behavior and act in ways that are contrary to God's Word – all the while excusing our actions as "living in the Spirit."

The bottom line is that as servants of Jesus, we must choose to live differently. Here is a popular saying I have improvised to fit my life: *When we read God's Word apart from his Spirit, we <u>dry up</u>. When we seek God's Spirit apart from his Word, we <u>blow up</u>. But when we read God's Word with the Holy Spirit's empowerment, we <u>grow up</u> into his character and likeness.*

Romans 12:2 says: "Do not be conformed to this world, but be transformed by the renewal of your mind, that by testing you may discern what is the will of God, what is good and acceptable and perfect." When you read the Bible, ask God to transform your mind through the power of his Word.

Never Lose Your Joy of Discovery

When life looks bleakest, God's Word shines brightest. It is through reading God's Word that all of our life's circumstances take on a full new meaning! That overtaxing boss at work suddenly fades to the background when we consider the true Master we serve. A financial loss pales in comparison to the riches God's Word promises in eternity.

Several years ago, Bible teacher Oletta Wald published a book on Bible study entitled *The Joy of Discovery*. What a fitting title! There should be no greater joy than to observe, interpret, and put God's Word into application through how we live! It gives us a whole new perspective on the God that we serve.

As we close out this section on the Bible, let me offer you a couple of warnings. First, never let God's Word become a drudgery to you. Keep it fresh. Mix things up and look for creative ways to allow the truth of his Word to come alive. Second, do not let your joy of discovery turn into pride. If you are not careful, your attitude will become very condescending. You will talk in such a way that says you know all the answers. Consequently, something inside of you begins to die, and others are not attracted to what you believe is so great. Third, never let your talk exceed your walk. Do not always speak about prayer if you pray little yourself. Do not blame others for petty inconsistencies when you refuse to allow God to confront you with your own.

Instead, read with a prayerful spirit, a humble heart, an obedient attitude, and always with a heart that wants to be better molded into the image of Christ.

Finally, get it settled in your mind that God's Word is the absolute authority for your life. As we have already covered in previous sections, *if you doubt the authority of God's Word, you will deny its message for your life.* You must get this issue settled. The moment you decide that all of God's Word is truth, you place yourself in a position to grow as never before.

The greatest joy in all the world is to discover and serve Jesus out of a heart of love.

Share with Others

God's Word has not fully worked in your heart until it is demonstrated by your life. You should treat others differently as a result of what you read! The greatest way to solidify God's Word in your heart is by sharing what you have learned with others. Through sharing, you begin to think more deeply and are able to better process what you have learned.

You may be thinking, "But how do I share God's Word? It is an intimidating task!" Charles Spurgeon was once asked, "How do you defend the Bible?" "Very easy" he responded. "The same way I defend a lion. I simply let it out of its cage." Too often, we get tied up on sharing God's Word with others because we think, "I just need to say this perfectly! Then they will be convinced!" But we must always remember that God's Word is alive, and it is much more powerful than any persuasive speech we can give!

I have found that sharing God's Word with others is often one of the best purifiers of theology. It is much harder to hold on to quacky, lifeless beliefs when we have to share them with others. Sharing God's Word with others moves us out of the world of theory and into the world of application. As we humbly accept the questions of others, wrong concepts of God will often fall by the wayside. Why? Because they do not work! But sharing God's Word God's way will do amazing things in the lives of others – and it will minister to us in ways we would not dream possible!

I want to wrap up this section with the words of former number one ranked tennis player, Arthur Ashe: "Start where you are, use what you have, do what you can." Then let the results be left up to God!

Action Points

1. What is your greatest fear in sharing God's Word with others?
2. How can you take steps to overcome this fear?
3. How does sharing with others ultimately change us as well?

Week 5

I Serve Someone Who Is Building Me a Kingdom

Day 29
You Are an Ambassador

"Each day brings us closer to death. If your treasures are on earth, that means each day brings you closer to losing your treasures."
—Randy Alcorn

You were born in this world for a reason, but you are not meant to live in this world forever. Every person you meet, every emotion you experience, and everything you do screams of this reality – you were made for another world!

In 2 Corinthians 5:20, Paul states that we are called to be ambassadors of Christ. Ambassadors are people who represent one country to another. They do not have equal allegiances. Their commitment is to the country they are representing.

For the believer, our citizenship is not of this world. Earth is not our final resting place.

An Ambassador Is a Stranger

This world lives under the curse of sin. Consequently, we live in hostile territory. The natural response for every man and woman is to reject God's authority and reign. *As servants of God, we are strangers in a foreign land. This world is not our home!*

Sometimes this is very difficult for us to understand. We like to think of our world as good. We like to think the best about people. We like to believe the house we have worked so hard to build will not come to an end. But this is just not the case.

Everything we have is temporary. From the moment we are born, life brings us the constant reminder that we are not of this world. It reminds us when our relative passes into eternity before us. It reminds us when our retirement collapses. It reminds us when we have a relational argument. We were made for something more!

An Ambassador Speaks on Someone Else's Authority

Being an ambassador of a country is a much higher position than just being a citizen. Ambassadors take an oath to uphold the rights of the country they represent. When you decide to become an ambassador of God, you are choosing to submit yourself to him and speak on his authority and not your own.

Take this example, as far-fetched as it may seem. As a Canadian citizen, say I want to be an ambassador of Canada to the nation of Australia. (I told you this was far-fetched!)

It is my first meeting with the Prime Minister of this fine nation. Wanting to impress him, I make it clear that Canada will do all that it can to please him. I tell him we will give Australia our half of the Niagara Falls. I tell him we will pay for all vacations taken by any member of the Senate or House of Representatives. I say we will work to immediately provide them with a 500 billion dollar stimulus. (I am quick to be on his good side!)

There is just one problem. I have no authority to execute every action I just proposed! I am not speaking on my own authority. I am speaking on behalf of the one who sent me. As a result, I am reprimanded heavily by the Canadian government.

Likewise as followers of Jesus, our authority does not come from ourselves. We do not have the right to run around making up whatever laws we want. Our responsibility is to uphold the best interests of the one who commissioned us.

We are not called to appease those living in sin. We are not called to do whatever it takes to make people like us. We are called to declare the authority of Jesus Christ to all nations of the world!

An Ambassador Must Be Entirely Loyal

Take another example. I am still ambassador. Only this time I decide to do things right. I declare my passionate belief that Canada is the greatest nation on earth. I tattoo the Prime Minister's name on my chest (much to my wife's dismay). I wear a little Canadian flag around my neck at all times. I have dozens of "I love Canada" bumper stickers all across the back of my Kia Soul. I even attend weekly "Keep Canada Awesome" rallies. By all external appearances, my total allegiance is to Canada.

Yet as the months roll along, it is suspected that I have been selling military secrets to the nation of Australia. This time I get a not-so-friendly visit from the Prime Minister. He begins to question my activity. In response, I hold nothing back. I tell him all I have done, but I am adamant I have done nothing wrong. I am quick to point out that I really do love Canada. I show him my "I love Canada" bumper stickers. I tell him that every night before bedtime I play the national anthem on the bagpipes. Strangely, all of this does little good! All of my statements mean little to him because I did not submit myself to the laws of the Canadian government.

Sadly, this is the exact game we so often play with God. We say, "God, I want to be an ambassador for you! Look at all the times I speak of you. Look at my 'I love Jesus' bumper sticker!" Yet through our actions, we represent the best interests of the world. We serve God in mouth but the world in deed. We reveal that our true allegiance is not to God but to men.

Attach this as a sticky note to your fridge: *Your stated loyalty to God means very little if your actions do not follow suit.* Being an ambassador of Jesus does not come through mere words. It comes through commitment and resolve behind those words – commitment that says, "Whatever my authority figure, King Jesus, says goes!"

Ambassadors Must Value What Their Authority Values

True ambassadors take on the values of those for whom they are speaking. It is not enough just to say, "I am on the team." You have to demonstrate through your actions that you value what your authority figure values.

This is a principle God taught me through being on staff at Eastlake Community Church. *Being on someone's team is not merely doing what they require; it is passionately pursuing what they value.* If you cannot pursue what your leader values, it is unlikely you will be on the team very long.

When it comes to following God, I fear we have many who claim loyalty and speak on God's behalf, but they do not value what God really values. They preach; they do ministry; they make an effort to lead their families, but their values are still a mess. As a result, their representation of Jesus is in shambles. They do not value what he values.

Take this thought to the bank: *What we value is determined by where we spend our time and how we use our resources.*

Time – Let's look at time. Every part of the day is to be lived for the glory of God (1 Cor. 10:31). There are no down spots. We must make time for that which matters most.

This can be tricky. It's like that illustration of being given the assignment to stuff rocks and sand in a jar. You only have so much jar to spare. If you start by pouring in the sand, you will have a tough time fitting in the rocks. The best way to start is by putting the big rocks in and then pouring the sand around them. When it comes to our lives, we must intentionally prioritize by putting the stuff that matters most in first.

Do you have a set time to communicate with God each day? Do you intentionally set aside time in your week to get around godly influences? What about your family? Are you intentional in leading them in the things of God? Do you spend time reading the Bible with your family? Do you take a Sabbath day to rest and focus on God? If not, why not? Could it be you do not really value the time God has given you?

Resources – You own nothing and have built nothing on your own. *Everything you own and have gained has all been made possible because of the graciousness of God.* In case that statement rolled by so fast you missed it, read it again. Everything you have is a result of the grace of God! What you have is not your own!

Resources come in many shapes and forms. They come through having land, connections, and financial access. Too often, Christians get caught up in the "If I just had what THEY have, THEN I would be in such a great position to give!" game. Ever heard this argument before? If I could just make $50,000 instead of $20,000, then I could give! If I just knew the people they know, then I could help. If I just had the building they have, THEN I could do what God wants me to do. All of these amount to a simple pile of excuses.

Money is obviously a big resource. When it comes to our money, I believe *the percentage of what we do with our income has more significance than the amount.* Everyone may not give equally, but we can sacrifice equally. Two people can give a thousand dollars to the work of God. Both mean well. Yet the person who only had two thousand to begin with was much more generous than the one who gave out of his $250,000.

Again, how you spend your time and where you spend your resources determine what you value.

Are You a True Ambassador of God?

Making a difference in this world is contingent on being an ambassador of the heavenly world. If you do not sell out to Christ's authority and commit to being loyal only to him and valuing what he values, everything you do in life will hold little weight.

Randy Alcorn makes this sad but telling statement:

Many Christians dread the thought of leaving this world. Why? Because so many have stored up their treasures on earth, not in heaven. Each day brings us closer to death. If your treasures are on earth, that means each day brings you closer to losing your treasures.

We are placed on this earth for a limited amount of time. It is up to you and me how we will decide to use it!

Action Points

1. How does "being an ambassador" help to guide you in the choices you make?
2. Would you say your actions characterize you as being an ambassador of the world or being an ambassador of God?
3. What are some ways that you need to better represent the God you serve?

— Day 30 —
God Is Building a Kingdom

"The Kingdom of God exists anywhere God is reigning as king."
—Ed Stetzer

Being an ambassador of God means having a commitment to his Kingdom. We are called to pursue after the Kingdom of God.

What is the Kingdom? This can be confusing, so let's walk our way through this step-by-step. I like Pastor Ed Stetzer's definition of the Kingdom of God. He says, "The Kingdom of God exists anywhere God is reigning as king." If Jesus lives in your heart, the Kingdom of God exists. If Jesus is in control of your church, the Kingdom of God is present.

Throughout the Gospels, Jesus spoke of the Kingdom over one hundred different times. Sometimes he spoke of the Kingdom of God, and other times he spoke synonymously of the Kingdom of Heaven. Over and over again, he taught us that the Kingdom is a big deal.

Having a Kingdom perspective is extremely important. Without having a Kingdom outlook we grow very territorial. We build our own little fortresses and burrow down. We mentally place people on teams. "You are on the liberal team, and you are on the conservative team. You are on my side, and you are on their side."

Here is an important news nugget: *The Kingdom of God is not based upon our differences. It is based upon what unites us as followers of Jesus Christ!*

How Do You Get into the Kingdom?

There are no magic passes into God's Kingdom. In John 3, Jesus outlined for Nicodemus what it takes. He says we must be born again. We all start off as a child of the kingdom of darkness and are in need of stepping into the Kingdom of Light.

We enter the Kingdom humbly. We realize we can do nothing to earn it. In the words of Jesus, we are to enter the Kingdom as a child (Matt. 19:14). Just as children cannot fully function on their own, so we are helpless without God. We approach him with humility, knowing that the Kingdom is not something we are entitled to attain. It is a tremendous gift and blessing from God!

Our humility in approaching God is the first step into becoming a Kingdom-minded follower of Jesus. God's process of turning us into Kingdom people is what we have already covered in previous sections. When we focus on glorifying God, enjoying him, loving him and others, having a holy character, and placing all our satisfaction in him, we are living as a Kingdom ambassador.

To be a child of God's Kingdom is to live like the King of that Kingdom – Jesus. Everyone can talk big and say the right things. Just because you speak eloquently about Jesus does not mean you will enter the Kingdom. In Matthew 7:21, Jesus shows us that a personal relationship is so much more important than the words we say. It includes the things we do!

We get into God's Kingdom by submitting ourselves to the King of that Kingdom – Jesus Christ.

The Kingdom Is Bigger Than You

The Kingdom is bigger than your church. God's Kingdom transcends time, location, and people. It is not contained in this world. *The Kingdom of God includes all God is doing to accomplish his purposes.*

In the grand scheme of things, our place in the Kingdom is relatively small. I am one of roughly twenty billion who have ever lived on this planet, and these twenty billion only encapsulate a small picture of God's greater Kingdom. Okay, I feel a little smaller just thinking about that!

Along with feelings of grief, it must make God chuckle when we place up our "kingdom palaces." We boast of OUR church, OUR organization, and OUR mini empire. And then to top this off, we have the gall to exclude people from our circles of power as though they were ours to begin with!

Make no mistake, God's Kingdom is not of this world (John 18:36). Several years ago, I began developing our Powerline Kingdom Network. Through it, we use the power of media to change people with the good news of Jesus Christ. I have chosen 1 Corinthians 4:20 as the foundational verse for this network. It says, "For the Kingdom of God does not consist in talk but in power." In context, Paul is saying to the church in Corinth, "You can talk big, but if you do not have the power of God in your life, all your talk is worthless!" This is a reality I remind myself of daily.

The Kingdom of God comes in ways and is in places we do not always expect (Luke 17:20-21). It is not all about me, and it is not all about you. And for our sakes, we can thank God it isn't!

The Kingdom Is Victorious

I love history. My favorite part to study is World War II. Aside from Great Britain, Hitler and the German army controlled all of Europe. But on June 6, 1944, D-Day changed this. Allied forces hit five beachfronts and were able to establish a stronghold. This was the turning point in the war.

On D-Day the war was essentially won. Yet there still remained many battles to come until the Allied forces conquered the streets of Berlin, and the Nazi's surrendered on VE Day – victory in Europe. Ed Stetzer writes, "On D-Day, the end of the war was inaugurated. On VE Day, the end of the war was consummated."

When it comes to our spiritual lives, Jesus Christ has already won the war. His death on the cross was our D-Day. From this we can take incredible confidence! Yes, there will be setbacks. Yes, the enemy will continue to kill. But we press on knowing that victory will indeed be ours! God's Kingdom will never be destroyed (Dan. 2:44) and it will never suffer defeat. We can have confidence knowing that God's Kingdom will remain forever (Dan. 4:34).

God Uses Us to Advance His Kingdom

One of the great marvels of God's Kingdom is that he uses us to advance it! He sovereignly works through finite men and women to take new ground from the enemy. This is incredible when you think about it.

Matthew 24:14 says, "And this gospel of the kingdom will be proclaimed throughout the whole world as a testimony to all nations, and then the end will come." How is this proclaimed? By simple men and women like you and me! Through declaring Jesus as king of our lives, we reflect his Kingdom to the world.

To be clear, it is not as though WE save anyone. Jesus Christ does the saving, but he works through us to speak to hearts and minds of those who are in rebellion against him. Jesus does it all. Contrary to what some would teach, nothing you do can force Jesus to return. We cannot magically usher in the return of Christ through winning the whole world to faith. Jesus will return when he chooses.

We are called to declare what Jesus Christ declared in Matthew 3:2: "Repent for the kingdom of heaven is at hand." We should follow his example and preach the Kingdom of God to everyone (Luke 4:43). When people reject our message, and many will, we are not to sulk. We do not whine that no one loves us. Rather, we do as Jesus instructed. We wipe off the dust from our sandals, so to speak, and move on (Luke 10:11)!

We continue to preach God's Kingdom with bold confidence knowing that nothing can or ever will compare to it (Luke 13:18).

God Wants to Give You the Kingdom!

God does not begrudgingly offer you the Kingdom. It is not one of those invitations where he invites you out of necessity but secretly hopes you never show up. (Invitations like that are always awkward!)

Jesus tells us in Luke 12:32 that it is the Father's good will to give us the Kingdom. The Father longs to give it to us. He sent his Son, so we could have the opportunity to participate in this Kingdom. Matthew 25:34 tells us that from the foundation of the world the Kingdom of God was being prepared for us.

Not only did Jesus speak of the Kingdom while he was alive, he spoke of it after his death and resurrection. When Jesus arose from the dead, he continued to make it a point to speak about the Kingdom of God (Acts 1:3). Jesus spoke much of the Kingdom because it is his intention for us to receive it.

This really excites me. I am invited to participate on God's team because he *wants* me to be a part!

Get Rid of Anything that Hinders You

The Kingdom is ours to receive, but it is also ours to reject. Jesus made it clear. We must get rid of anything that is keeping us from pursuing the Kingdom (Mark 9:47). If there are habits, attitudes, or behaviors that are hindering us, they have to go. If our circle of influence we hang around is holding us back, we must make a change. We are to be holy and set apart to a Kingdom calling!

WHAT KIND OF GOD DO I SERVE?

When we have made the decision to pursue the Kingdom of God, we must not look back! Jesus said in Luke 9:62, "No one who puts his hand to the plow and looks back is fit for the kingdom of God." You have enlisted in God's army, and there is no going back to the life you used to live! It's a new day and a new life.

Satan hates God's Kingdom. He works aggressively against the Kingdom (Matt. 13:19). Through pursuing the Kingdom of Heaven, we will encounter many tribulations (Acts 14:22). We will encounter serious opposition. It is a tremendous battle.

In Matthew 4, Jesus taught us the importance of pursuing the Kingdom. In this chapter, Satan was throwing massive temptations his way. One of these was taking Jesus up to a high mountain and showing him the kingdoms of the world. Satan promised to give Jesus all of this under the condition that Jesus fall down and worship him. But Jesus was not fooled. He realized that falling into this fleshly trap would keep him from pursuing the Kingdom of God.

When it comes to our lives, we must be actively on the alert against the attacks and temptations of Satan. There will be many things that will look very tempting and compete with our desire to pursue God's Kingdom. But it is in these moments that we must cry out to God and purposely readjust our focus. We are servants of the most high God and we refuse to be thrown off course!

Remember: *The key to staying focused on God's Kingdom is staying connected to the King of that Kingdom – Jesus Christ!*

Action Points

1. Why do you believe it is so easy to erect our own kingdoms in place of God's Kingdom?
2. How are you encouraged by knowing that the God we serve uses us to advance his Kingdom?
3. What is one activity in your daily life that you feel may be distracting you from pursuing God's Kingdom?

——••— Day 31 ——••—
What Does a Healthy Church Look Like?

"You never have to advertise a fire. Everyone comes running when there's a fire. Likewise, if your church is on fire, you will not have to advertise it. The community will already know it."
—Leonard Ravenhill

The organization God uses to grow his Kingdom on earth is the church of Jesus Christ. This church is the hope for our world. Without it, we might as well pack up our bags and go home.

When we talk about church, we must be careful to define our terms. First off, the word church was actually a German translation of the Greek word *"ecclesia,"* which simply means "assembly."

Broadly speaking, the church is both invisible and visible. *The invisible church is the church of Christ that has always existed from the creation of the world.* It includes all who have or ever will put their faith in Jesus Christ. It is universal and is not bound by geographical location. *The visible church is made up of local bodies of believers who assemble under the banner of Jesus Christ. We often refer to these as local churches.*

Every believer is automatically a part of Christ's invisible church. In addition to this, Scripture calls believers to assemble themselves together. Through this, the body is strengthened and encouraged.

So what does a healthy local church look like? Here are a few characteristics.

Healthy Churches Are Built on Jesus

Churches that are built upon Jesus do not just talk about him. They live him! God the Father has put all things under the feet of Jesus and established him as head of the church (Eph. 1:22).

Because Christ is the head of the church, every local church congregation must submit themselves to his authority (Eph. 5:23-24). If our theology and method of doing church does not line up with Jesus, we are the ones who are wrong, not him!

Submission is sometimes a hard concept for us to grapple with. How dare someone call me to submit to someone else! But the great news is that Christ is not some brutal dictator who formally hands down a list of commands to his subjects. Christ nourishes and cherishes the church (Eph. 5:29). He gave his life for the church. When I think about this reality, it sure makes it a whole lot easier to submit to his commands! Christ is the head of the body (Col. 1:18), and Christ is the one all churches must answer to.

Every church that wants to be healthy must decide to place Christ as the center of all that it does.

Healthy Churches Are Feeding Troughs

I will always remember the words of admonition that Bible teacher Stan Key offered to our ministry team during my days at Eastlake Community Church. They were simple, but they have stuck with me. They were some of the final words Jesus spoke to the apostle Peter in John 21:17. Just three simple words, "Feed my sheep." In context, Jesus is talking about sheep in reference to his followers. He wanted all those who served him to be fed even after he was gone.

This is a sad but truthful reality. The reason many believers, or sheep, are starving in churches today is because they are not being fed. However, healthy churches understand this and will have pastors and leaders who feed their sheep. The best way to feed followers of Jesus is by teaching them the Word of God. This is the best form of spiritual nutrition available!

Sheep that are not filled will grumble. But sheep and disciples of Jesus who are filled with God's Word will tend to be content and healthy!

Healthy Churches Have Spirit-Filled Leaders

You may have heard this saying, "Everything rises and falls upon leadership." I believe it is no different in the church. Local churches are to have pastors who serve as shepherds of their flock. These leaders should not be chosen with little thought. They should be appointed through careful prayer and fasting (Acts 14:23).

As leaders guided by the Spirit, they are to pay close attention to the flock the Holy Spirit gives them (Acts 20:28). Good pastors hurt when those in their congregation hurt. They rejoice with those who are happy and mourn with those who are sad. They bear the responsibilities and burdens those in their congregation carry. Just as a shepherd takes care of his flock, a pastor must take care of his congregation.

Take the apostle Paul. Here was a man who was busy, yet he directed most of his energy to building up local churches (2 Cor. 11:28). Some of the congregations had serious immoral problems and in-house church feuding. In fact, rivalries would often break out in local congregations where young upstarts would try to get the congregation to turn from Paul and to them. No doubt this must have caused him at times to wonder, "What in the world am I doing?" Yet through all of the pain, Paul still loved them!

A good way to tell if a leader will do well in the church is to watch how he does at home. True leaders take care of their families first (1 Tim. 3:5). If a leader is not good in the home, it is a telling sign he will not be good in your church.

Spirit-filled leaders develop Spirit-filled people. *If lives are not being transformed in your church, it may be a sign that the shepherd of your flock is experiencing little transformation in his soul.*

Healthy Churches Have Spirit-Gifted People

Spirit-filled believers are Spirit-gifted believers. By gifted I do not necessarily mean talented. 1 Corinthians 12 gives us a list of spiritual gifts that believers can have. Everyone has at least one gift, and many Christians have multiple gifts.

A healthy church will not be afraid to have people of diversified gifts. Rather, it will encourage this environment. The more spiritually gifted people we have in a local congregation, the greater we will display Christ's character, and the more impact we will have as a church.

Unfortunately, accepting everyone's differing gifts is often not the default mode for believers. We like to create a church where everyone thinks like us, dresses like us, and acts like us. As a result, we create self-destructing bodies. Everyone is content to plateau together.

Ultimately, our gifts are to be used with the purpose of building up the local body (1 Cor. 14:5). The more we squelch the gifts of others and the gifts God has given us, the less our churches and our lives have the anointing of God's Holy Spirit.

Read 1 Corinthians 12, and then ask yourself this question: Which spiritual gifts are emphasized and which ones are not emphasized in my church? Why is this the case? What can I do to make a difference?

Healthy Churches Are on Fire

Spiritual giant Leonard Ravenhill once made this tremendous statement: "You never have to advertise a fire. Everyone comes running when there's a fire. Likewise, if your church is on fire, you will not have to advertise it. The community will already know it." This fire is sometimes hard to define, but it is always marked with a fervency towards God.

A key attribute of this fervency is prayer. *A healthy church is a praying church.* In Acts 12, Peter is in prison. Yet what does the local church do? They fall on their faces and cry out to God on Peter's behalf. *The sooner a local body realizes the powers of darkness are beyond their control, the sooner God determines to show his power.*

Another part of this fervency is worship. It should be natural for believers to worship God (Acts 14:27). We should have hearts that want to declare all that Jesus is doing in our lives. Singing in a worship service on Sunday morning should not be a drag for us. It should be an incredible pleasure!

Healthy churches are churches that are on fire.

Healthy Churches Fear God

In connection with this, healthy churches have a healthy fear of God (Acts 5:11). *How we fear God is contingent on our standing with him.* Think of an Ontario provincial police officer. If you are doing 100 km per hour in a 45 km zone and you see a police officer, your fear of him or her will be one of dread. On the other hand, if you are walking down the street in a rough section of town, your fear of this same police officer will be one of respect. You realize he is there for your protection. Healthy churches fear displeasing God and look at God more with hope and respect than they do with dread.

Fearing God leads to willing obedience to his commands.

Healthy Churches Will Be Persecuted

Every healthy church will be on Satan's radar. He WILL come against it. All through the New Testament and down through the ages, the church of Jesus Christ has always suffered persecution. It comes in different forms. Sometimes persecution happens through death and torture. Other times it comes through ridicule and cynical resentment. But any healthy church you are a part of WILL suffer persecution.

Just yesterday I was convicted of this reality. I had to ask myself, am I really suffering for God? I was listening to a girl on the radio who had witnessed her brother and husband brutally shot before her eyes. Reason: They were followers of Jesus Christ. As I sat there and listened, my heart was checked. I don't know about you, but I fear I enjoy security way too much. Not just so much for my sake but for the sake of my family. Will my wife have to suffer persecution? Will my children have to suffer for the gospel? That is not always a comforting thought.

Yet I have hope, and you have hope. God's Word teaches us that through persecution, we can rejoice. As the apostle Paul showed us, we can rejoice when we suffer for the body and for Jesus Christ because there is no higher calling (Col. 1:24)!

The suffering our church may experience in this life is minimal compared to the joy that awaits us in the life to come!

Healthy Churches Give

Healthy churches are giving churches. The natural default of a church is to hoard. We give only to ministries that directly give back to us, and we certainly do not give to someone of a different denomination or theological background! Shamefully, when we do this we fail to take into account Jesus' words in Luke 14:14 when he points out we are blessed when people cannot repay us.

The church I pastor is committed to being intentional in church planting. We will always tithe off of our income. Always. With God's help, we will never become hoarders of all the resources God has given us.

Not only will we refuse to hoard resources, we will refuse to hoard people. My ministry mentor, Pastor Troy Keaton, always says, "The measure of success in our church will not be counted in how many people come to our church but in how many people go." This is hard to think about. I like keeping quality people in our church. But I also realize that sometimes the only way for believers to really grow is by sending them out from their comfort zone and empowering them to be all God wants them to be.

Healthy local churches should not fear giving away members, resources, or support. Because when you give, you will truly receive the greater blessing.

Healthy Churches Naturally Grow

The law of nature tells us that living organisms grow or die. A tree that is healthy will naturally yield branches and grow to new heights.

Read Acts 2. In verse 42, Luke pens these words about the local church body: "And they devoted themselves to the apostles' teaching and the fellowship, to the breaking of bread and prayers."

I believe churches that devote themselves to good teaching, have genuine fellowship with each other, break bread and live life together, and fall on their faces before God, will be healthy and growing. In verse 47, it says that God added to their number daily.

Keep reading Acts, and in chapter 16 verse 5 you get the same story. As the churches were strengthened in their faith, they grew. Note: This growth was in number, not just "spiritual maturity." Numerical growth was important. In the parable of Jesus, the reason the good shepherd realized one of his sheep was missing was because he had counted the other ninety-nine. *Numbers should matter to a local church because numbers matter to God.*

I believe Acts 9:31 really gives us the secret to having a church that multiplies. It says, "So the church throughout all Judea and Galilee and Samaria had peace and was being built up. And walking in the fear of the Lord and in the comfort of the Holy Spirit, it multiplied."

Churches that grow MUST walk in the fear of the Lord and step by step with the Holy Spirit. This means being intentional.

How Are You Engaged in Your Local Church?

God did not call you to be a loner. I believe *if I refuse to partner with other believers, it says more about me than it does about others.* Ouch! Because church means an assembly, worshiping God by yourself in the woods is not adequate. You must be connected to others.

How you participate in your local church says much about how you view Christ's universal church. With that being said, make a decision today to become involved. Be proactive. Do not wait for your pastor to beg you to participate. Join a ministry. Help in the kid's club. Be involved on the worship team. If your church is not healthy, work to make it that way! Be the change you wish would happen.

No, your local church is not perfect. But always remember that no matter what local church you serve, your service is ultimately to the universal church of Christ. It is upon Christ's commission that we assemble with others. He is our first allegiance.

The fact of the matter is that every local church on earth will one day perish. Nevertheless, the true church of Jesus Christ will last forever, and the gates of Hell cannot prevail against the church of Jesus Christ (Matt. 16:18).

A healthy local church is the means by which Jesus Christ brings hope to our world!

Action Points

1. Contrast the differences between a local church and the universal church.
2. How can you improve the way you serve in your local church this week?
3. Do you tend to be a loner? How many solid church friends do you have? What could you do to increase this number?

⎯•⊹••⊷⎯ **Day 32** ⎯⊶••⊹•⎯
YOLO, You Only Live Once

"He whose head is in heaven need not fear to
put his feet into the grave."
—Matthew Henry

Everything we do on earth is done with the overarching realization that one day we will die. (What an optimistic way to start a chapter!)

We can ignore this reality, but we cannot avoid it. You and I are on this earth for a short time. Everything on earth screams the word "temporary." We are in a world of constant decay. Rather than getting better, our world progressively gets worse. Buy a new item, and in just a short while it wears out. Let your yard go for a few weeks without upkeep, and it will soon turn into a jungle. Ignore your body, and it will soon begin to decay. Everything in life breaks down.

Our entire earth points to death. Death is the inevitable door which we all must pass through. It is that one-way street to which all paths lead. Death is inevitable.

As decaying human beings, we have two options: A) We can embrace death, or B) We can fear death. One reality is certain: death cannot be avoided. Matthew 24:14 reminds us that the end of this world will come after the gospel is proclaimed to the whole world. There are no ifs, ands, or maybes when it comes to death.

Death Is Not Final

The greatest hope for believers and the greatest dread for sinners is the reality that death is not final. Death is not a punishment for believers in Christ. Romans 8:1 says there is no condemnation for those in Christ Jesus. Death is swallowed up in victory. This led the apostle Paul to proclaim in 1 Corinthians 15:55 those famous words that we often cite at funerals today, "O death, where is your victory? O death, where is your sting?"

For believers, death is but a doorway to a greater picture. It is a necessary step in becoming like Christ. We have the hope that Christ will be honored in our bodies whether in life or in death (Phil. 1:20). Death issues believers into the very presence of Christ. 2 Corinthians 5:8 says that to be absent from the body is to be present with the Lord. In Luke 23:43, when Jesus spoke to the repentant thief on the cross he stated, "Today you shall be with me in paradise." (Note: This is one reason why a belief in soul sleep or purgatory just cannot be supported in Scripture.)

For unbelievers, their souls enter into eternal punishment. Luke 16 gives us a chilling account of a rich man who rejected God. In verse 26, Jesus talks of the great chasm that exists between those who have accepted Christ and those who have rejected him. There is no hint that those who have rejected Christ in this life can ever get a second chance in the life to come.

The Bible is repetitiously strong in this matter. In Matthew 25:31-46, Jesus is clear with a shepherding illustration that following death the righteous and the wicked will be separated. The sheep of Jesus Christ will receive eternal life with him while the goats will receive eternal punishment. In John 5:28-29, Jesus again speaks of those who will receive eternal judgment versus those who will receive eternal life. Acts 24:15 speaks of the resurrection of the just versus the unjust.

These two realities should cause us to view death with a whole new perspective. If you are a believer in Christ, it should cause you to become anything but arrogant. On the contrary, it should force you to your knees and give you a tremendous burden for those who do not know Christ. We should develop the heart of the apostle Paul. In Romans 9:1-3, Paul goes as far as to say that he would rather be accursed and cut off from Christ if by doing so he could see his friends come to faith and be saved. Think about that; he said he would rather face Hell than see his friends go there. Now that is love!

Christ Will Return

Our death and Christ's return are two undeniable realities. Hebrews 9:28 says Christ will appear a second time. This time will be different from his first appearance. He will not come this time to deal with sin, but he will come for those who are eagerly awaiting his return. James 5:8 says, "The coming of the Lord is at hand." In Revelation 22:20 Jesus says, "Surely I am coming soon."

There are several opinions as to when Christ will return. These are called Premillennial, Amillennial, and Postmillennial. All of these have numerous proponents supporting their view. Premillennialists believe Jesus will come before his prophesied thousand-year reign on earth. Amillennials deny that there is a thousand-year reign altogether, while Postmillennials maintain that Jesus Christ will come back after his thousand-year reign. I tend to lean more towards a Premillennial perspective, but I am readily open to those who hold differing viewpoints.

Rather than focusing on what we do not know about Christ's return, I believe it is more helpful to dwell on what we do know. For starters, we must understand that not even Jesus Christ knows the day and the hour of his return (Matt. 24:26). This means that all of the many predictions people give for Jesus' certain return are anything but certain. Matthew 24:44 says Jesus is coming at an hour when we will least expect him. We know neither the day nor the hour (Matt. 25:13), and we should run from those who claim that they do.

Check out some of these passages. 1 Thessalonians 5:2 tells us that Jesus Christ will return like a thief in the night. It will be sudden and unexpected. 2 Peter 3:10 echoes this promise with the words, "The day of the Lord will come like a thief." In 2 Thessalonians 4:16, the apostle Paul writes, "The Lord will descend from Heaven with a shout." This descent will happen in the twinkling of an eye (1 Cor. 15:51-52). Revelation 1:7 says, "He is coming with clouds, and every eye will see him." In other words, Jesus will come quickly, loudly, without warning, and in such a way that no one will be able to deny his return.

While there is a lot we do not know about Christ's return, we do know that his coming will be sudden and at an hour when we think not. A tip of advice for maturing believers: Rather than spending all of your energy *debating* when Christ will return, focus your time on *preparing* for his return.

Judgment Is Inevitable

The great wonder of death is that it levels the playing field. The whistle is blown. The game is up and everyone will stand before the judgment seat of Christ.

Following Christ's return, every person will come face-to-face with the judgment of God. Hebrews 9:27 tells us it is appointed for all to die and after that comes judgment. This judgment will separate those who believe in Christ and those who have rejected him. Those who have accepted Christ and lived by his commands will experience the resurrection of life, while those who have done evil will suffer the resurrection of judgment.

In 2 Timothy 4:1, Paul says that Jesus Christ is the judge of both the living and the dead. No one who has died or is here on earth when Christ returns will escape the judgment of God.

On the day of judgment, each of us will be called to give an account of our lives before God (Rom. 14:10-12). We are judged according to the Book of Life (Rev. 20:12). This Book of Life contains the names of all those who will experience eternal life. Those whose names are not written in the Book of Life are cast into a lake of fire (Rev. 20:15).

There Will Be Degrees of Punishment and Reward

How we choose to live on earth will determine our outcome on judgment day. For the unbeliever, a lifetime of sin will bring with it an eternity of punishment. For the righteous, a life lived like Christ will result in an eternity with him. A life sold out to Satan will suffer punishment; whereas, a life sold out to God will receive eternal life with him.

Revelation 20:12-13 teaches us that we will receive a greater amount of reward or punishment according to what we have done. Throughout Scripture, this theme is echoed. Luke 20:47 points out there will be degrees of condemnation. Colossians 3:25 tells us every wrongdoer will be repaid for the wrong they have committed.

Since this is true, it should cause us to sit up and think more clearly. Life suddenly becomes much more than just squeaking into Heaven. It is about living each day to the fullest, knowing that we will be rewarded for how we live.

It was biblical commentator Matthew Henry who wrote, "He whose head is in heaven need not fear to put his feet into the grave." As terrifying as judgment day may seem to you, we are given a great hope. 1 John 4:17 says we can have confidence on the day of judgment based upon our love for God and his love for us. We can approach it knowing that our judge is impartial (1 Pet. 1:17). He wants what is best for us.

YOLO

YOLO. Ever heard of this saying? It is a trendy way of saying, "You only live once." (Note: If you are older in age and want to impress your grandkids, this is the phrase you should use!)

As followers of Jesus, we only have one life to live. This should cause you and me to ask ourselves a very important question: Am I really making the most of the life God has given me? Are the decisions I am making today setting me up to receive a greater reward in Heaven?

I will never understand a believer who speaks more of retirement than they do of their hope in Heaven. Retirement is a terribly short-sighted goal to settle for in the grand landscape of eternity! As followers of Jesus, we are called to take our thinking deeper. Our decisions must not be made out of a desire to live well in this life, but to store up treasures for the life to come!

One of my personal hobbies is to study the lives of influential men and women who have lived and are still living today. I enjoy looking at people like Peter Mansbridge, Johnny Carson, Steve Jobs, Wayne Gretzky, and Mother Teresa to see what made them tick. What drove them to live and do what they did? If I had only one life to live, would I want to live it as they did?

It has caused me to evaluate what is truly important. Did these people I admire most live fulfilled lives, or did their lives consist of a lot of fluff? Did they position themselves to be spoken well of by people on earth but poorly of by their Father in Heaven?

The more I study, the more I ask God to help me to live a life of meaning and purpose. I hope that right now you will take some time to evaluate your place in life. Ask yourself some tough questions. Get on your face before God and beg him to show you ways to maximize your life on this earth, because after all – **You Only Live Once!**

Action Points

1. If you died today, would you be happy with the legacy you left to those around you?
2. How is judgment day a comforting and yet sobering reality?
3. Discuss the idea of "degrees of reward." Is this a new concept to you? If so, how might this change the way you live on earth?

Day 33
Hell Is Worse Than You Imagine

"Disbelieve Hell, and you unscrew, unsettle, and unpin everything in Scripture."
—J.C. Ryle

For an unbeliever, this life is the greatest blessing they will ever experience. That is an extremely troubling thought. Author Randy Alcorn writes, "For Christians, this present life is the closest they will come to Hell. For unbelievers, it is the closest they will come to Heaven."

Hell is without question the most troubling section I have had to tackle in this book. There are several reasons for this. One, it is troubling because its reality is horrendous. Second, I am troubled

217

in writing about Hell because of the need to make sure my words are correct. If we are really going to believe in Hell, we had better be certain we have the Bible's understanding on this issue. And third, I am troubled by Hell because so few people in our world seem to be troubled by it.

We have gotten so good at relegating Hell to being a theological debate or a flippant word to be used in conversation that we begin to desensitize ourselves and others to its meaning. Dare I say we have grown comfortable in speaking about Hell? Everything in me bucks against this way of thinking. Hell is anything but a comfortable topic.

Many years ago, a group of preachers were chatting, and one younger gentleman made the comment that he was getting to a place where he felt confident in how he talked about Hell. It was here that an older Irish preacher spoke up and asked this younger preacher a telling question. He asked, "Aye, but can you talk about it without a tear in your eye?"

I fear too many believers can talk big about Hell. We can use it to badger, abuse, and scare people into making a decision to serve God. The sad reality is that by our flippant attitudes we show we know little of Hell's eternal devastation. Hell is much more than a swear word, and it is high time we in the church lead the way in warning people of its horror.

Hell Is a Literal Place of Real Torture

The Bible does not give us any geographical location for Hell. This means that all those stories of people drilling down into the earth and hearing the sounds of screaming people are false. (This sure would have helped my fears if I would have known this as a kid!)

Hell, according to the Bible, is a place of eternal separation from God. As we go through Scripture, there appear to be differing degrees of Hell. The New Testament gives three different Greek words that are used to refer to Hell. These words are *Tartarus, Hades,* and *Gehenna.*

Tartarus is used only once in the New Testament in 2 Peter 2:4. It refers to a temporary holding place for fallen angels. There is not much else said about this place of imprisonment except for a minor reference to it in Jude 6.

Hades is a term that is probably most familiar to us. This is the word most people refer to when they talk about Hell. It is used ten times in the New Testament including an account of Lazarus in Luke 16:22-31. From this passage we can see that Hades is a place where spirits of the wicked go after they die (16:22). This passage and others point out that human beings will not spend eternity as spirits without bodies (Acts 2:27, 31; 24:15). There is no middle ground. You either spend your time on the new earth or in the lake of fire with unbearable heat (16:24). And yet it is also a place of darkness (Matt. 25:30). It is a place of memory and regret (16:25). It is a place of torment, agony, and without water (16:23, 24, 28). It is a separation from God and the righteous (16:26).

Gehenna is the lake of fire and the second death that swallows up those who were in *hades* (Rev. 20:14). *gehenna* is used twelve times in the New Testament and it serves as the ultimate destiny of all evildoers. The term *gehenna* is derived from the Valley of Hinnom, which was used as a burial place for criminals and for burning garbage. Matthew 25:41 tells us *gehenna* was created for the devil and his angels. It has unquenchable, eternal fire and brimstone (Mark 9:43-45). It is a place of weeping, wailing, and gnashing of teeth (Matt. 8:12). It is a place of eternal torment and death for both body and spirit (Matt. 10:28).

While not every biblical writer, such as the apostle Paul, directly mentioned Hell, the concept of Hell is a present theme all throughout Scripture. The prophet Ezekiel stated that the soul that sins shall die (Ezek. 18:20). The psalmist David spoke numerous times about Hell and the punishment of the wicked.

There are few people who hate the thought of Hell more than I do. I cannot bear the thought that many people I encounter on earth will go to this horrific place. Yet when I look at Scripture, I find its existence undeniable.

I readily admit that my fear of Hell is a key motivating factor in striving to share the good news of Jesus Christ with as many people as possible!

Hell Is the Home of Satan

Hell is the home of Satan, but Satan is not the master of Hell. I don't know about you, but I tend to think of Hell as Satan's palace where he and his evil demons rule and have dominion. It seems to make logical sense, right? God is the ruler of Heaven while Satan is the king of Hell. But Scripture does not support this view.

God is actually the Master of Hell. He alone has the power to send men and women there, and he alone will bind the hands of Satan and his demons. Hell is a place that was originally prepared for Satan and his demons (Matt. 25:41).

The reason Hell is Satan's home is because of his attitude toward God. Before God ever created the world, Satan reared up in rebellion against God. He attempted to usurp God's authority and to install himself as God. Isaiah 14:12-14 and Ezekiel 28:12-18 both point to this fact. In these passages, Satan is described as beautiful. In Revelation, Satan is referred to as a "star," and from piecing together different verses of Scripture we have good reason to believe that he was the highest of the angels and that one third of the angels joined him in his rebellion (Rev. 12:4).

One day Satan's power to kill and destroy will be taken away and he, along with his demons, will be cast into the eternal lake of fire. Revelation 12:12 tells us Satan knows his time is short. Because he knows it is short, he has determined to wreak havoc on God's creation. Satan's ultimate beef is not with us. It is with the one in whose image we are created. Because he cannot successfully attack God *directly*, he chooses to attack him *indirectly* through us.

Hell Is Eternal

There is no time limit on Hell. Matthew 25:46 makes it clear that whether we go to Heaven or Hell, both of these places are eternal.

In 2 Thessalonians 1:6-9, Paul is very adamant that those who reject the gospel of Jesus will suffer the punishment of eternal destruction away from the presence of the Lord. Mark 9:43 pictures Hell as an unquenchable fire. Once someone is sent to Hell, Scripture gives us no indication that there will ever be a possibility of leaving.

In recent years there has been a fresh push by some professing evangelical writers to deny the eternal nature of Hell. But as writer Randy Alcorn notes, "By denying the endlessness of Hell, we minimize Christ's work on the cross." We are saying that everyone has a get out of jail free card in their hip pocket.

In one sense, this is attractive to me, and I want to believe it. I would love to think that everyone I meet is going to experience everlasting joy and happiness. Still, everything I read in God's Word tells me otherwise.

WHAT KIND OF GOD DO I SERVE?

Hell Is What Everyone Deserves

The sobering reminder of Hell is that it is what we all deserve. (Rom. 6:23). I'll admit it, this thought has at times seemed crazy to me. I deserve Hell? I deserve eternal torture? I deserve everlasting separation from God? The answer is yes, I do.

I believe one of the reasons we struggle with this concept is because we have such a shallow view of sin. We believe sin is not as horrible as the Bible claims. Thus, our shallow understanding leaves us wide open to holding on to and excusing sins in our life, and we feel they are inconsequential. Just a little "cussing never hurt no one." A little dabbling in pornography is not a huge deal. Fudging slightly on our business ethics will not make or break us. In our eyes, these are small habits. But in God's eyes, they are willful and deliberate acts of hostile rebellion against him.

How you talk about Hell is often determined by what you think about sin. C. H. Spurgeon was right when he cautioned, "When men talk of a little hell, it is because they think they have only a little sin, and believe in a little Savior. But when you get a great sense of sin, you want a great Savior, and feel that, if you do not have Him, you will fall into a great destruction, and suffer a great punishment at the hand of a great God."

Understand that God takes no pleasure in sending people to Hell and seeing people punished (Ezek. 33:11). He will give everyone an opportunity to repent and receive Christ. God does not unjustly condemn men and women to Hell. It is their choice to choose Hell through refusing God's gracious gift of salvation (Heb. 2:1-3). Ezekiel 18:24-27 shows us that just as a sinful man can become a righteous man, a righteous man can become sinful and is then worthy of death.

Hell is what you and I deserve. Thank God that he has provided a way of escape and the hope of an incredibly different future!

Hell Is Not a Joking Matter

On a closing note, I have already mentioned how in more recent years there have been a good many debates over Hell. My fear is that if we are not careful, these will desensitize us to the real matter at stake. If Hell is really real, this should cause us to weep and mourn for those who are on their way to its doors. Hell is not a joking matter. There is not one single reference in Scripture of a biblical writer speaking trivially about Hell.

On the contrary, every reference to Hell is done soberly and with great thought. This is not by accident. Jesus said strongly in Matthew 10:28 that we must fear those who will destroy our soul and body in Hell. In Matthew 18:8-9 he instructs us to get rid of anything in our lives that might cause us to slip up and go to Hell. He never considered Hell a game or a debate. It was always a serious place with real souls at stake.

Many years ago overseas a prison chaplain came in to speak to a dying prisoner who did not believe in God. The prisoner stated these words:

> Sir, I do not share your faith. But if I did – if I believed what you say you believe – then although England were covered with broken glass from coast to coast, I would crawl the length and breadth of it on hand and knee and think the pain worthwhile, just to save a single soul from this eternal hell of which you speak.

Hell is serious and we must believe it if we will ever make a real difference in this world. Writer J.C. Ryle said, "Disbelieve Hell, and you unscrew, unsettle, and unpin everything in Scripture."

To this day, I remember the night when I gave my life to Jesus Christ. I was just five years of age when I had a vivid dream about Hell (not the most pleasant of nights!). Thankfully, God used this dream to stir up a spiritual realization in my life; a realization that I was in need of a Savior to deliver me from going to this awful place. At that time, I knew very little of God, but I knew my need for him. A tiny glimpse of Hell and a little understanding of my sin made me realize I needed a great big God!

Do you abhor Hell with everything in you? Do you really? I am not a fan of ending on "down notes." Today, however, will be an exception. I want you to take some time and think on the devastation Hell will bring for those who go there. Then let these sobering thoughts motivate you to seek after God and win others to Jesus as never before!

Closing thought: *How you really view Hell is evidenced by how you passionately pursue God and fervently forsake sin.* How do you view Hell?

Action Points

1. Based on that last statement, what would you say your view of Hell is today?
2. Why do people often find it difficult to speak about Hell?
3. How will you use this writing on Hell today to challenge you in your Christian journey?

Day 34
Heaven Is Better Than You Think

"When I've meditated on Heaven, sin is terribly unappealing."
—Randy Alcorn

Your best thought about Heaven pales in comparison to its splendor. Just think about that! Picture the greatest scenario, the most wonderful relationship, or the nicest vacation you could visualize. Now just realize, Heaven has this beat by a landslide.

If this is really true, if Heaven is really as good as some have claimed it to be, maybe we should know a thing or two about it! In fact, to not know anything about Heaven would be incredibly foolhardy if it is our desire to go there!

Picture going on a trip to France. In fact, your whole family is going. Everyone prepares for this trip for over a year. The proper airline tickets are purchased, and you call off work for two weeks. The kids all buy little French bracelets they wear with them every day to school. Everyone is excited. But as you are all settling down on the plane together, one of your family members asks, "Does anyone know anything about France?" You look around and realize no one has a clue. In fact, no one knows if it is any different from Asia, Europe, or Africa. Everyone is excited to go, but no one has any clue what it is like or even if it is worth going to!

Pretty ridiculous thought, right? Why on earth would you spend time and money to go on a journey with no understanding of the end goal? That is a good question.

When it comes to Heaven, I am afraid far too many Christians are on board for the ride but have no clue of their final destination. What a sad thought! We excuse our lack of understanding by saying Heaven is beyond our ability to comprehend. When truth be told, we are simply too apathetic and have very little expectation for what it will be like.

Consequently, our priorities reflect our level of excitement. Since we talk and think little of Heaven, we default to making decisions based from only an earthly mindset.

However, the Bible has something to say about this. Scripture does not support a dim view of Heaven. On the contrary, the Bible has quite a bit to say about what Heaven is like, and this should excite us greatly!

Heaven Is a Real Place

First off, we have to comprehend that Heaven is a real place. It is not a state of nirvana. It is not merely a heightened spiritual consciousness. Jesus said in John 14:2, "I go to prepare a *place* for you" (emphasis added). Heaven is a very real place that God is preparing for those who love him and obey his will. It is a place where there are physical items such as palm branches and robes (Rev. 7:9), the Tree of Life (Rev. 22:2), a temple (Rev. 15:8), and so forth. It is a literal, physical place.

Heaven is also not some cloudy utopia with angels playing harps on every corner. Scripture gives us every indication that Heaven will contain many of the same features we see here on earth – only to a much greater and perfected degree. There will be trees, grass, precious stones, and many of the same beauties we experience on earth.

In Heaven there will be streets of gold and gates of pearl (Rev. 21:21). All those gold bars that you no doubt have stored in your basement cellar are nothing more than blocks of concrete in Heaven!

Because Heaven is a real place, we will have real responsibilities. In John 5:17, Jesus tells us that the Father in Heaven works. If

God the Father works, we can expect to be doing the same. Read Matthew 25 and the parable of the talents. Through understanding this parable, we can see that we will be given positions of leadership and reign according to our level of commitment on earth.

I do not know about you, but this is a game changer for me. When I grasped this concept several years ago, I suddenly began to be more intentional in paying closer attention to the seemingly insignificant details of life. No task is insignificant. I am not pursuing an earthly reward, but a Heavenly reward!

Heaven Is Eternal Joy

The great, satisfying realization of Heaven is there is no reward that will not be great. This is difficult for us to understand because our minds tend to think in terms of reward versus loss. But true happiness and contentment does not come through attaining a certain reward. It only comes through delighting ourselves in God. There will always be someone who is rewarded to a higher degree than us and yet we all will experience eternal, satisfying joy!

I agree with Dr. Wayne Grudem when he writes:

> If highest status were essential for people to be fully happy, no one but God would be fully happy in heaven, which is certainly an incorrect idea. Moreover, those with greater reward and honor in heaven, those nearest the throne of God, delight not in their status but only in the privilege of falling down before God's throne to worship him.

In Heaven, there is no night (Rev. 21:25). There will be no pain or tears (Isa. 25:8-12). All sorrow will be wiped away. Because all sorrow and grief has sin as its ultimate originator, a sinless Heaven will be free from the torments of pain. The reason sin will be absent in Heaven is because our minds will be fully opened to the mind of Christ. Just as it was impossible for Jesus to sin when he had an eternal perspective, so realistically it will become impossible for us to sin when we have a similar vantage point. When we see sin for what it really is through Heaven's lens, our desire for it will vanish. Satan will be defeated (Rev. 12:8)!

In Heaven, we will never hunger, thirst, or endure the bitter heat from the sun (Rev. 7:13-17). There will be no more curse and no more night (Rev. 22:3-9). No more car payments, tax deadlines, or housing foreclosures. All of these will be no more.

Our arrival in Heaven will be the grand start of an eternity of joy. And it makes good sense to me that the more we pursue Jesus in this life, the fuller we will enjoy him in the next. We will have realized what our hearts have longed for in this life. Heaven does not magically bring an end to all growth. We will continue to expand in our knowledge. And as we expand, we will develop an even deeper appreciation for who Jesus is and thus expand in our personal joy.

Heaven Is Eternity with God

Would you still desire to go to Heaven if you realized God would be absent? This question, which I heard John Piper ask on one occasion, has really caused me to think. If you knew God would not be present, but you could receive all of the benefits of Heaven as you imagine them, would you still want to go?

Your answer and my answer to this question reveal much about the delight we take in God. Do we serve him because of what we can get from him, or do we serve him in order to find all of our fulfillment in him? There is a big difference! Heaven is not just about all of the beautiful new joy we will experience. It is about seeing face to face the originator of all beauty!

2 Chronicles 6:18 lets us know that God is so great that even Heaven itself cannot contain him. That is pretty great! Acts 7:49

says Heaven is God's throne and earth is his footstool. Just look around our world and its incredible majesty. In fact, earth is so small in comparison to who God is that it is viewed as his footstool. That is one big God that we serve! Jesus Christ, who came to this footstool, ascended into Heaven and now sits at the right hand of God the Father (Mark 16:19). And 1 Corinthians 15:49 gives us the hope that when we get to Heaven, we will fully bear Christ's image.

Ponder this for a minute. When I married my wife Janan, I realized it was a lifelong commitment. Because of this, we both took extra steps in getting to know each other at a deeper level before we were married. We wanted to know each other's passions, likes and dislikes, and generally as much about each other as possible. Why? Because we wanted to get an idea of what to expect for the rest of our lives!

It is the same way with God. *If you and I are really serious about spending an eternity in Heaven with him, we had better take serious steps forward in discovering who he is, so we can better enjoy him in the life to come!*

Heaven Is Perfect Relationships

There are a lot of problems in relationships on earth. People get offended; feelings get hurt; communication is broken down, and loneliness is experienced. But in Heaven, relationships will be profoundly deep and meaningful. We will be united with others in purpose and mission. There will be much we will have in common under our union in Christ.

Some people get very troubled when they read Jesus' words in Matthew 22 about there being no more marriage in Heaven. How in the world could God do away with the deepest form of union on earth? The reason is because our lowest level of union with another person in Heaven will be greater than our highest form of union on earth!

If you do not have a meaningful marriage, this might be difficult to picture. Yet regardless of the fact, just imagine the deepest relationship that you have with any person alive today. Now understand that this relationship pales in comparison to the connection we will have with others in eternity!

On earth we are really blessed if we have one or two great relationships with others. But in Heaven, our deep and meaningful relationships will be too many to count!

There Is Only One Way to Heaven

The deepest Christian lives are not built upon a longing for the pleasures of Heaven but the fulfillment in God. The road to Heaven is straight and it is narrow. The way we receive Heaven is to seek after God. Real eternal life is not found in a place, it is found in a person. When we pursue Jesus Christ with all our hearts, we will enter into Heaven.

Jesus made it clear in Matthew 7:21 that obedient living trumps big talking 100% of the time. You can talk all you want about your desire to serve God, but if it is not backed up through your actions, all your talk is for naught. Ultimately, Jesus promises us that when we acknowledge him on earth, he will acknowledge us in Heaven (Matt. 10:32). If we have accepted Jesus as Savior, we can rejoice because our names are written in Heaven (Luke 10:20).

There is only one route to Heaven, and that route is through Jesus Christ.

How Much Do You Long for Heaven?

The way we know if we long for Heaven is how we act on earth. In Mark 10, Jesus teaches us that in order to pursue after Heaven, we have to be willing to give up whatever is holding us back. J. C. Ryle said, "I pity the man who never thinks about heaven." I second his thought.

Colossians 3:1 says we are to set our hearts on things above (Col. 3:1). This does not mean we become disengaged down here on earth; we are not all called to huddle in a monastery. Rather, it means everything we do in this life should be done with the purpose of preparing ourselves for the life to come. In Matthew 6:20, Jesus calls us to lay up for ourselves treasures in Heaven. This means we do good here on earth knowing our Father in Heaven will reward us beyond what anyone else could compare.

While Heaven is open to all, it will not be accepted by all. Jesus tells us the way to Heaven is narrow (Matt. 7:13-15). There will be many who will not enter through its gates. From a strict percentage standpoint, it is against the odds to enter into Heaven. This says something to me. It tells me that you and I must develop a laser-like intensity. Going to Heaven will not happen by accident or through piddling our way mindlessly through this life.

Heaven must be our goal in the journey of life. It must be the clinching priority on our daily agendas. Our decisions are no longer made from a retirement perspective, but a Heavenly perspective. Should I buy this car? Should I purchase this house? Should I move to a new location? All of these questions become much clearer in our minds when we develop a Heavenly perspective.

Here is the reality. God sees everything you do from Heaven (Psa. 33:13). You cannot hide anything from him. He looks down from his throne and sees who is being faithful (Psa. 14:2). Nothing is hidden from his eyes.

But not only does God watch us from Heaven, he also provides us aid from Heaven. Psalm 121:2 gives us the tremendous hope that when we call out to God we can take confidence, knowing our help comes from the very one who is the maker of Heaven and earth (Psa. 121:2)! We take confidence knowing God promises to hear us from Heaven when we humble ourselves and pray (2 Chron. 7:14).

It is through the lens of Heaven that we see where our help comes from. Through the power that comes from Heaven we receive strength and sustenance for our journey through this life. Wickedness is no longer overpowering. As Randy Alcorn writes, "When I've meditated on Heaven, sin is terribly unappealing." *Temptation looks trivial when held up to the brilliant light of Heaven's wonder.*

Heaven is real, and Heaven is where God wants you to be. The choice is up to you!

Action Points

1. Why do you think Christians often talk very little of Heaven?
2. Meditate on how it makes you feel when you realize Heaven is a place of perfect relationships.
3. How much do you feel that you long to go to Heaven? Are you homesick, or are you fairly content living on earth?

Day 35
We Are in a Battle!

"Every inch of progress will have to be won by conquest,
for the enemy will never surrender."
—Robert Coleman

As believers, our conflict with Satan is not a difference of opinion. It is a war! We are in a battle, and unless we treat our spiritual lives like a battle, we will be defeated at every turn. We are warriors in God's army fighting an oppressive foe.

Because we are warriors, we must take on the mind of a warrior. 1 Peter 1:13 tells us to "gird up the loins of our minds." This metaphor Peter is using is a call to prepare our minds to action. Just as a warrior would gather up any loose ends of his robe to fight, so we are to prepare ourselves for spiritual warfare.

The way you prepare for spiritual warfare is to put on the armor God has given you to resist Satan's attacks.

Put on Your Armor

In Ephesians 6:11-13 the apostle Paul says these words:

[11]"Put on the whole armor of God, that you may be able to stand against the schemes of the devil. [12]For we do not wrestle against flesh and blood, but against the rulers, against the authorities, against the cosmic powers over this present darkness, against the spiritual forces of evil in the heavenly places. [13]Therefore take up the whole armor of God, that you may be able to withstand in the evil day, and having done all, to stand firm."

In the verses that follow, Paul gives us a list of armor to put on.

Belt of Truth (V.14)

In verse 14, Paul immediately calls believers to stand. The imagery here is of a soldier on guard. It is a call to action.

Typically, a soldier wore a lot of loose clothing that needed to be tied up before combat. The purpose of putting on a belt was to allow the soldier to move swiftly. It would be the modern day equivalent to a boxer throwing off his coat and stepping into the ring. It was a statement of intentional action. Game time!

Spiritually speaking, when we decide to put on truth we are tying together the loose ends of our lives. We are making a statement to God that all areas of our lives are coming under his control. We're getting serious about taking care of business. No area of our lives that are deceitful can remain!

If you are serious about fighting the Christian battle, you must get real about truth. It starts by accepting Jesus Christ as the only source of truth, and then it transitions into a commitment to let truth alone reign in your life.

Breastplate of Righteousness (V.14)

Paul takes a line from the prophet Isaiah by telling us to put on righteousness as a breastplate. This piece of equipment protected a soldier's most vital organs.

To put on righteousness is to put on God's character of holiness. Clothing ourselves in God's righteousness is the best form of protection. When Satan's darts of temptation are fired at our souls, we can reject them – not on the basis of our own merits but on what Jesus has done for us!

Shoes of Peace (V.15)

With the amount of walking a soldier would do, the type of shoes they wore was important. For instance, Alexander the Great and Julius Caesar had a great deal of success militarily due to their armies being able to travel with speed. Roman soldiers would even put nails in their shoes to give them extra grip in a battle. Good shoes were the key to balance and endurance for a soldier.

For the Christian, peace with God gives us confidence in every area of our lives. If we do not have peace, we will always doubt ourselves. I play hockey. My skates are critically important to me. If I do not have the right size, proper lace tightening, and blade cut, my whole game is off! Likewise, when we do not have peace, we feel insecure in every area of our lives.

Shield of Faith (V.16)

Soldiers' shields would often cover the whole front of their bodies. Shields often consisted of wood, linen and iron. To destroy these shields, enemy forces would shoot flaming darts. As a preventative measure, shields were equipped with a special metal plate that helped to extinguish the fiery darts the enemy would shoot.

A Christian's faith is a quenching defense. When Satan fires darts that would make us doubt the power of God, our faith not only repels these but extinguishes them as well. These darts of doubt can be extinguished because we have encountered the risen Savior!

Helmet of Salvation (V.17)

The head of a victim slain in battle used to be a soldier's prize possession. For instance, when King Saul was struck down, the Philistines immediately removed his head and touted it for all to see. Even in modern times we have seen instances in South America, Africa, and the Middle East where malicious people have celebrated the heads of their victims.

Our protective helmet of salvation is God's promise that no force can ever overpower us. John 10:29 gives us the assurance that no one can snatch our salvation away from us. This is the ultimate protection. As long as we stay completely in union with Jesus Christ, no force can take what God has done in our lives.

Sword of the Spirit (V.17)

Verse 17 switches us from a strictly defensive mode to an offensive mode by calling us to take up the Sword of the Spirit. A sword served both a defensive and an offensive purpose. On one hand it could ward off attacks when a soldier was getting pinched in a corner. On the other, it could be used as a major means of offense and devastate the opposition.

I like this: Paul lists this weapon alone as our only means of attack. He did not include clever strategizing or organized battle tactics. He just calls us to take up the Sword of the Spirit, which is the Word of God. I cannot stress this enough. You must get God's Word into your life.

In our next section we will discuss this in detail, but right now, make the decision to get God's Word into your life. Start memorizing it, meditating on it, and reading it. Pray it in your time alone with him. It is your only means of offense against Satan.

Who Do You Fight the Most?

Satan's number one goal is to destroy your relationship with God. His number two goal is to destroy your relationships with others. He has no problem if you are fighting, just as long as your battle is centered around someone else.

He is the great distractor. Think back with me to the story of Gideon in Judges 7. Here was a man with a small army of 300 men, and yet he defeated a much larger army of Midianites. Why?

Because God confused the Midianite camp, and they fought amongst themselves. In Matthew 12:25, Jesus said a house divided against itself cannot stand. Satan's goal for the body of Christ is to destroy it through division.

It is right now that I feel each of us need to stop and ask ourselves a very important question: *Are my main efforts in life focused on fighting the forces of Satan or dividing the body of Christ?* Do I enjoy spreading gossip and talking negatively about other believers? Do I talk more about taking ground for Christ or "holding the fort" against "worldly" Christians?

Often Christians become popular for what they oppose. We believe abortion, same-sex marriages, and racism are sinful behaviors. The real issues here are not what we oppose, but rather what we are for! We believe Scripture teaches that all life is sacred, and this is why abortion is wrong. We believe Scripture treats marriage and race as sacred, and it is out of this belief that we believe homosexuality and racism are wrong.

What we believe is right must always be the motivation for why we believe something is wrong. When your life is defined more by what you are against rather than what you are for, you are fighting the wrong battle!

As a follower of Jesus, I choose to spend my time warring against the forces of Satan. Yes, correction may be necessary for believers. Reproof may be in order. But I do this through love and compassion with the motivation to see them learn and grow.

Are You Engaged in the Battle?

The litmus test to determine your spiritual engagement level is the amount of demonic resistance you face. Chances are, if you receive little resistance from Satan, you are doing little to advance the Kingdom of God. Mark it down. When you take new ground for Jesus, Satan's forces will bear down on you in an instant!

Our defense against Satan's attacks is to be controlled and filled with God's Holy Spirit. Author Robert Coleman said: "Every inch of progress will have to be won by conquest, for the enemy will never surrender. Nothing less than the infilling of the Spirit of Christ will be sufficient to meet the challenge."

You and I are in a battle. Our eternal souls are the prize. Let's live life and serve God with passion in light of this reality!

Action Points

1. Take a moment to ask yourself this question: What stirs me up the most? What causes me to lose the most sleep at night?
2. Do you really believe this battle is really one that is worth fighting?
3. What step will you take to ensure that your efforts go towards fighting Satan as opposed to fighting fellow believers?

Week 6

I Serve Someone Who Will Journey with Me

Day 36
It's a Long Journey, Not a Short Sprint

Serving God is not a one-time event. It is a journey. There are a lot of ups and downs along the way. Good times and bad.

As a kid, I remember the long van rides my family would make from our small town of Cochrane, Ontario, down to visit my older siblings at college in Cincinnati, Ohio. It was usually about an eighteen-hour trip (give or take a few "necessary" shopping excursions). It was on these expeditions that I learned the value of patience! Mile after mile, hour after hour the trip would go by. It would take us a full ten or so hours to make it to the United States border, and at that point … we were just past halfway there … talk about a hike!

Here is something I realized though. The more I journeyed, the more I began to adjust and eventually enjoy the process. There was just a conditioning process that had to take place in my mind to get me from "Wow, this is awful" to "Hey, I kind of like this!" Similarly, in our journey with God, there is a conditioning process that has to take place. A process that prepares us to be a Christian for the long haul.

If you have been a disciple of Jesus for any period of time, you have no doubt seen fellow brothers and sisters in Christ fall by the wayside. They used to have a passion for God, but somewhere along the way they were overtaken with the fatigue of the journey. Now, they have little to do with God.

This should cause us to stop and ask ourselves a very important question: What practices do I need to implement in my life in order to be a Christian for the long haul? Here are a few habits that I believe distinguish the people who are in this journey for a few miles from those who are in it for eternity.

241

Run Versus Sprint

The first of these is the ability to run, rather than sprint. On the surface, these may seem like the same thing. But actually, they are very different. Runners must pace themselves, whereas sprinters do not have this same luxury. A good runner looks at a race from a bird's eye perspective. A sprinter sees the race develop very rapidly before them.

On our journey with God there are no sprints or fast tracks. Each of us has our own separate journey. God decides when our journey starts in this world, and he decides when our journey ends. This realization should change our mindsets. We create goals and growth patterns that are sustainable for the long haul versus short-term, whim ideas that we give up after a week of implementation.

In 1 Corinthians 9:24-27, Paul says we all must strive for the prize like a runner in a race. However, we do it through exercising self-control. We learn to discipline ourselves. Just as a boxer beats his body into submission, so we must bring our bodies under the authority of God's Word.

This takes a lot of sweat, hard work, and determination. However, the results are well worth it because the prize we receive will make all of our sufferings look like nothing!

Growth Versus Goals

Good runners set goals. They try to improve their time. They push themselves harder today than they did yesterday. Yes, goals are important, but goals without personal growth never come to pass.

I have found that daily growth always trumps daily goals. What does this look like? Let's take this writing project I am working on right now. This book has been about a year-long endeavor. Not long into this process I realized that I was going to need to grow as a writer before my goal of completing this book would become a reality. This caused me to study other writers, read writing books, and implement writing disciplines that were necessary.

In the Christian race, it is important to set goals for yourself. What are you going to do this year that you have never done before? How are you going to intentionally take your relationship with God to the next level?

The key to growth is action. Do you want to read the entire Bible through this year? Go online right now and get a plan that will help you do it! Is it your desire to reach out and touch your neighbors for Christ? Announce a barbeque in your backyard and invite people over! Have you never practiced the discipline of fasting but want to start? Pick a day in this coming week and do it!

Do you have a goal for where you would like to be as a believer? If so, set up some immediate growth steps that will put you on the path to reaching this goal.

Delay Versus Instant

Another characteristic of long distance people is they understand the concept of delayed gratification. Let's face it. Instant is everywhere. We have instant potatoes, instant microwaves, instant entertainment, and instant drive-thrus. We want everything now and on demand.

Thus, this affects our decision-making process. We make choices on what is easiest and most convenient. Just as a poured out glass of water follows the path of least resistance, so we default to following the path of least resistance in our lives. We give up when God asks us to complete a task that is difficult.

However, in order to grow in the journey with God, we must instill in our minds this concept of delayed versus instant gratification. Much of what God asks us to do does not see an instant result. We have to sow a lot of seeds before we will ever see a harvest of our work. We often have to wrestle in our desire to grow with God in order to press on to spiritual maturity.

This means that we do not get frustrated right away when we try to pray, and God does not seem to answer. We do not give up trying to study the Bible for ourselves just because we feel it is tough for us to understand. And we do not serve God one week and then quit the next when we run into hard times.

In Luke 14, Jesus made it clear that we should count the cost of being his follower. It is not always going to be easy. There are going to be horrendously tough times. There will be discouraging heart-breaks. But if we have a big picture mindset, we are focused on the prize to come and not on what will instantly gratify our desires.

Long Versus Short Term

Part of being a runner is having a long-term focus. While we continue to grow daily, we should dream widely. We must expand ourselves. Our vision should always be beyond our grasp. In fact, *any time our vision and current status become one, we begin to plateau.*

God modeled for us in Scripture what it means to think long term. In fact, being outside of the realm of time, God's perspective is entirely different from ours. We see things as past, present, and future. God sees them all playing out before him at once. We are like the child in a maze. All we can see are the walls around us. Yet on a grand scale, God has the panoramic view in sight and can see what paths will take us to the prize that awaits.

Have you ever flown in an airplane over a city that is bustling with activity? As you look down, people are as little dots on a massive Monopoly board. Out of the corner of your eye, you notice an accident on the freeway with cars lined up for miles behind. You can see it. You know why everyone is backed up for miles. Unlike the people at the end of the line who may be honking their horns in frustration, you can see everything from a big perspective. You realize what they cannot from their limited vantage point.

This is kind of like it is in our lives. Sometimes we go through trying times. It is here that having a long-term versus a short-term perspective makes all the difference.

Short-term thinking results in short-term decision making. The key to long-term thinking is to get a long-term perspective. The closer we draw to God, the more our thinking begins to expand.

Eternity Versus Retirement

The North American Dream tells us to live for retirement, but God calls us to live for eternity. As I have already mentioned, our goal is not to save up enough money so that we do not have to change our standard of living. Our ultimate goal is to spend eternity forever with Christ.

If this is really our goal, it should change everything. Sacrificing our physical bodies for the sake of spreading the gospel becomes worth it. Losing financially in this world is okay if it means eternal rewards in the world to come.

Retirement should not be the time when we quit our labors for God, but the time we give God our best!

Persist Versus Restart

Sometimes a runner is called to restart because of a lane violation. Restarts do happen. That being said, restarts are not the goal! No runner walks into an arena and says to himself, "My goal is to get as many restarts as possible today!"

Sadly, when it comes to the Christian race, I believe many believers get a certain thrill in restarting. Have an emotional service at church, and you can count on these same poor souls to repent, weep, and start over again with God. I believe constantly living in restart mode, while addictive, is extremely dangerous. It robs you of going deeper with God and soaring to new heights.

Have you recently come to Christ? If so, that is extremely exciting! But let me offer a word of warning. Do not fall into Satan's restart game. Satan wants to twist every mistake you make into a game ender. He will do all in his power to cause you to question your salvation experience. If he cannot get you to do that, he will try to set the bar so high you always feel God does not love you. "Oops, you did not pray today! God must be angry, so you might as well quit!"

To repeat, yes, there are definitely times for restarts! But never forget you are in a RELATIONSHIP! If you fail God, you should apologize and ask him to forgive you. If you did not walk in all the light God gave you, repent and move on. Just as one mistake should not end a friendship, so one slipup in your walk with God should not destroy your relationship.

God Is with You Each Step

So what about you? I challenge you to stop and take inventory of your life right now. Ask yourself some hard questions. Are you running at a pace that is unsustainable for the long haul, or are you developing a specific growth plan, so you will still be running strong twenty years from now?

The older I have gotten (I just passed a quarter of a century!), the more I admire "plodders." These are usually not very flamboyant people. They are not always seeking the highest position. They are not quick to speak their minds and blabber on about their accomplishments. Instead, they consistently go out, day after day, and get the job done! They have learned the great lesson of walking step-by-step with God and waiting patiently on him when others would get anxious and operate in their own strength.

God help us to be more like that! I connect with these words from Gloria Gaither: "God walks with us. He scoops us up in His arms or simply sits with us in silent strength until we cannot avoid the awesome recognition that yes, even now, He is there."

The pathway to Heaven and a relationship with God are not a sprint; it is a journey. Ask yourself, am I a plodder? Am I a journeyer? Do I run with God for a few days, lose my breath, and find myself checking out?

I dare you to run in such a way that brings glory to God, so you too can echo the apostle Paul's words from 2 Timothy 4:7 when he said, "I have fought the good fight, I have finished the race, I have kept the faith."

May God help us to be journeyers for the long haul!

Action Points

1. Are you a "restart" person? If so, what will you do to change this?
2. Contrast the differences between long-term and short-term journeyers.
3. What immediate action do you need to take in your life to ensure you will be a journeyer?

Day 37
Our Journey Requires Discipline

"The Disciplines allow us to place ourselves before God so that he can transform us…[they] are God's way of getting us into the ground; they put us where he can work within us and transform us."
—Richard Foster

Discipline. Not exactly the top inspirational word on many people's radar! When I think of discipline, I imagine staying up late to finish a paper in college. I visualize journaling, brushing my teeth, or doing the daily grind of work day in and day out. Discipline is, well, discipline!

For many, discipline is a negative. Nevertheless, from the Bible, I believe we can see that discipline is absolutely critical to spiritual growth. In 1 Corinthians 9:27, Paul says, "But I discipline my body and make it my slave, so that, after I have preached to others, I myself will not be disqualified."

When it comes to the Christian walk, there are several spiritual disciplines that are essential. In a study done by Lifeway Research, it was estimated that nearly 82% of Protestant professing Christians admit that they do not spend personal time with God on a daily basis. There are numerous reasons for this. One of them is because we simply get too busy with life. Another is that there is always so much going on around us, and it is hard to find some quiet time by ourselves. Perhaps the biggest problem is that people simply do not know where to begin.

Let's face it, when you have 66 books of the Bible, 1189 chapters, and 31,103 verses it is a little hard to know where to start! But discipline helps us overcome these mind barriers. It forces us to start throwing out excuses. It sets in place patterns by which we can grow and develop.

Discipline is not easy. There is no good way to sugar coat discipline. It takes a good deal of work, struggle, and intentionality for it to succeed. Still, I can testify personally that the rewards of having a good relationship with God are well worth it.

One of the greatest books on spiritual discipline is Richard Foster's work, *Celebration of Discipline*. In it he writes, "The Disciplines allow us to place ourselves before God so that he can transform us ... [they] are God's way of getting us into the ground; they put us where he can work within us and transform us."

Discipline is the framework that holds our spiritual house together. It does not save us, but it will transform us!

Internal Disciplines

Discipline starts on the inside. *If we are not disciplined internally, we will never be disciplined externally.* What makes internal disciplines challenging is that no one observes us while we do them. We do not get pats on the back or public acknowledgment. Yet what makes them so rewarding is they are done in the presence of God, who is the ultimate rewarder of those who seek him diligently (Heb. 11:6).

Study

It bears repeating that the discipline of studying God's Word must be top priority in the life of every believer. Through reading the Bible we are able to discern what his voice sounds like. Before you practice any of the other disciplines, start with taking time to read God's Word, and ask him to apply it to your life.

Prayer

I firmly believe prayer is the single most untapped resource available to a believer. The reason prayer can be difficult is because it requires discipline. It requires focus and determination. In Matthew 6:6, Jesus spoke of going into an inner room to pray. One of the practices my wife and I have implemented in our home is having an inner prayer closet. Nothing is in it except a chair and a blanket to kneel on. I challenge you to find a place in your house and develop the discipline of consistent prayer.

Fasting

Nothing will break you down more than the discipline of fasting. I would go as far as to say that almost every major breakthrough I have experienced in my life has come as a result of fasting. It was through fasting that I found a wife and went to my first church. Jesus fasted forty days (Matt. 4:2). In Matthew 6, Jesus spoke of fasting as the natural progression from prayer. He spoke of it as something that he assumed a Christian would do. Fasting is not so we can force God into our agendas. It is to clear our hearts and minds, so the Holy Spirit can fill us with his plan for our lives.

The longer I fast, the more I become aware of the battles in my life that are most important. Often when I start fasting, my focus is skewed. But the longer I wait on God, the more I experience a change in motivation. By choosing not to fast, you defraud yourself of a deeper work God wants to do in your life. I recommend fasting once a week for at least a meal. Take one day a month and take at least 1-3 weeks at the start of your new year to fast. When you do this, you will experience the onslaught of the enemy in different ways. However, it will enrich you, empower you, and prepare you for the battles ahead!

Meditation

We are a fast-action society. Take television for instance. On average, screen shots are changing every three seconds. It is hard for us to focus on one thing for any small period of time. We become so easily distracted. Now more than ever, the discipline of meditation is critical to spiritual growth. While Eastern religious meditation focuses primarily on emptying the mind, Christians focus on emptying to be filled with the Holy Spirit. We do not empty our minds so that we can think more clearly about how we can go about the day. We empty our minds to allow God to have total control. *Neglecting to stop and meditate on God is the quickest way to make your relationship with him lifeless and cold.*

Solitude

Question: How long can you sit still, without looking at something else, and focus on one thing? It is more difficult than you would imagine! Try practicing this with your spouse or friend (don't be weird about it though!). Just sit and focus all of your attention on them.

To do this effectively with God, you need a quiet place. Maybe it is a prayer closet, your backyard, or an overlook near your town. The place is not so important, but the discipline is.

External Disciplines

When we have allowed God to work inside of us, we are then ready for him to transform us on the outside. Here are a couple of ways to do this.

Stewardship

As Rick Warren points out, when we come down to the end of this life, God's two questions are going to revolve around salvation and stewardship. How did you respond to Christ's invitation, and what did you do with what he gave you?

Everything you have from God is a gift. You do not own your time or your resources. You are not free just to "check out" for a day or two. You are not entitled to live an extravagant lifestyle just because it has always been your dream.

Statistics say that right around 30% of believers in the church tithe. God is not poor. He will always take care of his bills. But the principle of giving money is similar to the principle of giving glory to God. Just as God does not need our glorification, he does not need our money. It is all a matter of demonstrating our level of dependency and trust in his provision. People and churches are hoarders by nature. This is OUR money, and these are OUR resources. Amazingly though, hoarding churches and hoarding people are often the most "broke" people physically and spiritually on the planet. Why? Because when you fail to give, you fail to receive. But on the flip side, the more you give the more you receive.

Failing to give God what is his will rob you of the blessing of God on your life!

Service

Genuine service for others starts by taking on the servant's heart of Jesus. He was the one who laid aside all he had and humbled himself in the form of a servant. He washed his disciples' feet and loved his abusers.

I believe every Christian should volunteer several hours of time weekly to serving the needs of others – no strings attached. *Service, in order to receive something in return, is not service. It is business.* Do this and you will begin to develop the heart of Jesus in a fresh way. You will be slower to judge others and quicker to give grace.

Service is not a step down. It is a step up. When we serve, we receive the greater rewards.

Health

Bodily exercise and nutrition do not make you spiritual. But they do remove unnecessary roadblocks that limit your ability to function alertly as a Christian. When I fail to eat right or exercise, I become irritable. Unconsciously I think less of myself. I over spiritualize problems in my life.

1 Timothy 4:8 says bodily exercise is of some value. During the time of Paul's writing, most people walked and naturally exercised much more than we do today with modern transportation.

My wife and I made the commitment to exercise at least four times a week, take daily vitamins, and do our best to steer clear of poor nutritional diets. As a result, we have noticed a big difference in our outlook on life. It helps to keep us focused on those battles in life that matter most.

Corporate Disciplines

Internal and external disciplines naturally overlap into what are called corporate disciplines. These are accomplished as we come into contact with others.

Evangelism

The first of these corporate disciplines is evangelism. Some would question if this can really be considered a discipline. I am convinced that it is. Speaking to others about your faith in God does not come naturally. There are far too many "secret Christians." Because sharing our faith does something huge in our lives, Satan will do all in his power to keep us from doing so. He will drive us to fear men more than we fear God.

Evangelism is not just standing on a street corner with a megaphone. It can be done in a lot of different ways. If you are new at this, *make it a practice to take one time a week to share your faith with someone else.* This will not come naturally at first, but it should develop into becoming a natural part of your life. Evangelism is a discipline, and it should grow to become a regular part of our spiritual life. It is exciting and very rewarding to our souls!

253

Accountability

The groundwork for creating a cult, becoming a loner, or staying immature spiritually starts with a lack of personal accountability. Mark it down, *the more you keep to yourself, the more like your self you will become.*

James 5:16 calls for us to confess our sins to one another and pray for one another. As the saying goes, confession is good for the soul. When we confess to others any faults or sins we may have in our lives, bonding occurs. Too often, we put our "social media face" on for others. In other words, we only say things that make us look better.

The problem in doing this is that it actually robs our fellow brothers and sisters in Christ. I have found that when we admit our shortcomings to others, it can actually be a unifying process. Confession is not just for you. It can actually be a bonding force with others! I like to say it this way: *We alienate when we exult our strengths, but we unite when we acknowledge our weaknesses.*

Do you have someone in your life who holds you accountable for your actions? If not, take on the discipline of finding someone who will help you in this area.

Worship

We have already looked at how there is tremendous power in worshiping together as a corporate body. Also, remember giving praise to God completes our enjoyment of him. When we worship in harmony with others, our satisfaction level goes even deeper!

When you attend church this week, I encourage you to take your worship deeper than it has gone before. Raise your hand in praise; sing with more passion; smile in such a way that reflects what God has done in your heart. Take your worship of God to the next level!

Celebration

Do you take times to celebrate what God has been doing for you? At our church, we intentionally create times of celebration. Baptism is a time to celebrate. Christmas, Easter, and special events are all times to intentionally step back and celebrate God's goodness to us.

I do not know how your church chooses to celebrate, but make the commitment in your life to celebrate what God is doing. If your church offers you no opportunity, tell someone else around you what God is doing in your life. Make an effort to intentionally celebrate the goodness of God every day of your life!

Start Viewing Disciplines As a Delight

Ultimately, your salvation is not based on spiritual disciplines, but they are instrumental in keeping you on track. Without disciplines, you will be all over the place in your daily growth with God. When you are feeling ambitious, you will read the Bible. When you are having good days, you may finally pray.

Spiritual disciplines help to prevent your emotions from governing your life. They move you forward even when you feel like going backward. When it comes right down to it, developing spiritual disciplines in your life is a purposeful and habitual choice you will have to make.

Discipline is way more than a list of dos and don'ts. Author Annie Downs writes, "The truth is that discipline isn't rules you have to live by or laws you have to obey; discipline is the work done on the practice field, so you are ready for the big game." So true!

Spiritual disciplines help us tremendously on our journey. *Discipline is a delight, and in the big game of life, the fruits of discipline far outweigh the pain of living without it!*

Action Points

1. What is it that often hinders us from being disciplined?
2. Which of these areas of spiritual discipline do you need to improve most in your life?
3. What are some ways you can make discipline more of a delight rather than a dread?

—— Day 38 ——
The Holy Spirit Is Our Navigator

"The Spirit does not live in us as a device we can use to achieve our own goals."
—John Oswalt

Who you listen to will determine where you end up. In the Christian journey the Holy Spirit is our personal navigation system. He tells us when to move, where to stop, and how we should continue on the path.

Of all the people in the Godhead, the Holy Spirit is the one our culture tends to understand the least. We can kind of grasp a Father and Son, but the idea of the Holy Spirit seems very different. Consequently, we find it difficult to discern the sound of his voice. And we often confuse our own thoughts and personal agendas as being the voice of the Holy Spirit. As a result, the Holy Spirit becomes an enabler to spiritually do whatever we want to in the flesh.

But God's Holy Spirit is the only voice that can guide us through this life safely into the life to come. We must take careful steps to hear his voice.

What Does the Holy Spirit Do?

If we are going to understand what the Holy Spirit sounds like, it is important to know what the Holy Spirit does. Scripture gives us several thoughts about this. As we walk our way through each of these take some time to meditate on what the Holy Spirit does and thank him.

He Reveals the Father

Through the Holy Spirit, God the Father draws us to himself. It is the Holy Spirit who knows our thoughts and knows the mind of God the Father (1 Cor. 2:11). He is the one who gives us access to God the Father (Eph. 2:18). Through him we are able to understand the deep things of God (1 Cor. 2:10), and it is he who proclaims the Father in our hearts (Gal. 4:6).

Through the Holy Spirit, we are able to understand all that the Father has given us (1 Cor. 2:12). *Everything the Holy Spirit says and does is with the purpose of revealing the Father and making us more like the image of his Son.*

Empowers Us to Be Like Jesus

This leads into the enabling power the Holy Spirit brings to our lives. *The Holy Spirit always speaks to us truth that will enable us to become more like Jesus.* It was Jesus himself who spoke of the coming of the Holy Spirit. He was the one who said it would be better for us if he went away, and the Holy Spirit came to us.

The Holy Spirit empowers us (Luke 24:49) and lets us know that Jesus Christ is abiding in us (1 John 4:13). He confesses that Jesus came in the flesh (1 John 4:2). And it is the Holy Spirit who empowers us with the ability to be conformed to the image of Jesus Christ. It is he who testifies of Christ (John 15:26), and he is the one who reveals Christ to us and in us (John 16:14-15). He is the agent by which we are baptized into the body of Christ (1 Cor.

12:13), and he is the one who continually transforms us into the image of Christ (2 Cor. 3:18). It is he who brings to our remembrance the things of Jesus (John 14:26).

The Holy Spirit is the key to understanding and becoming more like Jesus. *It is impossible to become like Jesus unless we are filled with the Holy Spirit's purity and power.*

Indwells Us with His Spirit

It's been pointed out that Jesus is often celebrated while the Holy Spirit takes a back seat. We celebrate Christmas and Easter when Jesus came to earth and died for us, but we do very little for Pentecost (the most common day of our calendar year to celebrate the Holy Spirit's work in the book of Acts). *We love the idea of someone coming and dying for us, but we are not as excited about someone coming and dwelling in us!*

But 1 Corinthians 3:9 says that when we give our lives to Jesus Christ the Holy Spirit indwells us. When the Holy Spirit is indwelling us, our speech becomes very different. We are empowered to speak as he desires (Matt. 10:20). Our actions and attitudes change.

Ultimately, as has already been pointed out, the Holy Spirit wants to fill us completely (Eph. 5:18). He wants to be our ultimate satisfaction. No more do we need to run to addictions in our lives that help us escape reality. The void in our lives has been filled! When we have the Holy Spirit, he becomes our teacher (1 Cor. 2:13). And we become so satisfied with him that he gives us joy (1 Thess. 1:6) and the ability to overcome fear (Acts 9:31).

The Holy Spirit's ongoing indwelling in our lives is the key to all that he wants to do within us in the future.

Strengthens Our Spirits to Overcome Sin

It is the Holy Spirit who convicts us of sin (John 16:8). Through Jesus Christ, the Holy Spirit sets us free from the law of sin and death (Rom. 8:2). After he convicts us and we make a change, the Holy Spirit strengthens our spirits (Eph. 3:16). Through him we are able to obey the truth God gives us in his Word (1 Peter 1:22). He promises to guide us into all truth (John 16:13), and he regenerates, washes, and renews us (Titus 3:5). He leads us (Gal. 5:18) and sanctifies us (2 Thess. 2:13). The Holy Spirit has the authority to cast out demons (Matt. 12:38), and nothing can stand against him. He gives new life to our mortal bodies (Rom. 8:11) and brings us the truest sense of liberty and freedom (2 Cor. 3:17).

Enables Us to Talk to God

The Holy Spirit bears witness in us that we are children of God (Rom. 8:16). He confirms in us what God the Father has promised to us and then produces in us the fruit of his work and presence (Gal. 5:22-23).

There are times when we do not even have the words to pray to God. Ever have one of those times? I know I have. Maybe the pain is too great to even speak. But it is in those moments the Holy Spirit functions as our great intercessor. He teaches us to pray and intercedes for us with groans too deep for human words (Rom. 8:26-27). God the Father specifically instructs us to pray in the Holy Spirit (Jude 1:20).

When we communicate with the Holy Spirit our words are issued directly into the very throne room of God.

Equips Us to Serve Others with Love in Unity

Ephesians 3:5 tells us the Holy Spirit reveals that all men, regardless of nationality or race, can come to faith in Jesus Christ. We are to love all people! Through him, the love of God is dispensed in our hearts (Rom. 5:5).

The Holy Spirit gives us spiritual gifts that we are to use to serve others (1 Cor. 12). Just as the Holy Spirit anointed Jesus for ministry, he anoints us for ministry today (Acts 10:38). He enables some to preach the gospel (1 Pet. 1:12), others to prophesy (2 Pet. 1:21), and some to be overseers of the church (Acts 20:28). He is the grand equipper.

Wherever the Spirit of God is in control, there is unity. Ephesians 4:3 tells us he brings unity and oneness to the body of Christ. The only way you will ever develop unified and meaningful relationships with others is through giving the Holy Spirit complete control of your life.

Assures Us of God's Work in Our Lives

Finally, the Holy Spirit is our granter of everlasting life (Gal. 6:8). Ephesians 2:22 says he makes us God's habitation. He comes in, cleans us up, and fills us, so God can actually come and indwell our souls.

The Holy Spirit bears witness to the truth in our consciences (Rom. 9:1) and seals us unto the day of redemption (Eph. 1:13). Through the Holy Spirit, we are assured that no one can ever take away the work God has begun in our lives (2 Cor. 5:5). It is impossible for someone to steal your salvation away. The Holy Spirit is the one who enables us to wait for Christ's promise that one day he will return for those who are waiting expectantly for him (Gal. 5:5).

How Must We Respond?

I hope this little synopsis of what the Holy Spirit does in our lives is helpful and causes you to have a greater appreciation for whom he is. I know it has for me. And it has challenged me to ask myself, how do I respond? If the Holy Spirit desires to be our personal navigator through life, what do we need to do on our end to allow him to do this work in us? Here are just three simple steps that I believe are essential.

1 – Turn On Your Receiver

You want the Holy Spirit to work in your life? Then you must make a decision to turn on your receiver to hear his voice. Every person has a spiritual nature, and this nature is either controlled by God or by self. Having the Holy Spirit direct your spirit is a decision you must make if you desire to have God as the Lord of your life. The way you turn on your receiver is by turning on a "Yes Sign" in your heart. Anything God says to do you will do.

2 – Tune to His Signal

A navigation system only works if it has the proper signal. I had an older GPS that would sometimes take several minutes to calculate. Until the right signal came through, we were stuck! Without the Holy Spirit directing your life, you will make wrong choices. But when you allow your spirit to be aligned to the same channel as the Holy Spirit, direction in life becomes clear. In order to live like the Holy Spirit wants you to live, you must be on his same wavelength.

3 – Obey His Direction

I am convinced the reason we see so little of the Holy Spirit's work in our lives is because we have so little passion to do as he says. Reality check: There will be many times when the Holy Spirit asks you to go somewhere or do something you might feel is unreasonable. There have been times like this in my life. Times when I have felt prompted to give people money, not go where I was going, or take another path in a relationship. All of these were unique situations, and some were very difficult.

Still, I am consistently reminded of this reality. A reality that reminds me God has big plans for my life, and the only thing hindering me from receiving his blessings is my failure to obey his direction.

Sadly, I have come to realize that average Christians are often not Spirit-led Christians. Average Christians will sense the Holy Spirit leading them to step out and do something, but they will pull back. They always tend to play it safe, keep their cards close to the vest, and operate only within the realm of what they can accomplish through their own strengths.

I do not know about you, but I for one do not want this to be the case in my life. I want to be bold. I want to go wherever and whenever the Holy Spirit calls me to go!

Your Decisions Determine Your Destination

When you are following a navigation system, every turn is important. Ultimately, it is the little turns that will determine your final destination. For every turn you ignore, you waste valuable time God has given you on this earth. Nothing breaks the heart of God more than to see his children wander about life in confusion and chaos.

Several years ago Darren Hardy, publisher of *Success* magazine, wrote a great book called *The Compound Effect*. In it, he points out that it is the small choices in life that determine our destinations.

In your spiritual journey, it is the little decisions you make that ultimately form you into who you become. You make decisions to skip church for weeks at a time to take your kids to sporting events, but then wonder why they want little to do with God. You start spending a little too much time developing a wrong attraction with a co-worker in the office and wonder why your marriage is not as intimate as you wish. You decide not to be obedient when God tells you to speak hard truth to a person and wonder why you never lead anyone to Christ.

It is the little decisions in life that make all the difference!

No Shortcuts

There are no shortcuts in walking with God, and getting to know the voice of the Holy Spirit might feel a little clumsy when you start out.

After using the same GPS for several years, I decided to make a change to another model. It was confusing to me. Everything felt a little different, and I was not used to the new turn-by-turn directions. There was an awkward phase where it felt like I messed up a lot! But now that I have adjusted, I like this new system much better.

Learning to be patient and listen to the voice of the Holy Spirit is different than anything you have ever done before. Waiting on the Holy Spirit's direction for a job when all of your friends tell you to make the "obvious" choice is sometimes tough. Deciding to give money when God directs, and you do not see how you will pay the bills is challenging. But it is so worth it!

God knows that when it comes to developing you into the person he wants you to be, there can be no shortcuts. I don't know about you, but I like to think I mature rapidly. I start praying prayers like, "God, I've already learned this experience! Can't you move me on to something else?!" Yet it is in those moments that God reminds me; we mature on his timetable and not our own. Oftentimes his lessons take us longer to learn than we picture in our minds. You cannot hurry in your relationship with God. As Kelsey Morton once wrote, "Hurry is not of the Devil; it is the Devil."

When you are traveling by GPS, there are times when you feel it is time to turn, but the GPS tells you to continue on for several hundred kilometers or a few more blocks. Likewise, it is easy to grow impatient in our walk with God. We think God is not moving, so we decide to force action. We get in the flesh and end up getting off course.

Two important lessons I have had to learn are that God does not work on my schedule, and God is not my puppet to manipulate. As John Oswalt wrote, "The Spirit does not live in us as a device we can use to achieve our own goals." He is not our gopher we order around. He is a person and longs to travel with us on the journey.

In closing (since this is what all pastors love to say!), there are no shortcuts in developing a relationship with God's Holy Spirit. While a navigation system is impersonal and mechanical, the Holy Spirit is a friend and personable. Get to know him. Study him. And through his strength become the person God wants you to be!

Action Points

1. How has your understanding of the Holy Spirit deepened as you have read this day?
2. How sensitive are you to the Holy Spirit? Are you obeying all he has called you to do?
3. What is one action you can take to better tune your life to the Holy Spirit's voice?

Day 39
Trials Refine Our Journey

"God is the only one who can make the valley of trouble a door of hope."
—Catherine Marshall

Salvation does not bring an end to our problems, but it does bring a new way of looking at them.

Often when someone gives their life to Christ, there is an intense spiritual battle that goes on the first week or two after their decision. Financial battles are harder than before, new relational problems emerge, or new pressures come to the surface.

These are to be expected. However, along with these added struggles, God's grace abounds! And God, if you will let him, will allow these circumstances to bring you closer to him instead of farther away.

I have personally found trials to be a true refiner. Like silver that is refined, so is a life that is dragged through the fires of pain. *Pain does not determine our character, but it has a unique way of revealing it.*

Why can some people go through years of struggle with cancer and yet remain astonishingly cheerful while others become bitter and harsh? Why does a sudden job loss kill one man's spirit while to another it motivates him as never before? Why does the abuse one woman has suffered leave her resentful of men the rest of her life while another finds healing and help?

The answer to all of these questions comes down to how each person decides to handle trials.

Trials Refine Our Dependency

We like to think of ourselves as independent. "I built my life." But trials have a way of making us look really small. Through them

265

we realize we did not have our lives in our hands as maybe we thought.

Trials always send us in one of two directions. We either isolate and become more self-absorbed, or we run to God and plead his protection.

Trials make a self-absorbed person more calloused. They will make statements like, "Well I'm never making that mistake again," or "See if I ever trust anyone in the future!"

On the flip side, *trials make a God-focused person more humble.* Through trials we realize this life is only a mere reflection of the new earth and new Heaven to come. The great missionary Amy Carmichael wrote, "Love accepts the trying things of life without asking for explanations. It trusts and is at rest."

Trials fine-tune the way we hear God's voice. C.S. Lewis eloquently stated, "God whispers to us in our pleasures, speaks in our consciences, but shouts in our pain." *Going through trials the right way will bring you closer to God than ever before.*

Trials Refine Our Character

Trials bring out our true character. Through pressure we say and act how our hearts really believe.

The greatest demonstration of human character was displayed through the life of Jesus Christ. As human beings we were created in his image, and it is God the Father's desire that we replicate his character well to people around us.

The problem is that comfort has a way of making us lazy. *Our motivation for becoming like Jesus is often small when our comforts in life are great.* We already have enough. We are self-sufficient.

But trials have a way of getting us back to those things in life that are most important. Through a trial, we suddenly value our families more. Read Romans 5:3-4. In these verses, Paul gives us a three-step outline. He tells us that suffering produces endurance. Endurance then produces character, and character produces hope. James 1:2-4 calls us to rejoice in trials. It says that trials come our way for a reason. They test us and make us steadfast.

Trials refine our characters.

Trials Refine Our Compassion

It is hard to hurt with a person when we have not hurt ourselves. Through trials we become more thankful for the blessings of life and more compassionate towards those who suffer.

When you suffer a financial trial, you become more understanding towards the homeless person on the street who struggles to make ends meet. Through experiencing a relational breakup, you go from being callous in your counsel with others to being sensitive to listen first and speak second. Suffering a close personal death puts a new perspective on eternity, and you become more urgent in touching others who have not heard the good news of Jesus Christ.

Trials refine our love for others. Mother Teresa once stated, "I have found the paradox that if I love until it hurts, then there is no hurt, but only more love." As our love for others increases, so does our compassion.

Trials Refine Our Destiny

It has been said that the life we live now is boot camp training for the life to come. The way we respond to trials in this life determines where we spend eternity in the life to come.

In John 16:33, Jesus offered these words, "In the world you will have tribulation. But take heart; I have overcome the world." No matter what trial we go through, we can take confidence that our God has everything under control.

I love these words from Catherine Marshall: "God is the only one who can make the valley of trouble a door of hope."

Trials Are Actually a Good Sign

I fear for the person who says they have no problems. Essentially, they are saying the devil is not after them, and unfortunately, they may well be right. They are so ineffective in their service for Christ that they are not even on the devil's radar.

On the flip side, a disciple of Jesus who has many trials might well be exactly where God wants them. The book of Job is a key example. It was because Satan recognized Job was such a devoted follower of God that he tried with all his energy to bring him down. If you feel Satan is coming after you nonstop, do not automatically assume you are doing something wrong. Often, this is a sign you are exactly in the right place!

How Are You Handling Your Trials?

So what about you? Do you have some trials and battles in your life right now? How will you allow God to use them to better shape you? Maybe you are going through the pain of a situation you have brought on yourself, so you feel guilt along with the pain. Perhaps someone has wronged you in a big way. What are you going to do about it?

I can confidently say trials are nothing when it comes to God. *The greatest question is not the size of your trial but the size of your God.* Do you serve a God who is greater than any situation you can imagine? A.W. Tozer said, "A low view of God is the cause of a hundred lesser evils. A high view of God is the solution to ten thousand temporal problems." He is exactly right.

The key to handling trials the right way is to continually discover your great big God!

Action Points

1. What is a tough trial you are going through right now?
2. How have you seen God bring you through trials in the past?
3. After what you have read, would you say you tend to have a bigger view of trials or a bigger view of God?

——·•·•·—— **Day 40** ——·•·•·——
God Reveals Himself Along Our Journey

"If you will go where you've never gone before, you will see God like you've never seen him before."
—Annie Downs

Have you ever taken a long route home just because of the scenery on the trip?

From time to time my wife and I will do this. We will be traveling and one of us will say, "Hey, let's take the scenic route." (She has also found out that sometimes this doubles for, "We're lost!") Why do we do this? What makes it so enjoyable?

I believe the reason is because we as humans have a natural appreciation for beauty. We genuinely enjoy journeys that are pleasant and refreshing to us along the way.

When it comes to our spiritual journey, we have already talked about how sometimes the road is tough. But here is an encouraging thought: *The road God takes us on is filled with spectacular revelations and manifestations of who he is.*

The problem is, sometimes we are just too busy to watch for them. We get so wrapped up in the cares and worries of life that we fail to check out all of the amazing wonders along the way. This is where I think back to God's words in Jeremiah 29:11, "For I know the plans I have for you, declares the LORD, plans for welfare and not for evil, to give you a future and a hope."

God has special ways he wants to reveal himself to us. We just need to be willing to stop and observe these blessings along our journey.

God Reveals Himself in Two Primary Ways

God reveals himself through two ways. These are what we call general and special revelation.

Special revelation refers to unique ways God chooses to reveal himself to us. These include God's workings with the children of Israel in the Old Testament, Christ's decision to come to earth, and the work of the Holy Spirit in people's lives throughout the centuries. All of these are special events in history. The primary means of special revelation we have available to us today is the Bible, which we have already discussed in previous sections.

General revelation speaks of how God reveals himself in nature. Psalm 19:1-2 tells us the heavens declare the glory of God and reveal his power. Every time we go on a nature walk and observe God's creation, we can see his general revelation on display. Nature itself points to God!

To summarize, *general revelation points us closer to God while special revelation lays out a plan for how we can accomplish this.*

God Reveals Himself Through Creation

A key way God reveals himself to us is through creation. Just by looking at our world, we can see his handiwork on display. Romans 1:20 tells us that from the very beginning of creation this world has pointed to God's divine attributes. The very fact that a universe like ours exists indicates there is a divine designer. Creation calls for a Creator!

Take this example. Say you are traveling down the highway and you happen to see a Tim Horton's coffee cup (the best coffee in Canada by the way!) lying alongside the road. Chances are you are not going to assume it happened to arrive there by chance. It makes logical sense that this coffee cup came from the place where it was manufactured.

Likewise, when we look around at our world with the sun, moon, and stars, these all point to a grand originator who oversaw their creation.

God Reveals Himself Through Design

Our world is incredibly designed and fine-tuned. Think about DNA for a minute (only a minute, I promise).

Christian apologist Werner Gitt estimates the amount of information that could be stored in a pinhead's volume of DNA is equivalent to a pile of paperback books 500 times as high as the distance from earth to the moon, each with a different, yet specific content! Not too shabby!

Want another example? Then think about gravity. "Gravity is roughly 1039 times weaker than electromagnetism. If gravity had been [1033] times weaker than electromagnetism, stars would be a billion times less massive and would burn a [million] times faster." Just a slight variance in our earth's rotation would throw our world into chaos.

These are two of the countless examples of God's amazing fine tuning!

He Reveals Himself Through Morality

At the very heart of man, there is something intrinsically moral. Even among notorious criminals, such as those in the mafia, there are many codes of conduct. (I've always found this ironic!) Lying, stealing, and killing are by and large considered wrong in our society. Why is this the case? Where does this standard of opinion and belief stem from?

Also, the very attributes of man seem to point to the fact that there is indeed a God. Attributes such as personality, emotion, guilt, compassion, and other natural tendencies point to something more than mere random chance. *Our lives call for something greater than ourselves!*

Those in opposition to the concept of God argue that the nature of evil in our world disproves his existence. I would respond by saying *the very fact we know something is evil points to the reality there is a God that condemns that action as evil.* Humanity's cry for moral justice calls for a moral standard giver.

He Reveals Himself Through Personal Experience

God chooses to reveal himself to each of us personally. He wants all people to know him. There is not one person whom God will not reveal himself to in some way.

For believers and disciples of Christ, he freely offers us a tremendous assurance of the work he has done in our lives. In Romans 8:16, Paul says, "The Spirit himself bears witness with our spirit that we are children of God." The Holy Spirit will confirm in the hearts of believers the solid reality that God is working in their lives. Sometimes this happens close to salvation. In other instances, it may take weeks or months. But God is faithful and keeps his promises.

This assurance is a tremendous faith builder in the lives of believers. It does not save them, but it confirms the saving work God has done in their lives. I can speak from personal experience that it is a wonderful reality. God wants and will reveal himself to us as we journey along with him!

The Key to Experiencing God's Revelations

Confession time. I feel like such a slacker when it comes to sitting down and marveling in all God has revealed to me. The phone is going off, distractions of work are on my mind, and pretty soon I am all wound up in the events of the day. So wound up that I fail to just sit and say, "Wow, God, you are awesome!"

With God's help though, I have made a concerted effort to make a change. The reason I am making a change is because I do not want to miss out on anything God wants to show me. I do not want to be so focused on my journey that I neglect to see the wonders God is revealing to me right in front of my nose!

I like this thought from Annie Downs: *"If you will go where you've never gone before, you will see God like you've never seen him before."* Not sure about you, but I want to see God as I have never seen him before.

So ask yourself this question: How is God revealing himself to me today? Start making a list. Appreciate how he shows himself through fine-tuning creation, people, and you personally.

This is not always easy, but it makes the journey incredibly better!

Action Points

1. Think about the various ways God reveals himself to us.
2. Ask how you can better appreciate his revelation.
3. What step will you take today to better appreciate your journey?

Day 41
Three Marks of the Journeyer God Blesses

"God doesn't bless us just to make us happy;
He blesses us to make us a blessing."
—Warren Wiersbe

More than anything in this world, I long for the blessing of God to be upon my life and ministry. Numbers, projects, and even people all fall below my passionate desire to have the blessing of God.

There are several reasons for this. One is that I have experienced life without God's blessing and have found it frustrating, discouraging, and meaningless. Another reason is I have observed others, in person and in Scripture, who have had the blessing of God upon their life and ministry, but through their actions have eventually lost his blessing. I read about men like King Saul, King Solomon, and others in Scripture who were blessed of God. Yet because of their actions, God removed his blessing from their lives.

On the flip side, I read about men and women like Noah, Abram, Sarah, Isaac, Jacob, Joseph, and many others who were blessed of God because of their service to him.

These examples and others have compelled me to stop and ask this question: How do people receive and maintain the blessing of God upon their lives? From looking through Scripture for every usage of the word blessing, I began to see a pattern develop.

On the Christian journey, here are three simple marks of the person I believe God blesses.

1 – God Blesses Total Dependence

The first of these marks is total dependence upon God. I cannot stress enough that total dependence upon God is absolutely critical to receiving God's blessing. Take the Old Testament patriarch Abraham. Here was a man who was so dependent upon God that he was willing to sacrifice his only son on an altar. He was so reliant on God's provision and character that he was willing to follow through with what was the unthinkable.

When it comes to our lives, *personal comfort is often the greatest enemy of total dependence upon God*. Comfort and stability are two facets of life we naturally crave. Few people enjoy living in a total state of discomfort! But if we are not careful we grow used to doing life without really needing to depend upon God. As a result, our lives become faithless and self-made.

A moment of transparency: Moving to Toronto to plant a church was a tremendous faith move for Janan and me. Yes, we knew beyond a shadow of doubt that God had called us, but still it was tough. Moving to a new city in a new country with a totally different culture was difficult. But through this process, it has compelled us to be completely dependent upon God. Yes, we work hard. Yes, we build relational connections and partnerships with others. Still, at the end of the day, the success of our ministry in Toronto will be built upon the blessing of God.

Question for you: What is an area of your life that you without question say is out of your control? What part of your life will fail miserably without God's intervention? If you do not have an answer to this, it is likely that your dependence upon God is not very high. The way you change this is by intentionally stepping out in faith in some new areas of your life. Start a new ministry that has the potential to fail. Put yourself out on the line in building a relationship with someone you might not feel entirely comfortable

275

with. Expand your comfort zone and move toward making your entire life completely dependent on God.

2 – God Blesses Absolute Obedience

In the later portion of the book of Exodus the Israelites are instructed to complete the tabernacle of the Lord. These chapters are amazing in their close attention to detail. From the color of garments, types of precious metals, and specific dimensions, the Israelites obeyed all that God commanded. This was no doubt an incredibly laborious task. Yet in Exodus 40:34 we see how the glory of God comes down and fills the tabernacle they had worked so persistently to complete. Through their obedience to do all God commanded, God's blessing was poured out upon their lives.

In 1 Samuel 15:22, the prophet Samuel put it well when he stated, "To obey is better than sacrifice." In those Old Testament days where the animal sacrificial system was so highly regarded, this was a strong statement. It should serve as a wake up call to us today. No amount of sacrifice we do for God can ever compare to the need to be completely obedient to his voice.

Without question the number one reason we miss out on blessings from God is our lack of obedience to do all that he commands. We do 95% but leave off something we feel is unimportant. We are not totally sold out to God. And so we wander through life, living decent lives, but without the manifold blessing of God on our souls.

The great Sir Winston Churchill rightly said, "Sometimes it is not enough that we do our best; we must do what is required." Christianity today has way too many "do what you can" believers. They are followers who make sacrifices for God based on *their* schedules and *their* desires. However, if you and I want to have God's blessing on our lives, we must stop "doing what we can" and instead start doing what God requires. There is a critical difference.

3 – God Blesses Radical Generosity

God blesses givers. A blessed hoarder is a contradiction of terms. No doubt you have observed people who are physical pack rats. (This is the way I tend to lean.) Walking into their house is like stepping into a second-hand shop. Stuff is everywhere!

Unfortunately, I have discovered there are many spiritual pack rats as well. "Give" is an evil four-letter word to them. This might be for a variety of reasons. Maybe they have had a poor experience in a money driven church. As a result, their radar immediately goes up when anyone speaks of the importance of giving. Immediately they become suspicious and assume something must be fishy.

But Acts 20:35 gives us that popular phrase we quote so often at Christmas time: "It is more blessed to give than to receive." If this is true, shouldn't this change the way we operate? Giving should become our natural instinct. Real generosity is not about me giving money to support another man or woman's ministry. Real generosity is giving of my talents, resources, and abilities to build up the Kingdom of God.

When we do give personally and as a corporate body of believers, we receive the blessing of God in a rich new way.

God's Blessing Brings Protection and Provision

God's blessings always protect and provide for his children. This does not keep them from persecution or even death. But God's blessing provides fresh strength and power to resist the attacks of Satan and energy to love God and others as never before.

When God's blessing is on our lives, his glory is manifested in an incredible way (Lev. 9:23). From passages like Leviticus 25:21, we can see that God's blessing on our lives leads to abundant living. This does not always mean financial or material gain. But it always

WHAT KIND OF GOD DO I SERVE?

leads to spiritual prosperity. Having the blessing of God on our lives leads to making clear decisions. Having God's blessing on our ministry makes it distinct from anything else in the world. There is a freshness and power that sets it apart.

As I write this, I am reminded that God's blessings often come in disguise. As song writer Laura Story wrote: "Sometimes our blessings come from raindrops." As you have probably experienced, sometimes what we picture as a curse from God can turn into our greatest blessing.

God's blessing is powerful. Go back in the Old Testament to the book of Numbers. In chapter 23, a man named Balaam is given the assignment by Balak the king of Moab to curse the nation of Israel. Balaam is promised wealth and prosperity, and he has every intention to fulfill this request. Only there was one problem. God said no. God's blessing was so richly upon the children of Israel that Balaam was unable to curse Israel in any way.

God's blessing upon our lives always leads to our protection and provision.

Talk Without Action Is ... Talk

It was Ralph Waldo Emerson who eloquently stated, "What you are stands over you the while, and thunders so that I cannot hear what you say to the contrary." A simpler and more modern version I have heard says, "What you do speaks so loudly that what you say I don't hear."

Go into a variety of church services today, and you will hear people praying, "Lord, give us your blessing." Enter a Christian home around meal time, and you will hear parents asking God to bless their meal and bless their family. These are fantastic prayers that I pray often. Nevertheless, I hope that as we pray these prayers

278

we ask God to search our hearts in the process. *I hope that before we ask for God's blessing, we have been obedient to his asking.*

Before you ask for God's blessing upon your life, take some personal inventory over your soul. Are you dependent in faith upon God? Are you actively obeying the sound of his voice? And are you being generous with what he has entrusted you with in this life? If so, you are in a great position to receive the incredible blessings of God on your life!

Make no mistake though. The purpose of God's blessing upon your life is not so you can live a life of extravagant prosperity. As biblical commentator Warren Wiersbe wrote: "God doesn't bless us just to make us happy; He blesses us to make us a blessing."

If you have God's blessing upon your life, thank him for it! Now go out and share that blessing with others around you.

Action Points

1. Dependence – What is one action you have taken recently that shows your complete dependence upon God?
2. Obedience – How well are you obeying all God has said to you?
3. Generosity – Do you struggle to give of your time and resources to others? Why is this the case?

Day 42
Never Walk Alone

*"The devil's number one priority is to isolate you from God.
His number two priority is to isolate you from others."*

We have covered some deep ground throughout the course of this book, and I hope it has been as great a blessing for you to read as it was for me to write!

That being said, I have a fear as we conclude our journey together. This fear is similar to what I experience every time I speak or share Jesus with another person. This is the fear of connection. I worry that what I have written will not travel the eighteen inches from your brain to your heart. In addition, I have concern that what you read will stay with you and you alone. I fear that you will mentally accept every word you have read, check this book off your to-do list, and stick it back on the shelf – never sharing these awesome discoveries of God with anyone around you.

The reason this concerns me so much is because our spiritual journey in this life is never meant to be a one-person expedition. It is designed to be walked arm in arm with your fellow brothers and sisters in Christ.

Ecclesiastes 4:12 is a passage that has repeatedly convicted me in times when I am tempted to walk alone. It says, "And though a man might prevail against one who is alone, two will withstand him – a threefold cord is not quickly broken." There is tremendous support in standing with others. *When we stand together with God alongside our fellow brothers and sisters in Christ, we cannot help but become stronger.*

Walking Without People Is Dangerous

I grow very concerned for the people who are spiritual loners. They slip in and out of services, doing their best to go undetected by others. Their lives have grown cynical and closed to others. They talk about all the hypocrites in church, a bad experience they had as a kid, a church that treated them poorly, or any other number of excuses. Meanwhile, their lives are falling apart as they wallow in loneliness.

The dark actuality of our Christian journey is that we will occasionally suffer serious hurts from our fellow brothers and sisters in Christ. Often, they will be the most painful hurts. In my life, I can still play back the memories of times I have been hurt by fellow Christians. This is just the reality of living life with imperfect people in an imperfect world.

However, just as one negative experience with a mechanic should not turn me off on all mechanics, so one or two negative experiences with fellow believers should not keep us from seeking out those who are truly genuine. Deciding to walk alone – just you and God – is exactly the opposite of his intent for your life. You were not created to walk alone!

To walk alone is a selfish choice. It is a choice that leads to loneliness, depression, and despair. But walking with others leads to joy, excitement, and edification.

Walking Without God Is Suicide

While walking without people is dangerous, walking without God is suicide. *The choice to walk without God is always "on us."* He is the one who never leaves nor forsakes us (Deut. 31:6). It is our choice if we decide to walk without him. This often happens very gradually. We start off excited to serve him, but then life happens, and we become distracted. *Rather than spending time WITH him, we do projects FOR him.*

It has been said: One day spent without time with God and I know it; two days spent without taking time with God and my family knows it; three days and my friends know it; and by the fourth day everybody knows it! There is a great deal of truth to this. Failing to stay connected to God is not just spiritual suicide for you. It brings discouragement to those around you as well.

Walking with God is in some ways similar to the start of a new project. Whenever you start a thousand piece puzzle the first 15% is the easy part because you're pumped up and ready to go! However, it is the remaining 85% that gets a little bit tougher. Similarly in marriage, the honeymoon period only lasts so long; the real commitment comes into play soon after the honeymoon is over. So it is with God. Some days are difficult. But it is on those days that we must press through, determined to grow in our wonder and awe of his holy and loving character.

To walk *without* God is suicide, but to walk *with* God is joy unspeakable.

What About Lonely Times?

I am aware as I write this that perhaps you are in a position where you feel all alone. Maybe it is a really dark time in your life. You long for someone to communicate with and talk to but feel trapped into a period of isolation. Perhaps no one around you has a passion to do good. If so, my heart goes out to you! Still, even in these times, you can take heart in the knowledge that God has preserved a remnant of people who are devoted to doing his will.

1 Kings 19 gives the story of the prophet Elijah. Here was a man who was living during some dark times. His life was in jeopardy; he was on the run in seclusion, and in verse four he exclaims that he

would rather die than continue on in his circumstances. He felt completely alone and abandoned. But just a few sentences later in verse 18, the Lord gave Elijah hope and encouraged him by telling him that he was not alone. In fact, there were seven thousand other people in Israel who were remaining faithful to God.

Are you feeling a little bit like Elijah today? If so, take heart. Ask God to bring other godly people across your path. Keep encouraged because no matter how strong the forces of evil, God always preserves a remnant of those who will continue to be faithful to him!

Walking with God and Others Is Joyful

Life will have many challenges, but walking with God and fellow believers will allow you to have joy when it seems impossible.

One of the great lies Satan has gotten many believers to buy into is that we must anguish our way through this life to get to the next. In other words, our focus becomes so much on the next life that we fail to be useful in the life we are in. We fall into "survival mode." We stop looking for lives to touch and selfishly focus on our eternal prize alone.

This is so contrary to the life God has planned for us! In Philippians 1:23-24, the apostle Paul admitted he longed to go to Heaven. And who wouldn't have in his shoes? Here he was suffering persecution and eventually preparing to face execution. He did not have the worldly comforts of life we experience to numb his hope for Heaven. Still, he realized his work on earth was not yet complete. He realized he needed to be a blessing to other believers. So he continued to write; he continued to encourage, and he continued to proclaim Christ with joy.

Until the God you serve calls you home, your work on earth is not complete! This means you can walk confidently, knowing the one true God of this universe stands by your side.

There will be many discoveries we will make in this life. But the greatest of these is walking hand in hand with the incredible God that we serve!

Action Points

1. Describe one practical way your walk with God has grown over these 42 days.
2. How has this book caused you to think differently about others?
3. Take some time and ask yourself, what kind of God do I serve?

Go All Out in Your Service

Wow, what a journey we have been on together! I cannot tell you what a privilege it has been to travel with you these past forty-two days.

It is my prayer that this will be just the beginning of your growth in God. I hope you will continue to use this book as a resource tool in your life. Don't just stick it on a bookshelf. Use it as a means of helping someone else. Take the knowledge you have learned *about* God and put it into *action!*

Briefly though, let me share with you a quick thought from my heart before we conclude. It was several years ago that God first placed within me a desire to write. I was sitting in a small pastor's meeting and a speaker named Keith Drury offered a convicting challenge to us pastors to author books. From that moment, God began to give me a burden for writing a threefold series on the basics of who God is, how we take him to others, and how we develop our personal lives. This book is the first step in that series.

I must confess that all through this writing process, I have wrestled with questions such as, "But God, why me? I'm too young and inexperienced. I feel like I know so little about you myself, let alone possess the ability to write a book on what you are like!"

Yet it was here that God stopped me in my tracks and said, "Ezra, you are not writing this book for you. You are writing this out of an act of obedience and service to me." That simple thought has kept me going through the days when I felt this task was impossible. It made me get up a little earlier many days and go to bed a little later on others.

Let me give you another example. My wife and I just recently moved to Toronto, Ontario, from where I pastored for three years in Moneta, Virginia. In many ways, I was comfortable where I was.

We had incredible people, a fantastic leadership team, and an awesome country atmosphere to raise a family.

Still, I remember the calling God placed on my life when I was just fifteen years of age. Through key influencers in my life and a book called *Fresh Wind, Fresh Fire* by Jim Cymbala, God began to stir in my heart a burning desire to do his will. He gave me a deeper love for others than I had ever experienced. He placed in my heart a longing to know him in prayer. And specifically, he gave me a heart for people who lived in the Toronto, Ontario, region. I do not remember every detail, but I remember committing to God in those days to follow him no matter the cost.

In some ways, moving to another country is extremely unsettling. How will we make it financially? Will we actually be able to grow a church? What if we fail? All of these questions and more have surfaced at times and yet I am also excited beyond measure. The reason for this is that *I have found God does his greatest work in our lives when we trust him humbly and obey him completely.* He works through people whose only safety net is him. He chooses to use people who burn the bridges behind them, step out in faith, and go "all in" no matter what he calls them to do or where he calls them to go.

Now, you might be saying to yourself, "So what does this have to do with me?" Here is why I believe this lesson is important. I have no doubt God wants to do something incredible through your life. He wants to use you in ways that you can barely imagine. Maybe he is calling you to write. Perhaps he is placing a desire in your heart to step out in faith and go somewhere you have never gone before. I don't know what it is.

My question to you is not: "What is God calling you to do?" My questions are: "What is holding you back from going for it? Why have you not chased the dream God has placed in your heart?"

If I were to answer for you, my guess would come down to one word – fear. You fear the opinions of men more than you fear the praise of the God you serve. You fear what others will say, how they will respond, and what may happen if you step out in faith. You are a servant of man more than you are a servant of Christ (so much for ending this book on a high note!).

This brings us back to the overarching theme of this book: *What Kind of God Do I Serve?* Have you locked in and settled the fact that you are going to serve him regardless of what it will cost you? Do you serve him with every part of your being, or is something held back?

It is my deep prayer for you that in all you do, your consuming desire and passion will be to serve God with total abandon. Focus the sights on your scope, and go all out in whatever he is calling you to do!

Ezra Byer is the lead pastor of Discovery Pointe Church in Toronto, Ontario (discoverypointechurch.ca).

He is also the founder of Powerline Kingdom Network (powerlinekingdom.com) – a ministry that seeks to use the power of media to help people discover Jesus, develop disciples, and deepen lives.

Currently, Ezra and his wife Janan live on the east side of Toronto. You can follow Ezra on Twitter: @ezrabyer

Bibliography

Week 1 – I Serve a God Who Wants to Know Me

Page 15: *The most portentous fact*: Tozer, A. W. *The Knowledge of the Holy: The Attributes of God, Their Meaning in the Christian Life.* New York: Harper & Row, 1961. I. Print.

Page 17: *Infinite and perfect spirit*: Strong, Augustus Hopkins. *Systematic Theology: A Compendium and Commonplace-book Designed for the Use of Theological Students.* Vol. 1. Philadelphia: Griffith & Rowland, 1907. 52. Print.

Page 18: *Our doctrine of God*: Torrance, James. *Worship, Community & the Triune God of Grace.* Downers Grove, Ill.: InterVarsity, 1996. 37. Print.

Page 18: *Where you start spiritually*: Audio of this can be found online at renewanation.org.

Page 19: *Let's Start with Jesus*: Kinlaw, Dennis F. *Let's Start with Jesus: A New Way of Doing Theology.* Grand Rapids, Mich.: Zondervan, 2005. Print.

Page 22: *Biblical scholar N.T. Wright*: Wright, N. T. *The Challenge of Jesus: Rediscovering Who Jesus Was and Is.* Downers Grove, Ill.: InterVarsity, 1999. 43-46. Print.

Page 26: *Discipleship can tolerate*: Bonhoeffer, Dietrich. *The Cost of Discipleship.* Rev. [i.e. 2d] & Unabridged ed. New York: Macmillan, 1959. Print.

Page 28: *Baptism separates the tire kickers*: This quote was taken from Max Lucado's online article *Baptism: The Demonstration of Devotion*

Page 29: *Faith in action*: Nee, Watchman. *The Normal Christian Life.* Grand Rapids, Mich.: Christian Classics Ethereal Library, 199. Print.

Page 31: *Prayer is the difference*: Batterson, Mark. *Draw the Circle: The 40-day Prayer Challenge.* Grand Rapids, Mich.: Zondervan, 2012. 226. Print.

Page 32: *The devil is not*: Cymbala, Jim, and Dean Merrill. *Fresh Wind, Fresh Fire: What Happens When God's Spirit Invades the Heart of His People.* Grand Rapids, Mich.: Zondervan, 1997. Print.

Page 33: *True prayer is the daily*: Taken from an email of Mark Cravens on prayer.

Page 38: *The New Testament was written*: Bird, Mark. Defending Your Faith: A Twelve Lesson Series on Apologetics. Hebron, Ky.: Answers in Genesis, 2007. 85. Print.

Page 39: *The time span*: Bird, Mark. Defending Your Faith: A Twelve Lesson Series on Apologetics. Hebron, Ky.: Answers in Genesis, 2007. 89. Print.

Page 39: *Most scholars believe*: This quote was taken from an online article entitled, *Updating the Manuscript Evidence for the New Testament*.

Page 39: *If we add up the total*: This fact was taken from an online article entitled, *Updating the Manuscript Evidence for the New Testament*.

Page 40: *Manuscript expert Dan Wallace*: This fact was taken from an online article entitled, *Updating the Manuscript Evidence for the New Testament*.

Page 40: *When it comes to the New Testament*: These facts were taken from an online article entitled, *Updating the Manuscript Evidence for the New Testament*.

Page 41: *There is not one doctrinal*: Schaff, Philip. *A Companion to the Greek Testament and the English Version,*. New York: Harper & Brothers, 1883. 177. Print.

Page 41: *Every translation has its own*: A more through list of Bible translation comparisons can be found at apbrown2.net.

Page 43: *Within one hundred years*: Dake, Finis. *God's Plan for Man*. Lawrenceville, Ga.: Dake Bible Sales, 1949. 731-734. Print.

Page 43: *Put your nose into*: Taken from a Facebook post by *The Way of the Master*.

Page 48: *There are roughly sixty*: McDowell, Josh. *More than a Carpenter*. Wheaton, Ill.: Tyndale House, 1977. 90. Print.

Page 49: *In his book Science Speaks*: Stoner, Peter Winebrenner, and Robert C. Newman. *Science Speaks; Scientific Proof of the Accuracy of Prophecy and the Bible,*. 3d Rev. ed. Chicago: Moody, 1969. Print.

Page 50: *You must make your choice*: Lewis, C. S. *Mere Christianity: A Revised and Amplified Edition, with a New Introduction, of the Three Books, Broadcast Talks, Christian Behaviour, and Beyond Personality*. San Francisco: HarperSanFrancisco, 2001. Print.

Page 53: *Nothing is objectively true*: Strobel, Lee. *The Case for the Real Jesus: A Journalist Investigates Current Attacks on the Identity of Christ*. Grand Rapids, Mich.: Zondervan, 2007. 234. Print.

Page 54: *The person who has*: McDowell, Josh, and Bob Hostetler. *Right from Wrong*. Dallas, Tex.: Word Pub., 1994. 131. Print.

Page 56: *The rule for doing*: Packer, J. I. *Knowing God*. Downers Grove, Ill.: InterVarsity, 1973. Print.

Week 2 – I Serve Someone Who Created Me to Glorify Him

Page 60: *A firm faith in*: Warfield, Benjamin Breckinridge. *Selected Shorter Writings of Benjamin B. Warfield,*. Vol. 1. Nutley, N.J.: Presbyterian and Reformed Pub., 1970. 671-672. Print.

Page 61: *God is God*: Elliot, Elisabeth. *Through Gates of Splendor*. New York: Harper, 1957. 267. Print.

Page 61: *A God wise enough*: Yancey, Philip. *Where Is God When It Hurts*. Grand Rapids, Mich.: Zondervan Pub. House, 1977. 106. Print.

Page 61: *You have made us*: Sheed, F. J. *The Confessions of St. Augustine*. London: Sheed & Ward, 1984. Print.

Page 62: *We never better enjoy*: Tiegreen, Chris. "The Pleasure of God." *The One Year Walk with God Devotional: 365 Daily Bible Readings to Transform Your Mind / Chris Tiegreen*. Carol Stream, ILL.: Tyndale House Pub., 2004. Print.

Page 62: *He who knows what it is*: Douglas, Charles Noel. *Forty Thousand Quotations, Prose and Poetical; Choice Extracts on History, Science, Philosophy, Religion, Literature, Etc. Selected from Thestandard Authors of Ancient and Modern Times, Classified According to Subject*. New York: Sully and Kleinteich, 1915. 835. Print.

Page 64: *the beauty of splendor*: Webster, Inc. *Merriam-Webster's Collegiate Dictionary*. 11th ed. Springfield, MA: Merriam-Webster, 2003. Print.

Page 65: *The beauty of his manifold*: Piper, John. *Desiring God: Meditations of a Christian Hedonist*. 25th Anniversary Reference ed. Colorado Springs, Colo.: Multnomah, 2011. Kindle Locations 565-567. Kindle Edition.

Page 66: *God is one Being*: Piper, John. *Desiring God: Meditations of a Christian Hedonist*. 25th Anniversary Reference ed. Colorado Springs, Colo.: Multnomah, 2011. Kindle Location 692. Kindle Edition.

Page 66: *The only thing that God*: Packer, J. I. *God's Plans for You*. Wheaton, Ill.: Crossway, 2001. 29. Print.

Pages 66-67: *God is infinitely happy*: This quote came from *An Unpublished Essay on the Trinity* by Jonathan Edwards.

Page 68: *The chief end of man*: This quote came from question 1 of the Westminister Shorter Catechism.

Page 68: *In commanding us to*: Lewis, C. S. *Reflections on the Psalms*. New York: Harcourt, Brace, 1958. 93-97. Print.

Pages 68-69: *If God told us*: This quote came from a Discovery Pointe radio program.

Page 69: *God will get glory*: Strong, Augustus Hopkins. *Systematic Theology: A Compendium and Commonplace-book Designed for the Use of Theo-logical Students*. Philadelphia: Griffith & Rowland, 1907. 398. Print.

Pages 73-74: *Here is his revised definition*: Brown, A. Philip. *Loving God: The Primary Principle of the Christian Life*. Cincinnati, Ohio: Revivalist, Ministry of God's Bible School and College, 2005. Print.

Page 77: *Love is the only fire*: Maclaren, Alexander. *St. Paul's Epistles to the Corinthians (to II Corinthians, Chapter V)*. London: Hodder and Stoughton, 1909. 101. Print.

Page 78: *The moral excellence of God*: Rowley, H. H. *Dictionary of Bible Themes*. London: Nelson, 1968. Print.

Page 79: *God defines his holiness*: Oswalt, John. *Called to Be Holy*. Nappanee, Ind.: Evangel Pub. House, 1999. 25. Print.

Page 81: *The only way we can*: This quote was taken from a class lecture Dr. Brown gave on the definition of holiness.

Page 81: *Holiness, as taught in the Scriptures*: Tozer, A. W. *Preparing for Jesus' Return: Daily Live the Blessed Hope*. S.l.: Bethany House, 2012. Print.

Page 81: *The will of God*: Graham, Billy, and Franklin Graham. "Billy Graham on God's Will." *Billy Graham in Quotes*. Nashville, Tenn.: Thomas Nelson, 2011. Print.

Page 84: *How little people know*: Lewis, C. S., and Clyde S. Kilby. *Letters to an American Lady*. Grand Rapids, Mich.: W.B. Eerdmans Pub., 1967. Print.

Page 84: *The act of God's grace*: Webster, Inc. *Merriam-Webster's Collegiate Dictionary*. 11th ed. Springfield, MA: Merriam-Webster, 2003. Print.

Page 85: *Sanctification means you have*: This quote came from a conversation I had with Darnell Wilson on this topic.

Page 88: *Turn your eyes*: This quote came from Helen Lemmel's song "Turn Your Eyes Upon Jesus."

Page 89: *It is much easier*: This quote came from a Tweet by Mark Batterson on March 9th, 2014.

Pages 98-99: *God is the highest good*: Edwards, Jonathan, and Edward Williams. *The Works of President Edwards*. New York: B. Franklin, 1968. 217. Print.

Page 99: *If you don't feel*: Piper, John. *A Hunger for God: Desiring God through Fasting and Prayer*. Wheaton, Ill.: Crossway, 1997. Print.

Week 3 – I Serve Someone Who Wants to Give Me Total Freedom

Page 103: *A man by his sin*: Tozer, A. W. *Gems from Tozer: Selections from the Writings of A.W. Tozer*. U.S. ed. Harrisburg, Pa.: Christian Publications, 1979. Print.

Page 114: *We have been playing*: This quote came from a sermon that he gave on sin.

Page 114: *When a person loses control*: Kinlaw, Dennis F., and John Oswalt. *We Live as Christ*. Nappanee, Ind.: Francis Asbury, 2001. 14. Print.

Page 116: *The prime purpose*: Torrance, James. *Worship, Community & the Triune God of Grace*. Downers Grove, Ill.: InterVarsity, 1996. 32. Print.

Page 123: *Will power will never*: Foster, Richard J. *Celebration of Discipline: The Path to Spiritual Growth*. Rev. 1st ed. San Francisco: Harper & Row, 1988. 5. Print.

Pages 123-124: *We have largely preached*: Kinlaw, Dennis F., and John Oswalt. *We Live as Christ*. Nappanee, Ind.: Francis Asbury, 2001. Print.

Page 132: *To say that someone*: Stanley, Andy. *The Grace of God*. Nashville, Tenn.: Thomas Nelson, 2010. Kindle Location 98. Kindle Edition.

Page 133: *God's grace is the outreaching*: This quote came from class notes that were taken in his class.

Page 134: *The law of God*: Stanley, Andy. *The Grace of God*. Nashville, Tenn.: Thomas Nelson, 2010. Kindle Location 1047. Kindle Edition.

Page 135: *Repentance is our response*: Torrance, James. *Worship, Community & the Triune God of Grace*. Downers Grove, Ill.: InterVarsity, 1996. 54. Print.

Page 135: *Faith's only function*: Stott, John R. W. *The Cross of Christ*. Downers Grove, Ill.: InterVarsity, 1986. 188. Print.

Page 137: *Sustaining grace promises*: Lucado, Max. *Grace: More than We Deserve, Greater than We Imagine*. Nashville, Tenn.: Thomas Nelson, 2012. Kindle Location 1209. Kindle Edition.

Page 138: *Tis grace that brought*: This quote comes from John Newton's hymn Amazing Grace

Page 138: *He himself is the treasure*: Lucado, Max. *Grace: More than We Deserve, Greater than We Imagine*. Nashville, Tenn.: Thomas Nelson, 2012. Kindle Locations 1687-1689. Kindle Edition.

Page 141: *It is the nature*: Kinlaw, Dennis F. *Let's Start with Jesus: A New Way of Doing Theology*. Grand Rapids, Mich.: Zondervan, 2005. 32. Print.

Page 141: *Death for a person*: Zizioulas, Jean. *Being as Communion: Studies in Personhood and the Church*. Crestwood, N.Y.: St. Vladimir's Seminary, 1985. 49. Print.

Page 144: *We are prone to being*: Bonhoeffer, Dietrich. *The Cost of Discipleship*. Rev. [i.e. 2d] & Unabridged ed. New York: Macmillan, 1959. Print.

Week 4 – I Serve Someone Who Reveals Himself to Me Through His Word

Page 151: *My definition of infallibility*: Strobel, Lee. *The Case for the Real Jesus: A Journalist Investigates Current Attacks on the Identity of Christ*. Grand Rapids, Mich.: Zondervan, 2007. 75. Print.

Page 151: *The Chicago Statement*: The full statement can be found online at bible-researcher.com.

Page 152: *The goal of redemption*: Oswalt, John. *Called to Be Holy*. Nappanee, Ind.: Evangel Pub. House, 1999. 34. Print.

Page 153: *The Bible is not*: Cox, John. *Googling God*. Eugene, Or.: Harvest House, 2008. 177. Print.

Page 155: *In Living By the Book*: Hendricks, Howard G., and William Hendricks. *Living by the Book*. Chicago: Moody, 1991. 21-24. Print.

Pages 165-166: *UP/SA Principle*: This thought came from class lectures.

Page 171: *Perhaps one reason is because*: This thought came from one of Dr. Ury's *Hour of Holiness* radio programs.

Page 172: *God's freedom always empowers*: Bahnsen, Greg L. *By This Standard: The Authority of God's Law Today*. Tyler, Tex.: Institute for Christian Economics, 1985. 114. Print.

Page 177: *Practice is the hardest part*: Voskamp, Ann. *One Thousand Gifts: A Dare to Live Fully Right Where You Are*. Grand Rapids, Mich.: Zondervan, 2010. Print.

Page 186: *The Joy of Discovery*: Wald, Oletta. *The Joy of Discovery in Bible Study*. Rev. ed. Minneapolis: Augsburg Pub. House, 1975. Print.

Page 188: *How do you defend*: This thought comes from one of Charles Spurgeon's sermons entitled, "Christ and His Co-Workers."

Week 5 – I Serve Someone Who Is Building Me a Kingdom

Page 196: *Many Christians dread*: Alcorn, Randy C. *The Treasure Principle*. Sisters, Or.: Multnomah, 2001. Print.

Page 197: *The Kingdom of God*: Stetzer, Ed. *Subversive Kingdom: Living as Agents of Gospel Transformation*. Nashville, Tenn.: B & H, 2012. Kindle Edition.

Page 199: *On D-Day, the war*: *The Kingdom of God*: Stetzer, Ed. *Subversive Kingdom: Living as Agents of Gospel Transformation*. Nashville, Tenn.: B & H, 2012. Kindle Locations 577-578. Kindle Edition.

Page 204: *Bible teacher Stan Key*: This thought came from a talk Stan Key gave to the staff at Eastlake Community Church.

Page 209: *The measure of success*: This quote came from a sermon Pastor Troy preached at Eastlake Community Church.

Page 217: *For Christians, this present*: Alcorn, Randy C. *Heaven*. Wheaton, Ill.: Tyndale House, 2004. Kindle Locations 818-819. Kindle Edition.

Page 221: *By denying the endlessness*: Alcorn, Randy C. *Heaven*. Wheaton, Ill.: Tyndale House, 2004. Kindle Locations 750. Kindle Edition.

Page 222: When men talk of: Spurgeon, C. H. "Joy Hindering Faith." *Spurgeon's Sermons*. Vol. 38. Grand Rapids, Mich.: Zondervan. Print.

Page 223: *Disbelieve Hell, and you*: Lowry, Malcolm, and Patrick A. McCarthy. *Malcolm Lowry's "La Mordida"* Scholarly ed. Athens, GA: U of Georgia, 1996. 162. Print.

Page 227: *If highest status were essential*: Grudem, Wayne A. *Systematic Theology: An Introduction to Biblical Doctrine*. Leicester, England: Inter-Varsity ;, 1994. 1144-1145. Print.

Page 228: *The question which I heard*: This question came from a sermon given by John Piper.

Page 232: *When I've meditated*: Alcorn, Randy C. *Heaven*. Wheaton, Ill.: Tyndale House, 2004. Kindle Locations 8623-8624. Kindle Edition.

Page 238: *Every inch of progress*: Coleman, Robert Emerson. *The Master Plan of Evangelism*. Westwood, N.J.: F.H. Revell, 1964. 115. Print.

Week 6 – I Serve Someone Who Will Journey with Me

Page 247: *God walks with us*: *God's Priorities for Your Life for Women*. Peabody, MA: Hendrickson, 2006. 156. Print.

Page 248: *82% of Protestant professing*: This stat came from the Lifeway Research website.

Page 249: *The Disciplines allow us*: Foster, Richard J. *Celebration of Discipline: The Path to Spiritual Growth*. Rev. 1st ed. San Francisco: Harper & Row, 1988. Print.

Page 251: *When we come down*: This thought came from a sermon he gave at Hillsong Conference in 2006.

Page 252: *Statistics say that right around*: According to and 2007 Barna study, 24% of Evangelicals tithe.

Page 255: *The truth is that discipline*: Downs, Annie F. *Let's All Be Brave: Living Life with Everything You Have*. 181. Print.

Page 262: *Several years ago*: Hardy, Darren. *The Compound Effect: Multiplying Your Success, One Simple Step at a Time*. New York, NY: Vanguard, 2010. Print.

Page 263: *Hurry is not of the Devil*: Kelsey, Morton T. *The Other Side of Silence: A Guide to Christian Meditation*. New York: Paulist, 1976. 83. Print.

Page 264: *The Spirit does not live*: Oswalt, John. *Called to Be Holy*. Nappanee, Ind.: Evangel Pub. House, 1999. 131. Print.

Page 266: *God whispers to us*: Lewis, C. S. *The Problem of Pain*. New York, NY: HarperOne, 2001. Print.

Page 268: *A low view of God*: Tozer, A. W. *The Knowledge of the Holy: The Attributes of God, Their Meaning in the Christian Life*. New York: Harper & Row, 1961. Print.

Page 271: *DNA is equivalent*: Gitt, Werner. *Dazzling Design in Miniature, Creation Ex Nihilo*. Creation 20 (1):6, 1997. Print.

Page 271: *If gravity had been*: Glynn, Patrick. *God: The Evidence : The Reconciliation of Faith and Reason in a Postsecular World*. Rocklin, CA: Forum, 1997. 27. Print.

Page 273: *If you will go where*: Downs, Annie F. *Let's All Be Brave: Living Life with Everything You Have*. 181. Print.

Page 278: *Sometimes our blessings*: This quote came from Laura Story's song "Blessings."

Page 278: *What you are stands*: Andrews, Robert. *The Columbia Dictionary of Quotations*. New York: Columbia UP, 1993. 185. Print.